M000030892

# AMERICAN FOREIGN POLICY AND NATIONAL SECURITY

# AMERICAN FOREIGN POLICY AND NATIONAL SECURITY

Paul R. Viotti

**Rapid Communications in Conflict and Security Series**
General Editor: Geoffrey R.H. Burn

CAMBRIA
PRESS

Amherst, New York

Copyright 2020 Cambria Press

All rights reserved.
Printed in the United States of America

No part of this publication may be reproduced, stored in or introduced
into a retrieval system, or transmitted, in any form, or by any means
(electronic, mechanical, photocopying, recording, or otherwise),
without the prior permission of the publisher.

Requests for permission should be directed to
permissions@cambriapress.com, or mailed to:
Cambria Press
100 Corporate Parkway, Suite 128
Amherst, New York 14226, USA

Library of Congress Cataloging-in-Publication Data on file.

ISBN: 978-1-62196-538-1

*To Paul Bowen*
*who motivates me and gives me the encouragement*
*I need in both good and challenging times.*

# TABLE OF CONTENTS

# List of Figures

# LIST OF TABLES

# PREFACE

This book seeks explanation for the making and implementation of American foreign policy—the decisions and actions the United States takes vis-à-vis state and non-state actors abroad. The latter includes international (IOs) and non-governmental organizations (NGOs), other groups and, in some cases, powerful individuals.

In this effort we are drawn to the decisionmakers themselves. Although precise or point predictions are elusive, deeper understandings of how policymakers tend to operate in the processes of making and implementing foreign policy can lead to greater accuracy in the practical expectations we develop for what may happen.

Although I do not present a *theory* of foreign policy, I do identify factors or essential elements that likely would be part of such a theory in chapter 1 (see figure 1). These structural and ideational factors (both domestic and international) influence the choices policymakers make—the ways and means by which they make and implement American foreign policy.

Ideas grounded in understandings of interest drive American foreign policy. We look to the understandings decisionmakers have about interests that drive their choices as well as material capabilities or power that facilitate or constrain these decisions. The international norms and understandings of how the world works that policymakers have internalized drive their decisions. How the policymaker sees international systemic *structure* (a material factor)—the distribution of power among states and the relative power position of the United States compared to other states—facilitates or constrains the making of choices.

We connect these material, ideational and other factors "out there" to the decisionmakers who incorporate them as part of their decisionmaking calculus "in here." We search for the root cause or causes in the subjectivities of individuals and the inter-subjective exchanges among them in both the policymaking groups to which they belong and the associations they have with counterparts and others abroad. What matters most are the understandings held by policymakers about domestic and world politics in general and how they play in particular contingencies.

Although global society lacks central or superordinate authority, there still is order to be found in what is essentially an anarchic world of sovereign states and non-state actors. We find this order in ideas, rules, or norms of conduct that decisionmakers customarily follow as well as the associations they form among themselves. Deviating from these norms undermines trust and typically results in pushback by counterparts and others abroad.

I focus on the nationalist or internationalist orientations of decisionmakers that affect the way they see the US role in making and implementing foreign policy. In this regard, nationalists are domestically focused and tend to deemphasize international involvement, minimizing to the extent possible government actions abroad. By contrast, I also identify three kinds of internationalist orientation—liberal, conservative, and militant. Broadly speaking, the range or spectrum of foreign policy options includes (A) diplomacy and other forms of peaceful or constructive engagement not just with allies, coalition partners, and other friendly countries, but also vis-à-vis adversaries; (B) containment of adversaries—

deterrence, coercive diplomacy, and other negative measures short of war; and (C) armed intervention or warfare with adversaries.

Given their domestic focus, *nationalists* tend to minimize international actions of any kind, not making or withdrawing from commitments overseas whenever possible. To them, the US need not be the world's "policeman." In the extreme, nationalists become isolationists. Although they may contain or intervene militarily when circumstances call for such actions, the preferred modality of *liberal internationalists* is diplomacy and other forms of peaceful or constructive engagement bilaterally, multilaterally, and cooperatively in alliances and international organizations. As with their liberal counterparts, *conservative internationalists* engage in diplomacy and armed interventions but are most comfortable with the stability that comes from efforts to contain adversaries. Finally, *militant* (or neoconservative) *internationalists* tend to contain or invade depending on calculations related to the contingency at hand. They are skeptical about what diplomacy can achieve when dealing with adversaries and thus engage diplomatically with adversaries primarily *after* attaining objectives sought through more forceful means.

## ORGANIZATION OF THIS BOOK

The three chapters in part 1 take up peaceful engagement, containment, and armed intervention. The discussion there refers to table 1 in chapter 1 that compares liberal, conservative, and militant internationalists in relation to their propensities to engage, contain, or invade. All three orientations resort to peaceful engagement, containment, and armed intervention or warfare, but each has a preferred modality.

In chapter 2, I explore peaceful engagement with China beginning with the Richard Nixon administration, the Soviet Union by the Franklin Roosevelt and, much later, the Ronald Reagan administrations, and institutionalizing peaceful engagement—institutionally embedding liberalism—in international organizations, particularly after World War II.

Peaceful or *constructive engagement* is the way both nationalists and internationalists prefer to deal with allies, coalition partners, and other "friendly" countries, groups and powerful individuals. Adversaries may be peacefully engaged, but containing or invading them is also possible.

Berlin and the Cuban missile crisis cases are the focus of chapter 3 on the ways and means of containment to include deterrence, coercive diplomacy, and the construction of rules or norms that set the bounds and expectations of adversarial relations. The use of force in armed intervention and warfare are the subject of chapter 4 to include the Spanish-American War, two world wars, and the Korean and Vietnam wars.

Part 2 takes a look back on the American experience since the eighteenth century. Chapter 5 takes up the understanding by many Americans who see the United States as exceptional—some alleging divine inspiration for the creation of a secular republic in the new world as a model for other countries throughout the world. Not all US decisionmakers have this view, but for those who do it may result in seemingly self-righteous claims to a higher moral or national purpose. Even those policymakers who do not see the US as morally superior to other countries may find value justifying American pursuit of national interest in moral terms that resonate well with public understandings. In this regard, policy makers also may be prone to use morally negative terms to describe the conduct of adversaries.

Beginning in the nineteenth century, chapter 6 again takes up armed intervention in greater detail—a high American propensity historically to intervene abroad with armed force, decisions made by policymakers driven by their understandings of national interest at different points in time. As noted in the previous chapter, they may cloak the rationale for intervention in moral terms. Humanitarian motives may indeed drive their decisions in some contingencies, but even in cases where interest and power considerations are predominantly at issue there is a tendency to justify actions in moral terms. Expanding territorial control in North America and enhancing hemispheric influence (fostering the establishment of republics in Mexico, Central America, the Caribbean, and South America) marked American foreign policy in the nineteenth and early twentieth centuries.

Beginning with the Spanish-American War (1898), policy focus initially expanded westward to Asia and the Pacific, later in two twentieth-century world wars to Europe, becoming global in the Second World War that included both European and Pacific theatres of military operations. The roots of internationalism in the Cold War and afterward have rested on the widely held understanding by policy elites that US security and the pursuit of commercial and other interests had become global, no longer constrained by protective barriers—the Atlantic and Pacific oceans on the country's east and west coasts. The nationalist challenge to this policy-elite consensus that resonates with much of the public, particularly in rural areas, holds that the country should revert to its historical position of tending primarily to domestic matters and withdrawing as much as possible from military and other commitments abroad.

Part 3 explores how domestic politics affect the making and implementation of American foreign policy—dubbed politics on the Potomac River where the executive, legislative, and judicial branches and private-sector actors operate. Chapter 7 focuses on *presidential power*—the ability to persuade in both domestic and foreign policy. Following Richard Neustadt's argument, presidential power is defined constitutionally, but the president's freedom of action (the ability to persuade) during any term in office varies in relation to both professional reputation and popular prestige. Although Congress has relatively more to say on domestic matters, the president's constitutional role as the principal decisionmaker on foreign policy affords the Congress a secondary albeit still-important role to play. Finally, chapters 8 and 9 address in greater detail the domestic political milieu and elite understandings of power that drive the making and implementation of American foreign policy.

## ACKNOWLEDGEMENTS

My debts are many, but this edition has depended upon the encouragement and help by Geoffrey Burn and Toni Tan of Cambria Press. Professor Thorsten Spehn of the University of Colorado, Denver, read the manuscript and offered constructive suggestions. I appreciate the insightful comments on my work of my good friend, Robert Guschewsky. My research associate, Kevin Jensen, also pitched in on the construction of the index and drawing of the important schematic in figure 1.

My appreciation also continues to those who helped me by reviewing or assisting me with the manuscript of the first edition—Carina Solmirano, then my research associate, Professor Dan Caldwell of Pepperdine University; Ken Jensen, then Executive Director of the American Committees on Foreign Relations; Ambassador George Lane; Curtis Cook of Colorado College, my friends Thomas Menza, Esq. and Warren Miller, and Louise Knight of Polity Press.

# American Foreign Policy and National Security

# CHAPTER 1

# EXPLAINING AMERICAN FOREIGN POLICY

When we try to explain foreign policy, identifying and relating the factors that *influence* its making and implementation, we are drawn to the decisionmakers themselves.[1] We look both internally and externally to ideas grounded in understandings decisionmakers have about interests that drive their choices as well as their understandings of material capabilities or power that facilitate or constrain these decisions. As depicted in figure 1, *foreign policy* refers to the decisions and actions the agents of a state take in relation to other state and non-state actors—the latter referring to inter-governmental and non-governmental organizations, other groups, and individuals.

States are commonly referred to as actors or agents in international politics, but these state units are abstract human constructions, not physical (much less human) beings. As a practical matter, we understand the existence of states, international and non-governmental organizations only in terms of the human beings who construct them or act in their name.

In figure 1, I specify structural and ideational factors—both domestic and international—that influence the decisions and actions of policymakers. They are driven by both ideas (such as internalized international norms and understandings of how the world works) as well as by how the policymaker sees international or systemic *structure*—the distribution of power among states (a material factor) and the relative power position of the United States vis-à-vis other states. Values and other ideas of domestic origin internalized by policymakers also matter, as does the domestic "structure" that defines the policymaking milieu—division of powers between federal and state governments and separation of powers among the branches of government.

## Figure 1. Structural and ideational effects.

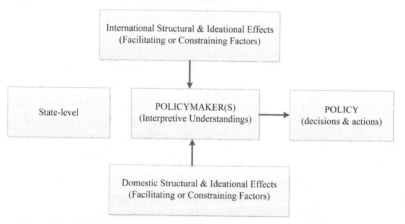

Figure 1 depicts a conceptual framework that helps us understand (perhaps providing practical expectations) on the making and implementation of American foreign policy. We focus on the process in which decisions are made and actions taken, searching for patterns as well as identifying anomalies or exceptions. Theories of international politics matter in the making and implementation of foreign policy to the extent that the insights they provide directly or indirectly contribute to policymakers' own understandings of how the world works. What matters most are the understandings policymakers hold and share with others within the policy elites of which they are a part.

## THE POLICYMAKERS

The *interpretive understandings* of policymakers are decisive in making decisions and taking actions in foreign policy. These understandings are grounded in the *psychologies* and *social psychologies* of individual policymakers—how they understand what they observe in the world around them and the group dynamics of how they relate to each other. The *ontology* or worldview—how one comprehends or understands the essence of the things we observe—varies from person to person, sometimes substantially. The "realities" we *perceive* are also highly subjective. *Personality* is yet another variable that influences how one thinks, acts or interacts with others.

In its idealization of objectivity, the rational-actor assumption sets all of these subjective factors aside. It is as if all policymakers were pre-programmed rationally to optimize desired outcomes by selecting objectively the best (or good enough) means to accomplish one's purposes or reaching one's objectives. As a predictive tool, the rational-actor model works primarily when the policymakers share interpretive understandings in common—often due to similar ontologies, perceptions, and personalities that are within a "normal" range of variation.

The worldview of presidents and those who advise them does make a difference on the course of American foreign policy. The liberal internationalism of Barak Obama was supplanted by the nationalism of his successor, Donald Trump, which marked a major shift in US conduct vis-à-vis allies, other "friendly" countries, and adversaries. Although differing on specifics, Obama's eight years in office sustained the *internationalism* of both Democratic and Republican administrations established by Franklin Roosevelt upon entry, during, and after World War II.

Trump's campaign and presidential "America First" and "Make America Great Again" ("MAGA") rhetoric was an echo of the non-entanglement, if not isolationist, thinking deeply rooted in the American historical experience. When Trump assumed office in January 2017, such rhetoric quickly took concrete form: (a) unilaterally imposing tariffs on trading partners in search of a better "deal" for the United States, (b) questioning whether the United States should remain in costly alliances like NATO and threatening withdrawal if allies did not increase their own defense-spending contributions, (c) withdrawing from the 2016 Trans-Pacific Partnership (TPP) free trade agreement that his predecessor's diplomats had negotiated with East Asian and Latin American countries, (d) demanding replacement of the 1994 North American Free Trade Agreement (NAFTA) that had been negotiated by the Bush and Clinton administrations with a new United States–Mexico–Canada Agreement (USMCA)—a set of trade arrangements seen as more favorable to the United States than those of NAFTA; (e) terminating US participation in the 15-year Iran nuclear deal made by the Obama administration along with the other permanent Security Council members, Germany and the European Union; (f) pursuing an immigration policy intended to deter or dissuade those seeking asylum (or for other purposes) crossing the US-Mexican border; (g) ending US participation in the United Nations Educational, Scientific and Cultural Organization (UNESCO) for its allegedly anti-Israel bias; (h) withdrawal from the 1988 Intermediate-Range Nuclear Forces (INF) Treaty with Russia; and (i) moving the US Embassy in Israel to Jerusalem from Tel Aviv, recognizing Israeli sovereignty over the Golan Heights, and legimating Israeli settlements in territories on the west bank of the Jordan River.

Referring to a president's personality as a disorder often leads to one's branding as a political opponent, a claim often rendered in partisan terms. For our purposes, however, we do need to take personality into account in any explanation of foreign policy. Indeed, it may be decisive when the policymaker's personality is outside of normal limits that psychiatrists establish in their *Diagnostic and Statistical Manual* (DSM).[2]

Thus, President Richard Nixon's *paranoia* led him to distrust "enemies" he saw inhabiting the State Department. Given this view, he excluded State from the policy-making decisions on his opening to China, relegating Secretary of State Rogers effectively to observer status while his National Security Adviser, Henry Kissinger, negotiated in Beijing with Premier Chou En-lai. By their actions, paranoids have a way of making their own enemies or, at least, sewing seeds of discontent among those who might otherwise have been their loyal followers.

President Donald Trump's personality influenced his foreign policy choices dramatically—his extreme narcissism an assessment rendered by 27 psychiatrists and other mental health experts, based as well on their reference to the profession's *DSM*.[3] According to these professionals, narcissistic personality disorder in its extreme form may exhibit antisocial behavior, paranoid traits, sadistic tendencies as in bullying behavior, and extreme hedonism.[4] *Solipsism* is another attribute of this extreme narcissism—seeing the world with oneself as the lens.[5] It may also manifest itself as a delusional disorder[6]—"facts" personally constructed and highly variable.

The DSM describes narcissistic personality disorder as "a pervasive pattern of grandiosity (in fantasy or behavior), need for admiration, and lack of empathy" and identifies nine characteristics: (1) "grandiose sense of self-importance"; (2) preoccupation "with fantasies of unlimited success, power [and] brilliance...."; (3) belief that one is "special"; (4) requiring "excessive admiration"; (5) "a sense of entitlement," thus demanding "favorable treatment or automatic compliance with his or her expectations"; (6) "interpersonally exploitative"—taking "advantage of others to achieve his or her ends"; (7) "lacks empathy" and "is unwilling to recognize or identify with the feelings or needs of others"; (8) "often envious of others or believes that others are envious of him or her"; and (9) "shows arrogant, haughty behaviors or attitudes."[7]

Playing to deeply held prejudices among many in his base of supporters, President Trump referred in his 2016 campaign to immigrants from

Mexico as "drug dealers, criminals, rapists." In office, he aggressively pursued his plan to build a wall to keep undocumented immigrants out. Separating children from their families and incarcerating immigrants within chain-link fences as their claims to asylum were processed were deliberate policy choices intended to deter or dissuade immigrants from coming to the border in the first place.[8]

The apparent lack of empathy for the plight of these people—a willingness to see them suffer in adverse conditions—underscores how personality matters in the crafting of policy, particularly when the personality at issue falls out of the normal range. Also indicative of a lack of empathy was the unilateral decision in October 2019 by President Trump to withdraw from northeastern Syria, abandoning an ally—the Kurds, who were instrumental in liberating territory from ISIS—without concern for their security in relation to invading Turkish and Russian armed forces.

To the President, the world is binary—composed of winners and losers, which is a perspective he apparently learned from his father who repeatedly put it that way. When deeply embedded in one's psyche as part of one's ontology, this zero-sum view (your gains are my losses and vice-versa) impacts profoundly both one's perceptions and how one deals with others. In this regard, the transactional, business, deal-making approach President Trump has celebrated[9] is one in which he seeks to extract the most from others engaged in negotiations—sometimes bullying them into submission. It is decidedly at odds with a conventional diplomacy in which the parties seek advantage but settle on an agreement in which the distribution of gains may be uneven or asymmetric. Dealing with allies or adversaries in this short-term, transactional way—bullying them both publicly and privately—is also a manifestation of how extreme narcissists deal with others.

Thus, ontology, perception, and personality bear directly on the interpretive understandings policymakers bring to the table. These are lenses through which both international and domestic structural and ideational factors pass into the psyche of those in authority, thus influencing their choices among alternative decisions and actions that might be taken.

Group dynamics are also part of the explanatory picture. The inter-subjective dimension of organizational processes and bureaucratic politics influence foreign policy outcomes. Conflicts among persons within the same or different organizations may be as dysfunctional as when all seem to agree in a "groupthink" mentality blind to what are, perhaps, more productive alternatives. A related dysfunction is "cognitive dissonance"—ignoring (or not even perceiving) facts inconsistent with what individuals or group members already "believe" to be the case.[10]

Given all of this complexity, then, our theoretical aim in this volume is rather modest—prediction only in terms of refining practical expectations while, at the same time, searching for better explanations of what we observe, however partial such understandings of foreign policy may be. It is also a *constructivist* effort,[11] thus taking into account the ideas and the subjective and inter-subjective processes by which rules, norms, and understandings of interest and capabilities take form in the minds of those who make foreign policy. Maybe it is enough for now to explore islands of partial or "middle-range" theory on foreign policy. As Ernst Haas (1924–2003) once put it, these theoretical "islands" are inherently non-additive, leaving us by default in a position at best of "creeping up" on the whole we are trying to explain.

## ENGAGEMENT, CONTAINMENT, AND USING FORCE

As noted in the preface, American foreign policy in practice takes one or more of three forms (or combinations of them): (1) constructive or peaceful engagement not only with "friendly" countries or other actors but also with adversaries; (2) containment, which includes essentially negative measures toward adversaries that fall short of going to war —deterrence, coercive diplomacy, punitive economic measures, and various forms of espionage or covert actions; and (3) the use of force through armed intervention or warfare. These are best understood as alternative *means* to achieving objectives not *ends* in themselves.[12] This set of choices—peaceful engagement, containment (negative measures short of going to war), and the use of force (armed intervention or various forms of warfare)—ranges across a spectrum from the most peaceful to the most hostile measures (see figure 2). The linkage between elite orientations and foreign policy actions is that orientations—relative preferences for peaceful engagement and diplomacy, containment, and armed intervention—influence directly how these policy makers position themselves when dealing with adversaries.

### Figure 2. Spectrum of foreigh-policy options.

| Peaceful/Constructive Engagement | Containment-Negative Measures Short of War | Armed Intervention or Warfare |
|---|---|---|

Even when containment is core to American foreign policy toward particular countries, peaceful engagement with these adversaries still may be an option. During the Cold War efforts were made to reduce tensions between policymakers in Washington and Moscow through various forms of peaceful engagement that included on-going arms control negotiations. In the 1970s, American policymakers across several administrations also pursued a normalization process in relations with officials in Beijing, effectively adding peaceful engagement to the long-standing policy of containing China. By contrast, following the defeat of the Iraqi Army, forcing its withdrawal from Kuwait in 1991, peaceful engagement with the Iraqi regime under Saddam Hussein was never really part of the mix; instead, for the following decade, American officials and their British counterparts opted for a combination of both containment and armed intervention.

Such policymaking takes place in what decisionmakers generally see as an increasingly complex world in which people find themselves. Although global society lacks central or superordinate authority, there still is order to be found in what is essentially an anarchic world. We find this order in ideas, rules, or norms of conduct that decisionmakers in both state and non-state actors customarily follow as well as in the associations they form among themselves.

The agents who speak authoritatively in the name of states that have been constructed in this anarchic global society still claim the rights of states as *sovereign* entities both to exercise complete jurisdiction in domestic matters and to be independent in the way they conduct their foreign affairs. Like them or not, states or, more precisely, the policymakers or their agents—decisionmakers who decide and act in their name—are still the principal actors in international politics.

To explain the making and implementation of American foreign policy at the "unit" or state level, then, we need not stray too far from the consciousness of decisionmakers as they relate to others around them in the country as a whole and abroad—the world outside the territorial confines of the United States. Ideas are shared directly, even globally. Policymakers come to know what is happening in the world subjectively by themselves and inter-subjectively through exchanges with others, whether they happen to be in the same room or tens of thousands of miles away—communications that nowadays can occur instantaneously no matter where individuals may be.

The anarchic world in which policymakers are immersed not only provides them with opportunities but also is the source of the threats they perceive. As countries pursue opportunities, of course, actions taken for these purposes can be threatening to others. Threats made to others can reverberate as threats of one kind or another are received in return.

The security dilemma that policymakers confront is that when they put more resources into the security sector, others—their counterparts in adversarial countries—likely will respond in kind, thus reversing any relative security gains and perhaps even undermining the security they originally had.[13] To avoid a threat, counter-threat spiral of conflict, decisionmakers may decide not to pursue a certain course of action or, alternatively, try to find a common ground or compromise that takes the interests of all relevant players into account. By contrast, unilateral actions taken in disregard of these external actors can lead others to try to find a diplomatic remedy, impose costs of one kind or another, or block actions through coercion or the use of force.

The attention throughout this volume, then, is not so much on states as abstract entities, but rather upon the decision or policymakers themselves as agents of the states they represent. To explain the making and implementation of American foreign policy, we search for the root cause or causes in the subjectivities of individuals and the inter-subjective exchanges among them in both the policymaking groups to which they belong and the associations they have with counterparts and others abroad.

In our search for explanation we find not surprisingly that what matters are the understandings held by policymakers about domestic and world politics in general and how they play in particular contingencies. Although precise or point predictions are elusive, deeper understandings of how policymakers tend to operate in the processes of making and implementing foreign policy can lead to greater accuracy in the expectations we develop for what may happen. Our search leads us to look inside the heads of those who make foreign policy. If only we readily could do so! Alas, in most circumstances we will have to be content empirically with indirect indicators and measures of what leads decisionmakers to the choices they make.

We miss quite a lot when we speak only about material or ideational factors—interests and the distribution of power or norms as exogenous global factors that lie somehow outside of human space. Domestic interests are also problematic when we cast them abstractly as external to the decisionmakers and somehow discoverable by anyone of "right" mind—the rational-actor model.

The making and implementation of foreign policy remains a very human, voluntarist enterprise at the individual and small-group levels of analysis. The theoretical challenge is how we connect material, ideational, and other factors seemingly "out there" to the decisionmakers who incorporate them as part of their decisionmaking calculus "in here." Interests, norms, and the distribution of power in an anarchic world—one lacking central authority over states and their policymakers—take on meaning when they are incorporated as part of the understandings policymakers take to the decisions they make or implement. Our focus, then, is not on exogenous, abstract factors, as if somehow they are external forces operating on their own in a world of their own making. No, internalized considerations of power and interest along with other ideas are the motive forces that facilitate or constrain the decisions and actions of policymakers.

Policymakers seem always to face tension between the material and the ideational—power and interest, on the one hand, and the ideas or ideals they wish to advance, on the other.[14] It is as unrealistic to think that power and material interests are the only things that matter as it is utopian to think that ideals alone can drive politics and policy choice. How, then, do decisionmakers ground in interests the ideas or objectives they wish to advance, using the capabilities they have in efforts to achieve these ends? The answer to this theoretical challenge lies not "out there," but rather "in here"—within and among the decisionmakers themselves.

## POLICY ELITES: IDEAS GROUNDED IN INTERESTS AS MOTIVE FORCES

In the ideas they form—usually in relationships with others—and the exchanges they have with one another are forged the consensus that also defines a particular policy elite. The consensus is not just on the issues of the day but also on the underlying shared meanings, understandings, and interests that connect them with others as fellow "travelers" making their way through the complexities of the policy-making world.

Personal connections matter. Indeed, it is their personal networks that not only link individuals within particular policy elites but also connect them with those in other policy elites in cross-cutting alliances or coalitions that form and sustain relationships. In some instances these networks dissolve over differences or changed circumstances that no longer give substantive grounds for them to coalesce.

Ideas in one or another of these policy elites are not static, of course. Nor are the individuals we count in a particular policy elite necessarily permanent party. Human beings learn, adapt, and even alter their under-standings that directly affect the positions they hold, decisions they make, and actions they take. People come and go, but some also stay—truly committed members of a particular policy elite and what its members advocate. This commitment is particularly strong, of course, when the ideas advanced are grounded in interests—not just standing alone in the abstract. It is when ideas are grounded in interests[15] that they cease to be "out there" but instead become humanized by the identity people establish with them.

Integral to explanation of foreign policy, then, are the understandings that decisionmakers hold and that typically are shared in the policy elites of which they are a part or with which they identify. We look to the ideas, shared meanings, and norms accepted in particular by individuals in leadership positions and positions of influence at particular points in time. Material and ideational factors—the American position in the global distribution of power and both domestic and international norms—matter to the extent that policymakers take their understandings of them into account and use them as guides to decisions and actions, exploring the art of the possible.

The term policy *elite* is truly variable. We not only see significant vari-ation among policy elites in different places and at different points in time as they circulate in and out of power but also observe changes that occur in a particular policy elite as identities shift and its "members" come and go. When policy elites can be identified with a particular area of expertise, we can refer to them as knowledge-based, epistemic communities.[16] The specialists who constitute these epistemic communities are typically attentive publics[17] for at least the issues that concern them most, but they also may enter policy-elite ranks on matters relating to their expertise.

Attentive publics are consumers of information who rely on personal contacts and the mass communications media, Internet, social networks, and the "blogosphere" as their sources. Although all members of attentive publics are consumers, many are also producers of information—making their views known through mass communications, publication, or personal contacts and on-line social networks, perhaps also making direct inputs to policymakers. Policy elites in positions of power (or influencing those who are) emerge from the attentive publics of which they still remain a part. To become part of policy elites, members of attentive publics draw on the personal connections or networks that link individuals.

The complex communications and interpersonal networks that link members of policy elites with each other are also the mechanism for exchanges that occur between one policy elite and another. The subjective takes or understandings by members of one or another of these policy elites vary substantially. The contrast between policy positions advocated by liberal internationalists and militant internationalists is quite striking. The former are more prone to constructive engagement policies even with adversaries. The latter, meanwhile, tend to limit such engagement to "friendly" countries, preferring military strength and global presence in policies toward adversaries that are rooted in one form or another of containment or armed intervention. Between the two are the conservative internationalists who, if they have a choice, prefer containment to armed intervention and are far less skeptical about the gains to be had from diplomacy than the decidedly more "hawkish" militant internationalists.

## Figure 3. Spectrum of foreign-policy-elite orientations.

| Liberal Internationalist | Classical-Realist or Conservative Internationalist | Neoconservative Internationalist | Nationalist / Isolationist |
| --- | --- | --- | --- |

## LIBERAL INTERNATIONALISM

The worldview shared by members of a policy elite does influence the foreign-policy positions its members adopt and the choices they make. At one end of the spectrum depicted in figure 3 are the more "dovish" *liberal internationalists*, who generally prefer peaceful engagement, often coupling such policies to containment of adversaries. Their agendas typically include advancing human rights and human security, socioeconomic welfare, and other liberal values as ends worthy in themselves not just for the United States but also for the world as a whole. To them, although adversaries may need to be contained while on-going efforts are made to reach out and engage them constructively, armed intervention or warfare is reserved more as a last-resort option employed only when more pacific measures seem insufficient to achieve objectives at hand.

If one is to choose an iconic label, *liberal internationalism* is essentially Wilsonian. Driven by what he saw as necessity, Woodrow Wilson brought the country into World War I, but he did not abandon liberal-internationalist commitments. Indeed, in the war's aftermath he used the opportunity to continue multilateral efforts and constructed a new international organization—the League of Nations—to advance the rule of law internationally.

A Republican-led Senate blocked Wilson's vision, choosing not to ratify the League of Nations Covenant. Liberal internationalism receded further in the inter-war period (1919–1939), which was marked by nationalist, more isolationist sentiments. Its revival became clear in policies advanced by Franklin Roosevelt, who normalized relations with the Soviet Union and promoted an anti-interventionist "Good Neighbor" policy toward Latin American countries (1933).

In the depths of the Great Depression the president took a more nationalist, short-term position on policies intended to promote American exports and dampen domestic demand for foreign products. Nevertheless, Roosevelt's deeper commitments to liberal internationalism became apparent as he began bringing the US out of isolation after the outbreak of World War II (1939). The Lend-Lease agreement designed to help the British war effort against Germany (1940), the US-UK Atlantic Charter, and his "Four Freedoms" speech (both in 1941) are all indicative of this shift.

Even in the midst of war, plans were put in place to construct a new post-war order based not just on the rule of law and the institutionalized multilateralism one finds in international organizations preferred by liberal internationalists but also compatible with conservative-internationalist understandings of the role that national power and balance-of-power policies can play in providing and maintaining international security.

## CONSERVATIVE INTERNATIONALISM

"Conservative" internationalists typically are willing to try constructive- or peaceful-engagement policies that rely heavily upon diplomacy with adversaries but tend to be more skeptical about the efficacy of diplomatic efforts in any way disconnected from such power considerations as the threat or use of force. To them, adversaries are more prone to be influenced by *containment* policies and, if necessary, armed intervention or warfare. Members of policy elites holding this conservative position tend to accept the world as they see it and are likely to distrust schemes designed to change the order or value systems in the world "out there," often seeing and portraying liberal internationalists as perhaps well-intentioned but utopian—divorced from reality.

Conservative internationalism is a worldview or realist orientation we can identify iconically with Theodore Roosevelt's classic representation of US foreign policy as speaking softly while carrying a big stick.[18] At the same time, however, the president was not hostile to peaceful engagement, speaking eloquently from time to time about what could be gained from extending the reach of international adjudication of disputes and other international institutions committed to extending cooperative relations and the rule of law.

Until the George W. Bush presidency that took office in 2001, foreign-policy elites in power positions during the post-World War II period tended to be drawn primarily from either liberal-internationalist or conservative-internationalist ranks in both political parties, the former more prevalent in Democratic and the latter in Republican administrations.

## "NEOCONSERVATIVE" OR MILITANT INTERNATIONALISM

We find in the George W. Bush administration, however, a departure from conservative internationalism—the ascendancy to power of a neoconservative, more militant hybrid that drew from both nationalist, US-first, and liberal-internationalist commitments to advancing democratic and other liberal values, sometimes combining the threat or use of force to advance an otherwise liberal but always American-focused agenda.

To neoconservatives, advancing liberal or democratic ideas in the Middle East and elsewhere was an ideational component fully compatible with the simultaneous pursuit of security and other more materially oriented interests. This combination of using force while, at the same time, trying to advance liberal ideas defined the neoconservative position in favor of military intervention as the means to effect Iraqi regime change in 2003.

Elites in liberal-internationalist circles were appalled. Portraying neoconservatives as using liberal values as a cover for more power-oriented purposes, they were deeply skeptical of alleged attempts to advance democratic values through the use of force. Although in popular discourse many referred to President Bush's policies as neo-Wilsonian, many liberal internationalists objected strenuously to labeling such policies as in any way "Wilsonian," much less "liberal."

World War I may have been intended as the "war to end all wars" and to make the world "safe for democracy," as Woodrow Wilson claimed, but President Wilson did not start World War I to advance democracy. The US did not send troops to Europe until late in the war and only then when doing so was seen by Wilson and his administration as an imperative in the national interest.

For those in attentive publics listening closely, the George W. Bush administration's advocacy of armed intervention in Iraq in 2003 was a not-so-distant echo of earlier neoconservative calls in 1991 not to be weak-kneed but rather to go beyond merely liberating Kuwait and to use the opportunity to push the war all the way to Baghdad. Exercising this more hawkish option clearly exceeded the agreed multilateral goal of liberating Kuwait from Iraqi aggression, an extension rebuffed at the time by policy elites in the George H. W. Bush administration (to include his National Security Adviser Brent Scowcroft) who identified themselves more with classical-realist or conservative-internationalist understandings.

After all, through conservative-internationalist, balance-of-power lenses, either going unilaterally beyond agreed coalition objectives in 1991 or initiating armed intervention in Iraq in 2003 could destabilize the regional balance and unleash forces adverse to US interests. Thus, many conservative internationalists objected to what they understood as unnecessary risks the more militant neoconservatives seemed so willing to take without first having exhausted other, seemingly less dangerous remedies. Notwithstanding these clear differences among them in their foreign policy positions, liberals, conservatives, and neoconservatives did exhibit an internationalism or internationalist focus they all share

—one not found among elites favoring a strictly nationalist or, in the extreme, an isolationist orientation toward world politics.

## NATIONALISM AND POPULIST MOVEMENTS

The nationalist perspective is deeply rooted in the American experience. It was by no means an invention of the Trump administration. George Washington's address, drafted for him with substantial inputs by James Madison and Alexander Hamilton, made clear that the new republic should avoid foreign—mainly European—entanglements. Although in the nineteenth century the United States became fully engaged in Latin America (advancing its commercial interests and political values to some 20 republics carved out of the Spanish and Portuguese colonial empires), Washington's advisory defined foreign policy vis-à-vis the rest of Europe until entry into World War I (1917). The post-war years were marked by a nationalist withdrawal from European affairs until entry into World War II (1941).

The US also promoted its commercial interests in Japan and China during the late-nineteenth century, victory in its war with Spain (1898) giving American territorial control over not just Cuba and Puerto Rico in the Caribbean but also extended to the Philippines—the Hawaiian and other islands added to enhance US naval power projection across the Pacific. An "America First" policy for advancing commercial interests while avoiding foreign entanglements in Europe was the order of the day.

Nationalist policies then and now have rested on a populist foundation— the view from the countryside consistently less prone to engage the world "out there" than those in urban, more cosmopolitan settings. The success of Washington in the revolution against Britain depended upon a rural support base for the insurgency, particularly since Britain controlled the cities. Although a majority in the colonies at the time favored the *status quo* and opposed the campaign against British authority, the insurgents led by Washington depended upon a populist support base in the countryside for the success he and his followers finally achieved.

Populism in the late-nineteenth century took the form of a left-oriented movement advanced famously by such leaders as Nebraska populist William Jennings Bryan. To Bryan, maintaining the gold standard—tight money—served the interests of the owners and managers of capital (what I call the OMC) but was adverse to agricultural interests in the rural areas Bryan represented.

Rural discontent stemmed economically from government-imposed tariffs on non-agricultural goods that kept prices artificially high while their agricultural commodities traded in a free-market competition particularly subject to downward pressures on price. Moreover, railroad, telephone and telegraph, oil, and other industrial monopolies were by Supreme Court ruling legal *persons* with due process protections of the 14th amendment.

Notwithstanding this claim that inhibited their regulation by government, post-Civil War agricultural groups challenged the dominant positions held by monopolies. The Granger movement in the 1870s (later the "Alliance," another farmer organization) and other labor groups lobbied against monopolies that kept prices of their goods and services artificially high—a steep challenge particularly to cash-poor farmers. One outcome of this populist movement was the Sherman Antitrust Act (1890) that outlawed conspiracies in restraint of trade in interstate commerce. It would not be until the progressive, "trust-busting" Republican administration of Theodore Roosevelt (1901–09), however, that the Act was used to break up monopolies.

Rural groups from different parts of the country came together in 1891 in the first people's or Populist Party national convention. Their nationalist focus was on domestic prosperity that appealed to their rural, agricultural base. Among other things, they complained about the "money changers of Wall Street" (the OMC) and sought to replace gold as monetary standard with free coinage of the more abundant silver valued in a 16:1 ratio with gold.

Populists favored bimetallism (both silver and gold) as monetary standard—silver in greater supply, thus allowing for a more expansive money supply beneficial to labor interests. Not surprisingly, the OMC of the day saw growing the money supply in this way as inflationary and thus contrary to their capital-owning interests. Populism remained essentially a rural, nationalist movement notwithstanding efforts to accommodate urban worker interests in a party agenda that called for an eight-hour workday, limits on immigration that otherwise would drive wages down, and an end to strikebreaking tactics used by the OMC against labor interests.

For the rural constituency were proposals to ease borrowing by farmers, restricting use of public lands to settlers and away from urban and other speculators, "fair and liberal pensions" for military veterans, a graduated income tax and, on a more socialist turn, government ownership—confiscation "in the interest of the people" of railroad, telegraph, and telephone interests. Direct election of US senators rather than their selection by state legislators would bring power to the people.[19]

On the urban-rural (OMC-agricultural) divide, Bryan put it this way: "You shall not press down upon the brow of labor this crown of thorns, you shall not crucify mankind upon a cross of gold." Bryan delivered this historically famous "Cross of Gold" speech in Chicago to the Democratic Party's national convention on July 9, 1896—symbolically a high point for the left-oriented populism of his time. Bryan, the Democratic nominee, lost the election to Republican William McKinley who kept the country on the gold standard.

The populist agenda continued to be a substantial influence in twentieth-century American politics, particularly in the Theodore and Franklin Roosevelt and Truman administrations that saw substantial gains for both agricultural and labor interests. Trust busting, farm subsidies, the right of labor to bargain collectively for wages and other benefits, progressive income taxes intended to reduce inequality, social security, and conservation—the protection of national parks and other public lands from unregulated development—were among their progressive, essentially populist achievements. As president (1963–69), Lyndon Johnson—a Franklin Roosevelt "New Deal" southern Democrat—carried the progressive legacy forward through Medicare and Medicaid legislation.

On the nationalist side, however, the Smoot-Hawley tariff legislation (1930) in the Republican Herbert Hoover administration, coupled with Democratic Franklin Roosevelt's 69.3 percent devaluation of the dollar in 1934 (changing the exchange rate from $20.67 to $35 per ounce of gold) were intended to serve agricultural, labor,and OMC interests in the Great Depression—a decidedly nationalist, "America First" position. In fact, tariffs and competitive devaluation designed to dampen imports and promote exports vis-à-vis other countries resulted in an extraordinary reduction of world trade that did not benefit OMC, labor, or agricultural interests.

It was also a nationalist period of relative isolation from world affairs. Woodrow Wilson's liberal internationalism was repudiated. Citing the Washington advisory to avoid foreign entanglements, isolation was the order of the day—particularly toward European countries. This continued through the Republican Harding, Coolidge, and Hoover years (1921–31) and into the Democratic Roosevelt administration.

Although Roosevelt and British Prime Minister Churchill forged the liberal-internationalist vision in the bilateral Atlantic Charter and the conservative-internationalist, military-assistance Lend-Lease agreement in 1940, it would take the Japanese attack on Pearl Harbor on December 7, 1941 to bring the country into its World War II great power alliance with the UK, Soviet Union, France, and China. Preparations for a post-war order made during the war, the United Nations and its system of international organizations was the landmark achievement of what had become a decidedly internationalist Roosevelt administration. From Roosevelt to Obama, internationalism had become the new constant in American foreign policy—whether in its liberal, conservative, or neoconservative, more militant variants.

Both in his campaign and in office, President Trump embraced a nationalist position even as his national security advisers and secretaries of state and defense tended to remain wedded to internationalism, whether of conservative or militant orientation. The president's rise to power was facilitated by a recurrence of populist sentiment, a right-oriented political movement. As in the nineteenth century, this populism has a decidedly southern, mid-western, and predominantly rural base. Workers in so-called "rust-belt" states that have lost industries and the jobs that went with them have also been receptive to populist appeals led by Donald Trump. Feeling left behind by an increasingly technological society in which traditional, labor-intensive agricultural, industrial, and mining jobs are increasingly scarce (and underpaid), they have gravitated to the right —responsive to "America First" and "Make America Great Again" appeals.

To them, internationalist promotion of increasing globalization advances capital but not labor interests. Although twenty-first century circumstances are different, the conflict between capital and labor is a common populist thread. As rural areas fall behind the cities in this newly globalized world, their discontent is palpable. Populists in the nineteenth century, then as now, whether politically left or right, have contended that the US should be concerned primarily with jobs and other domestic matters—not the world "out there." The convergence of populism and nationalism is nothing new, deeply rooted as it is in the American experience.

## POLICY ELITES, ATTENTIVE PUBLICS AND DIVERSE INTERPRETIVE UNDERSTANDINGS

The policy elites that come to power or hold positions in government have obvious salience, but we also have to take account of their influence when out of power, whether confronting elite counterparts in power or operating more quietly behind the scenes. The history of American foreign policy is filled with examples of members of policy elites advocating positions and forming coalitions and counter-coalitions with others to influence policy outcomes. Some succeed. Others fail. Sometimes they are successful even after an extended period of failing to chart the overall direction or course policy takes, their tenacity or patience finally rewarded.

Members of policy elites also cultivate and find support from the attentive publics of which they are a part—those who have or take the time to study the issues of the day, observing closely the work of policy elites and the actions they take. Although some may move from being part of one or another attentive public into a policy elite, most do not. They are content to pay attention to what they see happening, often sharing the perspective commonplace within the consensus that defines a particular policy elite or, perhaps, standing in critical scrutiny of it. A policy elite identified with a liberal-internationalist perspective may find support from attentive publics of similar mindset, much as a conservative or neoconservative policy elite will have its own support base among attentive publics sharing their orientations.

In addition to less formal, ad hoc meetings that occur from time to time, policy elites communicate or aggregate within or among particular governmental or nongovernmental organizations to which they belong or at attendance-restricted conferences or gatherings to which they are invited. I define policy elites as either making policy while in power or seeking to influence it when out of power. As a practical matter, of course, the line distinguishing policy elites from others in attentive publics is often a very thin one with considerable movement back and forth between the two. Indeed, Washington is replete with centers and institutes that bring policy elites together with attentive publics that include scholars who conduct policy-oriented research often from a particular point of view consistent with the organization's overall orientation.

Internationalists of all stripes usually are quite comfortable engaging peacefully with allies, coalition partners, or other "friendly" parties in official state-to-state contacts or in international organizations as well as in the full range of private-sector commercial and other contacts that link non-state actors within and across societies. What concerns us here, however, is how different internationalist policy elites prefer to deal with present or potential adversaries—a multiple choice of overlapping options that varies in application from country to country. Combining the spectrum of options in figure 2 with internationalist policy-elite orientations in figure 3, table 1 provides us with a way to anticipate in general terms the course policy elites in positions of power or influence may take toward present or potential adversaries.

Changing circumstances in the world around them force policymakers to grapple with their understandings of threats, opportunities, and interests as they make choices or modify their decisions. These choices are moderated by the understandings of contending elites even within the same administration. In the first rounds of a bureaucratic battle on the Potomac during the lead-up to the Iraq War (2003), the conservative internationalism of Secretary of State Colin Powell and his supporters lost out to a neoconservative, more militant coalition led by Vice President Richard Cheney and Secretary of Defense Donald Rumsfeld. National Security Adviser Condoleezza Rice navigated between the two camps.

Even with battles won, the bureaucratic "war" was not over as contending elites continued to vie for the president's ear. In the first two years following the 2004 election, neoconservatives who had been dominant in the first years of the Bush administration gradually were supplanted in and around power positions by those of a more conservative-internationalist persuasion, including Condoleezza Rice who became the new Secretary of State. Although the vice president still had the president's ear, his personal influence appeared more muted in the last years of the administration. Given these shifts, the skepticism concerning negotiations with adversaries early in the administration yielded over time to attempts to engage, particularly in the Middle East, whether dealing with Iran or other trouble spots in the region.

**Table 1. Practical expectations and courses of action for different policy elites.**

| | BROAD, OVERLAPPING OPTIONS FOR DEALING WITH ADVERSARIES | | |
|---|---|---|---|
| **POLICY ORIENTATION** | **PEACEFUL ENGAGEMENT** | **CONTAINMENT** | **ARMED INTERVENTION** |
| LIBERAL INTERNATIONALIST | center of gravity: preferred option | will seek to contain adversaries while also engaging them | willing to invade or intervene militarily as a last resort |
| CONSERVATIVE INTERNATIONALIST | will engage with adversaries when expectations of net gains from doing so are clear or seem particularly likely and thus warrant doing so | center of gravity: preferred option | willing to invade or intervene militarily, but likely to revert to containment sooner rather than later |
| NEOCONSERVATIVE OR MORE MILITANT INTERNATIONALISM | highly skeptical of any net gains to be realized through engagement diplomacy, much less arms control | center of gravity: straddles containment and armed intervention options—will contain, but most willing to intervene militarily when expectations of net gains are clear and thus warrant doing so | |

Decisionmaking contexts, then, are often very dynamic. Not only do understandings of circumstances change but also the players and the policy elites of which they are a part may shift within the same administration. Nevertheless, we still have a degree of predictability, assuming we can gauge accurately both what policymaker and policy-elite orientations are (or the courses of action they generally prefer) that are captured in our nationalist and liberal-, conservative-, and neoconservative- or militant-internationalist categorizations. Knowing the positions of power or influence members of policy elites have or likely will hold gives us a predictive handle we can use to anticipate how they likely will relate to adversaries in particular contingencies or, more generally, as part of the broader foreign policy they formulate.

Most dramatic in this regard were the shifts in policy-elite orientations that occurred beginning in 2001 between liberal internationalists in the Clinton–Gore administration and neoconservatives coming to power in the first Bush–Cheney administration (2001–2005) and the shift to conservative internationalists in the second (2005–2009). The Obama administration reverted to liberal internationalism when it came into office (2009). Following that in 2017 the Trump administration moved to a nationalist, "America-First" position that clearly marked a significant departure from the internationalism of all of his post-World War II predecessors. When policy elites in or near power positions shift as sharply as they did in this period, we also observe substantial changes in policy that follow.

In the internationalist post-World War II period, echoes of earlier nationalist sentiments were heard from time to time, particularly during presidential elections. Some questioned why the United States should be the world's "policeman"—a role that often meant committing US troops to foreign wars. Nationalists (often referred to as "nativists") also tended to be anti-immigrant. On trade and capital flows, they often were more protectionist. The advent of the Trump administration built on these themes—questioning alliances, withdrawing from diplomatic agreements, imposing tariffs, seeking to close borders and limit immigration.

In earlier decades policy changed, if not to the same degree, when the liberal internationalism of President Jimmy Carter gave way to the conservative-international presidencies of Ronald Reagan and George H. W. Bush. Even then, the more strident rhetoric and confrontational policy toward adversaries of the early Reagan years gave way over time to engagement with the Soviet Union and Warsaw Pact countries on arms control and other initiatives.

During the George H. W. Bush presidency (1989–93), these efforts finally culminated in the end of the Cold War, breakup of the Warsaw Pact, and dissolution of the Soviet Union! After the liberal-internationalist Clinton years (1993–2001), neoconservatives in the George W. Bush administration (2001–2009) identified themselves with and sought to revive what they saw as the essence of a "Reaganite" foreign policy premised on the supremacy of US national power—a successful challenge in their view to the Soviet "evil empire"—buttressed by a strong national economy and accompanied by commitment to robust strategic defenses to complement nuclear and conventional military forces.

Winning the November 2008 election and bent on restoring public perceptions abroad—engaging not just with friendly countries but also with adversaries—President Barack Obama and other members of his administration quickly repudiated torture and other "harsh interrogation" techniques at the Guantánamo base in Cuba, Abu Ghraib in Iraq, Bagram in Afghanistan, and other secret prisons on the "dark side" (Vice President Cheney's reference). In breaking sharply with the previous administration and adopting constructive or peaceful engagement combined with containment as its first-line approach toward present or potential adversaries, the new administration underscored its renewed commitment to multilateralism.

The pursuit of arms control and other cooperative-security agendas that, for the most part, had been set aside by the Bush administration now had a new lease on life. At the same time, of course, the new Obama foreign-policy team, which included Secretary of State Hillary Clinton, still had to balance their understandings of intelligence and other national-security requirements with moral and legal constraints they felt had not been accorded proper emphasis by their predecessors.

## CONNECTING POLICY ELITES, ATTENTIVE PUBLICS, AND THE GENERAL PUBLIC

Mass communications—both print and electronic media—connect policy elites with their respective attentive publics and with the general public. The Internet, on-line social networks, e-mail, text messaging, and "Skype" live audio and video transmissions personalize, expand, and facilitate efforts by policy elites that also rely on television and radio, newspapers, published articles and books, and special mailings.

Selective-membership groups such as the Council on Foreign Relations in New York, the Chicago Council on International Affairs, the Atlantic Council, and the Pacific Council on International Policy in Los Angeles recruit from among both policy elites and attentive publics, providing both actual and virtual meeting places for their members. American Committees on Foreign Relations (ACFR) and World Affairs Councils in cities across the United States recruit from attentive publics, providing them with limited access to members of policy elites and others whom they invite as speakers or participants in panels and workshops or connect by Skype or teleconference links.

Academics who participate as part of attentive publics on foreign-policy matters may be drawn into any of these organizations, but they also participate in meetings of such professional organizations as the International Studies and American Political Science associations or their organized sections dealing with international politics, foreign policy, or national and international security. On the latter, organizations like the International Institute for Strategic Studies (IISS) operate both globally and nationally, bringing policymakers and policy-oriented scholars together in meetings and through widely distributed print and electronic publications.

By contrast, the general public lacks even this limited degree of connectivity to foreign-policymaking elites that members of attentive publics enjoy. In part this is due to a generalized preference to leave foreign policy to the experts—a tendency one also finds in other countries. Terrorism, foreign wars, or economic challenges that stem from abroad may capture the public's interest for a while, but for the most part public attention, if on foreign policy at all, tends to be short-lived.

Given elimination in 1987 of the Federal Communications Commission's fairness doctrine, the television and radio networks are not legally required to present balanced treatment on the issues of the day. Public Broadcasting (PBS) and National Public Radio (NPR) explicitly do seek to present multiple sides of the issues they cover. Although major commercial networks (ABC, NBC, and CBS) also seek balanced, more centrist treatment of the news of the day, cable networks like Fox position themselves on the right, MSNBC on the left, CNN somewhere in between.

The president and other officials express their views on Twitter feeds followed by millions. Facebook and other electronic sources provide additional means for the exchange of views. Many manipulate these platforms presenting one-sided, often factually incorrect arguments. The proliferation of television, radio, and social networks has allowed people a high degree of selectivity—many watching, listening, or engaging only with those sharing their own views. If not hermetically sealed, these separate compartments or "silos" ("echo chambers") contribute to the polarization of the general public. Facts compete with "alternative facts" in this milieu that focuses on opinions that often lack either evidentiary support or analytical validity.

Because of their greater importance to the average citizen, the politics of domestic issues generally occupy a more prominent place in their lives, although for a variety of reasons many do not participate at all even in these political processes. Contacting representatives, joining groups, writing letters to the editor, sending email messages, tweeting, or posting blogs are activities left to others. They may doubt the efficacy of their involvement—the difference they can make—in domestic (much less foreign-policy) issues, the complexity of which can be bewildering. Besides, daily personal concerns may matter more than political participation to any meaningful degree. Even voting may be too much of a chore, hence the relatively low turnouts we observe in most elections. Relatively high voter turnouts (60% or more of the electorate) tend only to occur when the stakes people see themselves having in the outcome or commitments to particular candidates or causes as being especially strong.

It is from the general public, of course, that attentive publics are drawn. Interest and formal or self-education in international affairs are the ingredients that produce attentive publics on foreign-policy matters. In turn, some of the people in these attentive publics may gravitate to policy-elite circles. Although foreign policy thus remains primarily the preserve of policy elites and those who follow them in attentive publics, the general public does matter as a source of support for presidents and their administrations—policy elites in power—that have the primary responsibility for making and implementing American foreign policy.

## NOTES

1.  Richard C. Snyder, H.W. Bruck, and Burton Sapin, *Foreign Policy Decisionmaking* (New York: Free Press of Glencoe, 1962).
2.  A reader-friendly, abbreviated version (just under 400 pages) of the DSM is readily available. See American Psychiatric Association, *Desk Reference to the Diagnostic Criteria from DSM-5* (Washington, DC: American Psychiatric Publishing, 2013).
3.  More precisely, *malignant narcissism* is a term used in psychiatry to specify an extreme (or pathological) form of this disorder that is beyond (rather than within) normal limits. Bandy Lee, M.D. (ed.), *The Dangerous Case of Donald Trump: 27 Psychiatrists and Mental Health Experts Assess a President* (New York: St. Martin's Press, 2017). Psychiatrists and psychologists are usually loath to diagnose personality disorders outside of the doctor-patient or counselor-patient clinical setting. On the other hand, contributors to *The Dangerous Case of Donald Trump* reasoned that Donald Trump's public display of behavior over decades provided a sufficient empirical basis for them to render their professional diagnoses.
4.  Ibid., pp. 44 and 94-95.
5.  Ibid., pp. 114-115.
6.  Ibid., pp. 102 and 110-112.
7.  See *Desk Reference to the Diagnostic Criteria from DSM-5*, op. cit., p. 327.
8.  The president was allegedly dissuaded by his advisers from pursuing even more extreme measures to include shooting migrants in the legs to slow them down, electrifying and putting spikes on the border wall, and building a water moat stocked with alligators or snakes. See Michael Shear and Julie Davis [*New York Times* journalists], *Border Wars: Inside Trump's Assault on Immigration* (New York: Simon & Schuster, 2019).
9.  Donald J. Trump and Tony Schwartz, *The Art of the Deal* (New York: Random House, 1987).
10. On *organization process* and *bureaucratic politics*, I refer to the work of Graham Allison among others, *groupthink* to Irving Janis and *cognitive dissonance* to Leon Festinger.
11. On constructivism, see Mark V. Kauppi and Paul R. Vioti, *International Relations Theory*, 6th ed. (Lanham, MD: Rowman and Littlefield, 2020), ch. 6.
12. I owe this means-ends distinction to a question raised by Justin Brakke.

13. John Herz , "Idealist Internationalism and the Security Dilemma," *World Politics*, Vol. 2, No. 2 (January 1950): 157-80.
14. E.H. Carr, *The Twenty Years' Crisis, 1919-39* (New York: Harper Torchbooks, 1940, 1964).
15. I owe this point to my mentor, Ernst Haas (1924-2003).
16. Peter M. Haas, *Knowledge, Power, and International Policy Coordination* (Columbia, SC: University of South Carolina Press, 1997).
17. Gabriel Almond, *The American People and Foreign Policy* (New York: Harcourt Brace, 1950).
18. On Wilsonian idealism vs. Rooseveltian realism, Henry Kissinger, *Diplomacy* (New York: Simon & Schuster, 1995), ch. 2.
19. Robert E. Riegel and David F. Long, *The American Story* (New York: McGraw-Hill, 1955), vol. 2, pp. 101-02.

# Part I

# Peaceful Engagement, Containment, and Armed Intervention

CHAPTER 2

# PEACEFULLY ENGAGING "FRIENDS" AND ADVERSARIES

We start with the story of US relations with the rising power of China beginning with President Richard Nixon's outreach in 1971 and 1972. Nixon departed from his customary position in his reassessment of China policy, reaching a very different conclusion on what the future direction of US policy toward the most populous country in the world should be. A self-styled realist, he could not have anticipated just how far peaceful engagement would take the two adversaries. His legacy of peaceful engagement remains a model for managing what have become competitive relations between the US and China, the world's largest and second-largest economies respectively.

Ronald Reagan, who shared Nixon's conservative internationalism and Republican credentials, later took a page from Nixon's constructive or peaceful-engagement book in his own outreach as president to his Soviet counterpart, Mikhail Gorbachev, the latter a proponent of greater openness (*glasnost*) and institutional reform or reorganization (*perestroika*) within the Soviet Union. Reagan's willingness to engage with Gorbachev, connecting with him in 1986 at a summit meeting in Reykjavik, Iceland, was consistent with his earlier support in 1971 as governor of California for Nixon's outreach to China. After overcoming his own doubts about the change in policy, he visited Taiwan on behalf of the Nixon administration to explain the policy change and reassure Chiang Kai-shek and other government leaders in Taipei of the continuing American commitment to Taiwan's security.

Reagan shared Nixon's understanding of American interest, informed as it was by the realist balance-of-power thinking they held in common. "Playing the China card" in the on-going "game" with the Soviet Union through peaceful engagement with both countries appealed to them as effective means to serve their understandings of American interest. Whether of conservative- or liberal-internationalist stripe, present-day policymakers find that, when coupled with containment, constructive or peaceful engagement has positive potential for advancing their understandings of US interest in dealing with adversarial regimes with which they have been at odds.

The enormous economic, diplomatic, military, and other capabilities the United States enjoys give it a particular advantage in playing the peaceful-engagement card, whether dealing with North Korea, Cuba, or Iran. The liberal-internationalist Obama administration had difficulty dealing with the regime in Pyongyang but made important gains in relations with Cuba (moving forward on normalization of relations) and Iran (negotiating a multilateral nuclear weapons-development arms control agreement). The nationalist Trump administration that took office in 2017 quickly reversed these gains by walking back US-Cuban trade and other agreements, withdrawing from the agreement with Iran and re-imposing sanctions on Tehran. Having relinquished American leadership, Russia, China, the UK, France, Germany and the EU remained in the Iran accord.

We take up here in greater detail one illustrative case: peaceful engagement with a Chinese adversary beginning in the 1970s that effectively cut through several decades of hostility. The long-established containment policy remained in place even as improved US–China relations became the new order of the day. Peaceful engagement was a positive complement that proved fully compatible with continuing pursuit of containment. The case exhibits the value added that may come from combining peaceful engagement with containment of adversaries. In time, sustained peaceful or constructive engagement has the potential (though by no means certainty) of transforming relations with adversaries to a more positive standing in which policymakers gradually rely less on containment and armed intervention as options.

In the US–China case that I explore, effective diplomacy was essential to starting and later sustaining the process leading to normalization of relations and subsequent expansion of economic, cultural, and other forms of peaceful engagement between the two countries. Although criticized roundly at the time, particularly by those on the right who saw the change in policy as a betrayal of long-standing commitments to Taiwan, it remains a remarkable success for Nixon and others in his administration who sought to serve their understandings of US interests through peaceful engagement with China.

The conservative-internationalist Ford and liberal-internationalist Carter administrations continued Nixon's normalization process. Embassies were established and ambassadors exchanged in 1979 during the Carter administration. Subsequent administrations managed relations with China in an effort to bring the PRC into the rule-based trade-and-investment order in which the US held a leading role. Admission to the World Trade Organization occurred in December 2001 during the George W. Bush administration.

The period was not without disputes with China for not respecting intellectual property rights and, on trade, to undervalue their currency to advantage their exports and reduce imports. Beijing was accused of pursuing mercantilist policies—accumulating capital from substantial trade surpluses—that also resulted in increased employment in China at the expense of American workers. At the same time, use of less-expensive labor by US firms producing in China and other Chinese-manufactured imports meant reduced prices in the American consumer market. Failure to correct these commercial disagreements led the "America-First" Trump administration to impose tariffs on Chinese exports in an effort to negotiate what Washington saw as more equitable trade relations.

On China's relations with Taiwan, the US sustained over the decades a policy of discouraging Beijing from any intent to invade Taiwan while, at the same time, encouraging Taipei not to provoke China unnecessarily. Balancing China's increasing naval strength with US Seventh Fleet, army, and air force assets in the region have remained central to the US containment policy. Nevertheless, Beijing has pursued an expansionist policy in the South China Sea, asserting its claims to disputed islands and enhancing its capacity to use these islands for naval and other military purposes.

We turn now to the origins of the shift in policy from containment to containment plus peaceful engagement.

## ADDING PEACEFUL ENGAGEMENT TO ADVERSARIAL RELATIONS WITH CHINA

The Sino-Soviet split that became apparent in the early 1960s was followed later in the decade by a territorial dispute and even armed conflict between the two countries along the Amur and Ussuri Rivers in eastern Siberia on the Chinese border. Toward the end of Richard Nixon's first term in office the Vietnam War was still underway under successors to revolutionary leader Ho Chi Minh, who died in September 1969, nine months after Nixon took office. Relations with the Soviet Union in the late 1960s and 1970s were marked by occasional periods of relaxed tensions or détente alternating with a return to heightened tensions.

In themselves these circumstances did not trigger changes in overall policy. It took realist, balance-of-power thinking on Nixon's part to consider playing what he saw as the China card.[1] Although a substantial departure from policy pursued over more than two decades, constructive or peaceful engagement with China was also consistent with efforts at the time to achieve this relaxation of tensions with the other US adversary, the Soviet Union.

Since coming into office in 1969 Nixon had continued pursuing arms control agreements with the Soviet Union that had been initiated in the Kennedy–Johnson years. On this separate US-Soviet peaceful-engagement track, a strategic arms limitation (SALT) agreement on offensive missiles and an anti-ballistic missile (ABM) treaty were signed in May 1972 just three months after Nixon's late-February visit to China. Given his balance-of-power lens, Nixon saw peaceful engagement as a means to develop relationships with policymakers in both countries, playing one off against the other as need be.

But these events and the balance-of-power rationale for them get us ahead of the US-China rapprochement story. I begin with the long struggle in China between communists and nationalists in the 1920s and the 1930s that was suspended during the common effort in World War II against the Japanese occupation of China. Fighting resumed after the war. Notwithstanding American efforts to prevent a communist takeover, Mao's victorious revolutionaries displaced US-backed nationalists under Chiang Kai-shek, who took refuge on Taiwan in 1949.

The government of the Republic of China in Taipei continued its post-1949 jurisdictional claim over all of China—a legal fiction that also served understandings of American interests then held by US policymakers. Taipei continued to represent China in all organs of the United Nations, including holding its position as a permanent member of the Security Council. Relations between the US and the Republic of China already institutionalized diplomatically with exchange of ambassadors and embassies in each other's countries, the parties agreed to a bilateral alliance with US forces under a Taiwan Defense Command as the military component that defined the *status quo*.

Soon after taking office, President Nixon shared his ideas on altering US-China relations with Henry Kissinger, then his national security adviser. An ardent anti-communist with an established record on the political right, Nixon saw himself as better able than others to make a 180-degree turnabout. People, he thought, might challenge his wisdom but not his patriotic commitment to his understanding of the American way. Change coming from the Republican right ironically was more feasible in his view than for a left-of-center Democratic president, who might have been accused of selling out not only Taiwan, but also US interests.

Under White House direction, US Ambassador to Poland, Walter Stoessel, and other officials from State established contact with their Chinese counterparts in January 1970 on prospects for a presidential visit to Beijing. Although China-trip planning stalled after the US invasion of Cambodia in May and June, the process was restarted in October through the good offices of Pakistani President Yahya Khan. Events moved slowly but in July 1971 Nixon sent Kissinger on a secret trip to Beijing via Pakistan to explore further the possibility of a presidential visit.

While visiting Pakistan, Kissinger reportedly took ill and was taken to a mountain retreat for needed rest—all a cover for his actual departure by air for China. The secret trip was on the heels of an April 1971 American ping-pong team visit to China accompanied by journalists, which officials in Beijing arranged during the team's scheduled visit to Japan. It was taken by officials in Washington as a signal of greater openness by officials in Beijing to the United States, an interpretation underscored by Premier Chou En-lai's personal acceptance of the "ping-pong" diplomats in the Great Hall of the People in Tiananmen Square.

Nixon and Kissinger (the latter initially reluctant to move out of the customary foreign-policy box vis-à-vis China) put in place the ground-work for an entirely new policy course. As carriers of the institutionalized consensus—that there is only one China and its legitimate government is in Taipei, the national capital—officials in the State, Defense, and other government departments and agencies were perplexed. Secretary of State

William Rogers and senior diplomats and staffs initially resisted White House efforts even to consider altering this *status quo*.

Learning this, Nixon cut State out of the process. It was relatively easy for him to do this, given his long-standing personal suspicions of bureaucracy in general, and the State Department in particular. Personal perspectives or bureaucratic prejudices do matter. Indeed, Nixon's lack of trust toward the State Department had been exhibited throughout his career, going back to the late 1940s, when he was a junior member of Congress on the House Un-American Activities Committee. Well before the McCarthy period, he had built his right-wing credentials with anti-communist rhetoric directed against his opponents in successful 1946 and 1948 election campaigns for the US House as well as against the high-ranking former State Department official Alger Hiss—accusing him of espionage. Predispositions internalized by policymakers do count, however idiosyncratic they may appear.

After initial contacts through diplomatic third parties in Poland and Pakistan, Nixon directed Kissinger to make his secret visit to Beijing. In July 1971 Kissinger met with the Chinese premier, Chou En-lai, to discuss what became a new policy of peaceful engagement. This was a major departure from the existing policy of trying to isolate China—all the while trying to deter and contain the exercise of any Chinese ambitions outside of the mainland. American commitment to Taiwan, including defense of these islands, became a central point of focus in Nixon's 1960 presidential campaign debate with then-Senator John F. Kennedy. Central to American policy was deterring attack on Taiwan or the islands just off shore from the Chinese mainland—Quemoy, Matsu, and the Pescadores.

To Nixon and Kissinger, however, containment through deterrence pursued on the one hand did not preclude peaceful engagement on the other. The secret conversations occurred even as both parties supported opposite sides in the war then still underway in Vietnam and elsewhere in Indochina. Mao Zedong and Chou En-lai saw important opportunities for China in exploring the possibilities of improving relations with the United States. Developing consensus across Chinese policy elites, however, could by no means be assumed.

It was indeed a period of great political turbulence in China, marked not only by the cultural revolution but also by the September 1971 death of Mao's chosen successor, Lin Biao, in a mysterious plane crash in Mongolia. Although the facts remain unclear, some speculated that the crash was due to sabotage, as Lin had been involved in serious anti-regime activity—coup plotting and an alleged attempt to assassinate Mao. Others saw Lin's demise as perpetrated by opponents in reaction to his leadership of the cultural revolution.

Not all senior party members were of the same mind on so radical a departure from the *status quo*. Some in Shanghai vehemently opposed these moves and allegedly attempted to derail preparations for the Nixon visit, giving American officials the cold shoulder in a follow-on trip led by Kissinger's deputy, General Alexander Haig. When notified about what was happening, Chou En-lai intervened personally and, apparently with Mao's concurrence, weighed in decisively to put preparations for the state visit back on track.

Nixon's visit finally took place in February 1972. Kissinger and others in the American delegation to China also understood the president's perspective on "playing the China card" in three-way relations between officials in Washington, Moscow, and Beijing. Keeping a wedge in place between China and the Soviet Union was understood by them to be advantageous to the United States. It was this internalized balance-of-power understanding that clearly motivated the president. Under-standings of American and Chinese interests led both sides to set aside commitments to their respective allies (Taiwan and North Vietnam) that might be compromised by their turn to peaceful engagement.

Albeit initially in secret, merely meeting with the communist Chinese was interpreted by Chiang Kai-shek's regime as a betrayal. Similarly, Mao and Chou faced understandable opposition by North Vietnamese officials then still at war with the United States. Making this somewhat easier for the Chinese, however, was the death of Ho Chi Minh in September 1969. Seen not as a personal betrayal of Ho, Chinese leaders finally agreed to a meeting in Beijing with Nixon, which set them at odds with Ho's successors in Hanoi. Leaders on both the American and Chinese sides obviously saw expected gains from talking as outweighing risks of compromising their relations respectively with Taiwan and North Vietnam.

During the state visit in February 1972, Nixon was received by Mao and Chou and negotiators on both sides went to work trying to find common ground, finally hammering out a joint "Shanghai Communiqué" that acknowledged "progress toward the normalization of relations between China and the United States" as being "in the interests of all countries." US officials affirmed the position that "there is but one China and that Taiwan is a part of China" and indicated their intention to withdraw forces from Taiwan.

In this agreed statement negotiated by Kissinger and his team, the US listed its bilateral defense alliances in East Asia, but omitted reference to its commitments to Taiwan. Secretary of State William Rogers, who had been deliberately left out of the negotiations, was livid. The American delegation was splitting apart. Whatever agreement had been reached was in jeopardy of becoming unglued when Nixon and his divided team finally returned to the United States, particularly given deep concerns by fellow Republicans distraught by the apparent betrayal of Taiwan.

It was at this point that Chou intervened to help patch up the Kissinger-Rogers divide. In an unprecedented visit to Rogers' personal quarters that broke conventional protocol, the Chinese premier thus honored the secretary, urging him to accept the compromise that negotiators had reached—eliminating all references to American alliances, thus not singling out Taiwan for silent treatment. It was a creative ploy by Chou: a head of government reaching out one level down directly to the secretary—in effect "stooping to conquer." It worked, and the way was clear for both sides to announce on February 28th their agreement on the terms of the Shanghai Communiqué, which set in motion a seven-year process of normalizing relations between the US and China.

The process leading to the Shanghai Communiqué was a model of the getting-to-yes formula.[2] The parties quickly got beyond arguing from positions, focusing instead on both substantive interests and professional relationships among the negotiators on both sides. They were willing to think outside the box, looking for creative approaches to problems or obstacles blocking their reaching agreement. Agreeing on criteria for carrying out any agreement was also part of the process—the US, for example, premising any withdrawal from Taiwan on the future security situation.

Following the Nixon visit, relations began with establishing liaison offices in Beijing and Washington in 1973. President Ford visited China in 1975, recommitting to full normalization of relations, but that would not occur until the Carter administration, when both sides finally agreed in January 1979 to establish embassies in their two capitals effective in March. The US ended official relations and, much to the dismay of conservatives in Congress, terminated the defense treaty with Taipei, which was challenged unsuccessfully in the Supreme Court case *Goldwater v. Carter*. The Taiwan Relations Act (1979), however, did provide for establishing an American Institute on Taiwan with unofficial, quasi-diplomatic functions in relation to the government in Taipei.

It was the kind of calculated ambiguity that made full engagement with China possible. As Beijing assumed the Chinese seat in the United Nations and other international organizations previously occupied by the government on Taiwan, officials across several administrations in Washington and Beijing cultivated economic, social, and cultural ties that extended well beyond the political realm. Even as these relations expanded dramatically in the decades that followed rapprochement, American policymakers did not abandon the containment policy toward China. Peaceful engagement was clearly a positive addition to this policy, which had relied almost exclusively on American naval and other military presence in the region.

US policymakers across succeeding presidential administrations from time to time found themselves in the middle of disputes between officials in Beijing and Taipei. In 1995 and 1996, Chinese missile tests conducted in waters around Taiwan produced understandable alarm among officials in both Taipei and Washington. It was to them an exercise of coercive diplomacy by the PRC intended to dissuade officials in Taipei from moving away rhetorically from the one-China understanding, which was interpreted by officials in Beijing as steps toward establishing a separate Taiwanese state. Defusing the crisis quickly became the objective for US policymakers.

The norm internalized by most US policymakers and generally shared by members of diverse policy elites across both Republican and Democratic administrations is, when necessary, to use leverage on Beijing officials not to threaten the security of (much less invade) Taiwan while, at the same time, keeping Taipei officials from unduly provoking their counterparts in Beijing. It is an essentially conservative understanding of US interest—urging caution and trying to keep the lid on disputes between the PRC and Taiwan. A show of force—establishing greater US presence during such crises by directing more ships from the 7th fleet to sail to positions in the South China Sea—is a mild form of America's own coercive diplomacy, signalling continuing US resolve to resort to armed intervention if necessary.

US policy toward China has combined peaceful-engagement efforts with containment and the shows of force in naval exercises and other deployments either to deter or compel officials in Beijing and similarly to dissuade their counterparts in Taipei from taking provocative actions that would upset the *status quo*. In the meantime, commercial ties expanded to an extraordinary degree. Notwithstanding some saber-rattling episodes, policymakers have tended to opt for a more productive course, managing conflict through continued peaceful engagement with both sides in the

China-Taiwan conflict. For them, too much has been at stake to do otherwise.

Unilateral imposition by the Trump administration of tariffs against PRC exports in 2019 marked a substantial change in US policy. One can expect on-going tensions in both commercial and military relations. China is the rising power that ultimately can challenge US dominance in East Asia that provides extended deterrence and protective cover to Japanese and South Korean allies and Taiwan while, at the same time, containing and engaging China.

## CONFLICT MANAGEMENT—THE U.S., TAIWAN, AND THE PEOPLE'S REPUBLIC OF CHINA[3]

Resolution of conflict among the three entities seemingly remote, I explore conflict management through construction and maintenance of an international security regime in relation to Taiwan. In this regard, the US, PRC, and Taiwan do share a common interest in war avoidance even as they remain in conflict over questions of sovereignty and relative power in East Asia. That common interest leads them to maintain the *status quo* rather than push their conflicts to the brink of war.

Visions of departures from the *status quo* in relation to Taiwan vary across a wide spectrum. On one extreme is full integration with the PRC and on the other is complete independence—Taiwan becoming a sovereign state like Singapore. Not surprisingly, Taiwan is vehemently opposed to full integration with the PRC, much as the PRC actively resists thoughts of Taiwan becoming recognized globally as a sovereign state. At the same time, Taipei understands the danger of declaring *de jure* independence.[4] Thus, "*status quo* ambiguity" remains Taiwan's position, regardless of changes in government. In between these extremes is a future with some degree of autonomy within the PRC for Taiwan, the status Hong Kong enjoys—the "one country, two systems" model. The more Beijing constrains or interferes with Hong Kong, however, the less attractive this alternative appears on Taiwan.

Finally, there is the loose association between Taiwan and the PRC option that a commonwealth or common market provides—well-developed ties based on cultural exchange, commerce, and the free movement of people, resources, and capital. Although this is the most likely peaceful option, any such departure from the *status quo* cannot be realized in the absence of extensive government-to-government political communications that foster continued expansion of economic, socio-cultural, and even military-to-military ties between Taiwan and the PRC.

## SPECIFYING THE US-TAIWAN-PRC SECURITY REGIME

We can identify a security regime that has emerged, documented by a set of internationally constructed, agreed rules, understandings, and perspectives, developed over time, that influences choices made by the parties (see table 2). The regime has as its purpose to avoid war by putting off to another day resolution of differences that divide them.

The US-PRC-Taiwan regime remains intact even as Taiwan and the PRC differ on the one-China policy. Indeed, upon taking office in May of 2016, President Tsai (DPP—the Democratic Progressive Party) broke with the position held by the previous KMT[5] government in Taipei, rejecting Beijing's and the KMT's interpretation of the outcome of bilateral talks between Taipei and Beijing, the latter then under the leadership of President Jiang Zemin. That there is only "one China" (the interpretation of what that phrase means left to each of the parties) had been the so-called "consensus" between the two capitals. To President Tsai and other DPP members, however, the outcome of the 1992 meeting in Hong Kong between Taiwan and PRC surrogates and subsequent contacts was a "non-consensus"—a non-agreement.

The KMT's position did align Taiwan with the US-PRC understanding in the Shanghai Communiqué that there was "one China." Calculated ambiguity is the stuff of diplomacy—often the only means of "getting to yes." That China was a state or country was left undefined. The vague reference to Taiwan as part of "China" in the Communiqué allowed both sides to hold their separate grounds. Beijing saw Taiwan as an integral part of the PRC while Washington could keep Taiwan's options open, allowing Taipei to maintain its claim at the time to be the *de jure* or legitimate government of all of China, albeit *de facto* at most a government in exile.

Consistent with this agreement and part of the Washington-Beijing normalization process, in 1979 the US and PRC signed a communiqué, the US formally recognizing Beijing as the legitimate government of China and severing formal diplomatic relations with Taiwan. The US also terminated the combined US-Republic of China (ROC) Taiwan Defense Command (TDC) originally established in 1955 during the Eisenhower administration a half decade after Mao's insurgent force successfully defeated Chiang Kai-shek's nationalist forces.

### Table 2. The Taiwan-US security regime.

**Foundational Documents:**

(1) Shanghai Communiqué between Washington and Beijing (1972)

(2) Communiqué normalizing US-PRC diplomatic relations (December 15, 1978, effective January 1, 1979)

(3) Taiwan Relations Act (April 10, 1979)

(4) President Reagan's Six Assurances to Taiwan (July 1982)

(5) US-PRC "August 17 Communiqué" (1982)

(6) 1992 "consensus" or "non-consensus" on the meaning of "one China"

Nevertheless, the US did retain economic and cultural ties with Taipei. Over the succeeding decades, Taiwan-US relations were sustained by liaison missions in each other's capital, consular functions still performed *de facto* by administrative units—dubbed "economic and cultural offices" headed by Directors (as opposed to Consuls) in various cities to the present day. What had been the Republic of China's embassy in Washington was replaced by the Taipei Economic and Cultural Representative Office. For its part, the US closed its embassy in Taipei, replacing it with the American Institute in Taiwan, career state-department officers and others filling positions as if it were an embassy.

The change in US policy was seen by many in Congress as the betrayal of a stalwart ally. Efforts to reassure Taiwan of ongoing American support took two forms—the Taiwan Relations Act and subsequently President Reagan's "Six Assurances" to Taiwan. These two initiatives are still seen in Taipei as the "cornerstone" of US-Taiwan relations.

The Taiwan Relations Act passed by the US Congress and signed into law in 1979 assured Taipei of the US commitment to its security by making "available to Taiwan such defense articles and defense services in such quantity as may be necessary to enable Taiwan to maintain sufficient self-defense capabilities," further asserting that the US will "consider any effort to determine the future of Taiwan by other than peaceful means, including by boycotts or embargoes, a threat to the peace and security of the Western Pacific area and of grave concern to the United States."

The first "assurance" by Washington was that there would be no date certain for ending arms sales to Taiwan, which have continued over the decades to the present day. Second, the US would not assume a mediation role between Taiwan and the PRC, thus leaving Taiwan in the driver's seat without interference by the US in any negotiations it might have with the PRC. Third, the US would not pressure Taiwan to negotiate with the PRC. Fourth, there would be no change in the US position on sovereignty over Taiwan, leaving the matter to be settled later by the parties—Taiwan and the PRC. Fifth, there were no plans to revise the Taiwan Relations Act, which gave Taipei substantial assurance of its right to determine its own future. Finally, the US would not consult with the PRC on arms sales to Taiwan, thus allowing this matter to remain exclusively in US-Taiwan hands. Washington also negotiated with Beijing for some eight months what became the US-PRC "August 17 Communiqué" (1982) in which they agreed to enhance economic, cultural, educational, scientific, and technological ties, the US also stating an intent gradually to reduce arms sales to Taiwan as the two parties peacefully settle the dispute between them.

Taiwan had had no role in crafting the Shanghai Communiqué, which was entirely a US-PRC matter. The Taiwan Relations Act and Reagan's Six Assurances were in Taiwan's favor and were a response to Taipei's concerns but were entirely US constructions. Finally, a decade later negotiators for Beijing and Taipei (then under the KMT party-led government) held diplomatic discussions leading to the 1992 "consensus" on the meaning of the "one-China" principle—that both sides were free to interpret its meaning.

Not everyone—least of all the DPP on Taiwan—agreed with the notion that a binding consensus was actually reached with the PRC in 1992. Indeed, polls now indicate that the majority of people on Taiwan, though ethnically Chinese, see themselves as Taiwanese—decidedly not part of China. Matters came to a head in the 2016 elections when the newly elected government under President Tsai and the DPP rejected the notion that there ever was a 1992 consensus on the "one-China" principle. To the DPP it was a "non-consensus." Furthermore, the DPP explicitly rejects the PRC's interpretation of "one China" as "one country, two systems." Taiwan should not be construed as another Hong Kong, particularly given the measures Beijing has taken to curb the degree of autonomy within the PRC that Hong Kong was promised.

Reaction by the PRC was immediate. Official communications with the new DPP government in Taipei were suspended on May 20, 2016, and remain so. Beijing, which often refers to Taiwan as a "renegade province" of China, insists that talks with Taiwan through the Mainland Affairs Council (MAC) in Taipei will not resume until there is official Taiwanese acceptance of the one-China principle. In the meantime, however, Beijing remains in contact with the opposition KMT party that continues to accept the 1992 consensus.

Communications with non-governmental organizations (NGOs) also remain intact, as do commercial transactions. By doing so, Beijing has limited its quarrel to the DPP under President Tsai and other party leaders who see themselves as carrying out the will of the people on Taiwan. Nevertheless, DPP leaders clearly favor maintenance of the *status quo* rather than seeking fundamentally to alter the China-Taiwan-US security regime.

## CONFLICT MANAGEMENT AND INTERNATIONAL SECURITY REGIME MAINTENANCE

Avoiding armed conflict depends on the US military presence in the region —particularly the US Navy's 7th Fleet—coupled with Washington-Beijing diplomacy to dissuade Beijing from ever taking military action against Taiwan. US-PRC cooperative security relations—through diplomacy successfully managing economic, military, and other conflicts—also discourage Beijing (or, for that matter, the US) from taking actions that alter or threaten the *status quo.*

For its part, the Mainland Affairs Council in Taipei oversees both governmental and non-governmental relations with the PRC. Operating as an office separate from Taiwan's Ministry of Foreign Affairs, the MAC is a construction that has allowed Beijing to communicate with Taipei without conveying recognition of any separate sovereignty that direct contacts with the foreign ministry would suggest. An "office" is not a "ministry"—a useful ambiguity that facilitates this unofficial diplomacy.

Even so, well aware of the MAC's political focus, Beijing's suspension of communications with that entity on May 20, 2016, over disagreement on the 1992 "consensus" (or "non-consensus") did not extend to other entities. Working (not high-level) contacts have continued with Taipei's ministries of economic affairs, transportation and communication, and justice that are in Beijing's interest to maintain in service of some 23 PRC-Taiwan agreements.[6]

Notwithstanding the suspension of communications with the MAC, commercial relations between the PRC and Taiwan remain in place. Civil aviation links are highly developed to an even higher degree than maritime contacts that also are quite substantial. Taiwan's principal PRC trading ports, Hong Kong and Macau, also are transit places for movement back and forth for some nine million passengers annually.[7] Taiwan's islands just off the mainland have been opened up for people on both sides to connect—their military function downgraded (the number of soldiers there reduced sharply)—a significant confidence-and-security-building measure (CSBM). Taiwan also limits naval presence there to Coast Guard units on Taiping and other islands in the South China Sea.

Although capital investments by Taiwan firms on the Chinese mainland are long standing, PRC investments on Taiwan are still increasing, notably in semiconductors. The Investment Review Commission on Taiwan has the responsibility to assure investments are not supporting PRC military or other governmental purposes.

A tacit understanding that military aircraft and warships not cross and thus respect the median line in the Taiwan Strait is an established CSBM integral to the international security regime. Military-to-military contacts between Taiwan and the PRC are decidedly underdeveloped. Active duty contacts are essentially non-existent. Nevertheless, a modest CSBM survives the current suspension of PRC-Taiwan communications through the MAC—a little-known annual golf tournament in which retired senior military officers from the mainland and Taiwan get together (most of those from Taiwan having a KMT identity). Bolstering its international position and commercial relations, Taiwan (as Republic of China) still maintains its diplomatic relations through embassies in 17 countries and some 120 Economic and Cultural offices worldwide—80 in the capital cities of host countries.

Nationalist policies pursued by the People's Republic of China (PRC) lay serious claim to disputed islands in the South China Sea, creating still others, and militarizing the region through naval expansion. The PRC has enhanced its military spending and, in particular, its naval capabilities that challenge the long-standing prominence of the US Navy's 7th Fleet in East Asian waters—an essential part of US commitments to the security of Japan, South Korea, and Taiwan. Taipei also has increased military outlays in its own defense interest. Nevertheless, it is the common interest in stability that preserves the peace. Put another way, the *status quo* remains the "core security foundation."[8]

## REFLECTIONS ON CONSTRUCTIVE OR PEACEFUL ENGAGEMENT AND DIPLOMACY

Constructive or peaceful engagement, then, is the set of policy options that may be part of relations with adversaries but more commonly occurs when dealing with non-adversaries, relations that can be competitive, cooperative, or collaborative depending on time and circumstance—choices made by government officials and private-sector participants. It's a mixed bag. Collaboration with allies or coalition partners may occur even as governments and private-sector firms compete in global and regional markets.

Peaceful engagement is also the stuff of classical diplomacy—a search for outcomes that accommodate not only the interests understood by American policymakers or purposes sought by them but also those of other countries. Diplomats share communicative understandings and meanings among themselves and with their counterparts abroad. One such norm is the notion that—as the British diplomat Harold Nicolson (1886–1968) once put it: "Sound diplomacy is based on the creation of confidence and that confidence can be inspired only by good faith." Diplomats learn to think and act differently than others external to their professional culture. Nicolson observed how historically "they [even] tended to develop a corporate identity independent of their national identity."[9]

Characteristic of this common identity are a set of expectations—"confidence in each other's probity and discretion" bolstered by "a common standard of professional conduct." Moreover, there is a shared "assumption that negotiation must always be a process rather than an episode, and that at every stage it must remain confidential."[10] There clearly has been erosion in the universality of these attributes as the diplomatic world has expanded to include more countries with substantially greater diversity among them, thus becoming decidedly more complex than when norms and expectations among diplomats were more uniform. Nevertheless, the expectations of proper diplomatic conduct that define this corporate culture remain largely intact.

Breaking these norms—as has occurred during the Trump years—is not without its costs. Reaching new agreements through diplomacy requires some degree of trust that the parties will keep promises made in prior negotiations. When short-term, transactional calculations lead to immediate decisions to withdraw from or displace arrangements negotiated earlier, often with little if any notice, other countries not surprisingly react negatively. Moreover, rebuilding trust—so essential to maintenance of existing arrangements, much less forging new agreements—is by no means an easy task.

Career diplomats constitute a professional (or epistemic) community— a set of elites unto themselves differentiated from the less knowledgeable "others" in the political world. The latter, looking in from the outside, quite simply know less about understandings among these career specialists. Nicolson observes how the professional diplomat "is so inured to the contrast between those who know . . . and those who do not know . . . that he forgets that the latter constitute the vast majority and that it is with them that the last decision rests."

These "politicals" are quite capable of trumping the professional diplomats and often do, sometimes, but not necessarily, to the good.

The two groups often read from very different sheets of music and act accordingly. Career diplomats in this sense tend to be the more patient and to have a higher tolerance for ambiguity than others, muddling on as need be through the most complex of circumstances. On the other hand, they also may be more resistant to major policy changes that substantially alter the *status quo*, as occurred when Nixon reached out to China.

As a policy option, peaceful engagement is by no means confined to "friendly" countries or those transactions that occur bilaterally or multilaterally in ad hoc arrangements or within established institutionalized settings of international organizations. It can be pursued with adversaries even as containment or deterrence relations remain in place. Indeed, peaceful engagement has particular salience for managing adversarial relations, if not converting the leaderships of these countries into allies or partners over time, then at least keeping relations from deepening levels of conflict that can lead to the outbreak of war.

Success in diplomacy often requires extraordinary patience over long periods of time—years, if not decades—to manage conflicts and work toward satisfactory agreements among competing parties. Certainly this has been the experience with the Arab-Israeli peace process, where US policymakers for more than half a century have assumed an intermediary or third-party role in negotiations between opposing sides. Comprehensive solutions have been elusive, diplomats having to be content with only incremental progress toward their goals.

Policymakers distrustful of such peaceful engagement with adversaries typically set preconditions—establishing clear positions prior to any talks. Tending to discount any value to be found in such communications or in engagement processes, their preference is to rely on military strength or economic capabilities to contain, sanction, deter, coerce or, if necessary, attack or invade.

## PEACEFUL ENGAGEMENT AND AMERICAN LIBERALISM

Nixon's outreach to China and Reagan's peaceful engagement with the Soviet Union, though dramatic, were by no means historically unprecedented as shifts in the orientation of American foreign policy. After bringing the country into World War I, Woodrow Wilson sought a new world order based on respect for law and institutionalized within a League of Nations committed to maintaining international peace and security. For his part, Franklin Roosevelt departed from an established interventionist script vis-à-vis Latin American countries, opting instead for a "Good Neighbor" policy of non- intervention and the building of cooperative and collaborative ties.

Roosevelt and many of the people he drew into his policy-making elite thought in revisionist terms, whether in designing a "New Deal" to bring the country out of the Great Depression or in institutionalizing peaceful engagement and other essentially liberal ideas. During World War II his administration (continued by his successor, Harry Truman) put in place building blocks for yet another new world order, based this time not only on a Wilsonian legal framework of *collective security* but also on two other features: defensive alliances consistent with balance-of-power, *collective defense* understandings of security coupled with institutionalizing peaceful engagement in international organizations— a decidedly liberal design.

The sentiment of a new liberal world order is contained symbolically within the Great Seal of the United States, designed at the time of independence in 1782, to which Roosevelt's administration gave greater prominence by featuring an image of both sides of the Great Seal on the back of the dollar bill. The eagle grasps both arrows and olive branches— the instruments of war balanced by those of peace. It was an invocation of an eighteenth-century design on its obverse side that looked explicitly to a new order of the ages[11] as being of world importance, not confined just to the United States. Peaceful engagement was also core to the design, not just the use of force.

Peaceful engagement is the core of an American foreign policy grounded on liberal principles—to construct and sustain a world in which human rights are respected. The vision is itself a projection onto the world of a pluralist American domestic society. People are free to express their ideas, form with others in groups or organizations, travel or move, buy and sell, import and export, invest and enjoy gains (or suffer losses) therefrom. Interactions across national borders become routine not only among individuals who serve as agents of governments but also among those in the nongovernmental sector, particularly in countries sharing similar or overlapping interests, objectives, or traditions.

Extensive political, economic, social, and cultural connections and transactions define peaceful engagement not only with capital-rich counterparts but also with capital-poorer, low- and middle-income countries throughout the world. Such peaceful engagement occurs not only bilaterally but also multilaterally within international organizations, alliances or security-related coalitions, and nongovernmental organizations in which Americans participate.

Enhancing international commerce is a core economic objective in the Group of Seven (G-7) countries to which Russia was added, making it the G-8 (Russia subsequently suspended in 2014 after its invasion of Crimea in Ukraine) and to the larger number of G-20 countries. North American free trade is a regional example of peaceful engagement with both a capital-rich, high-income country in Canada and a comparatively capital-poorer, middle-income country in Mexico. Also, a significant part of peaceful engagement are capital transfers by US government aid programs for development, security assistance, or other purposes and investment by multilateral and private banks, corporations, and others.

Peaceful engagement may also occur with adversaries either out of perceived necessity or, more positively, in an effort to influence each other's agendas over time. In such circumstances peaceful engagement typically is combined with the pre-existing containment and deterrence postures one finds between or among adversaries. Covert actions and

coercive diplomacy remain viable options, although liberal internationalists tend to take efforts, when possible, to avoid coercive diplomacy,
much less armed intervention.

US relations with Russia and China have combined peaceful engagement with containment through deterrence and intelligence-related
covert actions that were decidedly more prominent during the Cold
War. As transactions and state and non-state connections are enhanced,
peaceful-engagement relations tend to displace the threat of force, adverse
economic measures and other negative actions with the passage of time.
Nevertheless, these still remain part of the equation so long as the other
party is understood by policymakers to pose a current or potential threat
or security-related challenge. The effort, on the other hand, is aimed at
building connections and trust and confidence over time, thus sustaining
peaceful engagement.

The Obama administration's shift in policy orientation from the conservative (and earlier militant) internationalism of the Bush administration
to peaceful engagement toward adversaries began in 2009. Until Obama
took office, peaceful engagement had not been core to US relations
with Cuba since 1959, Iran since 1979, and North Korea since 1950—
short-term efforts pursued with Pyongyang from time to time without
much success. US relations with these countries combined containment
through deterrence with coercive diplomacy, covert actions (the "dark"
or secret side of American foreign policy), and the prospect (or reality) of
armed intervention. Indeed, throughout the country's history, American
policymakers have not been reluctant to intervene abroad or use force
when such actions are understood by them to be in the US interest or
in service of national objectives they have set.

## INSTITUTIONALIZING PEACEFUL ENGAGEMENT IN INTERNATIONAL ORGANIZATIONS

Following World War II, peaceful engagement finally had replaced the policy of neutrality and, as George Washington had advocated, non-involvement in European entanglements. The necessary elements were present this time for sustaining the new internationalism. "The world has grown smaller" narrative was accompanied by increasingly shared understanding that security was now to be found through involvement in world affairs, the US assuming leadership in security, international commerce, and human rights. It was an opportunity to advance American understandings of liberalism—a world in which people are free to move, assemble and form groups, exchange their ideas, and make money through trade and investments if not totally unfettered, then at least less constrained, by national borders.

In American eyes it was constructing a world just like the then-48 continental United States—a view held widely across most policy elites with varying degrees of acceptance in the general public. Given the relative power they now had at their disposal, policymakers tended to see themselves as using that power to set the world on the right track. Even with war still underway, both bilateral and multilateral discussions were initiated and plans were put in place in 1943 and 1944 for a new and different liberal world order.

Occupying and reconstructing Germany was a central part of planning among the American, British, and Soviet allies who met in London beginning in 1943, well before landings at Normandy the following year by American, British, and French forces and ultimate defeat of Germany by the Soviets at Berlin in 1945.

Inboxes were full of pressing, day-to-day wartime concerns, but decisionmakers still found time to plan in depth for the post-war period that would follow later victories over Germany, Italy, and Japan. This kind of in-depth planning—finding alternative ways and means to meet anticipated post-war needs while, at the same time, fighting a world war —was truly remarkable, particularly in light of the subsequent American experience in more recent decades in which foreign policy often has seemed to lack such preparation.

Although war issues were understandably the focus of summit meetings, peacetime principles stated in the bilateral Atlantic Charter became multilateral commitments among wartime allies who dubbed themselves "united nations." Garnering support among policy elites in different countries for liberal principles to guide the post-war international order was one of the agenda items American policymakers pursued, as did their British counterparts. At Tehran in 1943, the US, UK, and USSR acknowledged the "supreme responsibility resting upon [them] and all the United Nations to make a peace which will command the goodwill of the overwhelming mass of the peoples of the world and banish the scourge and terror of war for many generations." They sought "the cooperation and active participation of all nations . . . dedicated . . . to the elimination of tyranny and slavery, oppression and intolerance" in the construction of "a world family of Democratic Nations" in which "all peoples of the world may live free lives, untouched by tyranny, and according to their varying desires and their own consciences."[12]

These threads were brought together in bilateral and multilateral meetings of national representatives. In July 1944, diplomats and economic experts from the US, the UK, and some 42 other countries gathered at Bretton Woods, New Hampshire, to design international monetary arrangements within a broader international economic framework then under construction. Two significant multilateral institutions in which the US would play a decisive role resulted from Bretton Woods and other policy-related exchanges—an international monetary fund (IMF) to maintain international liquidity, so essential to trade and other forms of commerce, and an international bank for reconstruction and development (the IBRD or "World Bank") to make loans, thus transferring capital for economic recovery or development programs.

Delegates from the US, UK, USSR, and China also held meetings in 1944 at Dumbarton Oaks, a 19th-century Georgetown mansion in Washington, DC. Formally dubbed "Conversations on International Peace and Security Organization," participants at Dumbarton Oaks developed consensus among themselves on important details that were incorporated in drafting a charter for a new United Nations organization in San Francisco the following year. Agreement was reached in these "conversations" or diplomatic exchanges on creating an institution that not only provided bases for maintaining international peace and security but also multilateral approaches to "international economic, social and other humanitarian problems"—the latter an institutionalization of peaceful engagement. A UN system or network of international organizations tied directly or loosely linked to the United Nations organization in New York was the form this institutionalized multilateralism took.

US elites participating in this process saw themselves as making the world over as much as possible in the American image. Ethnocentrism and hubris aside, this liberal American ideological vision also was advanced on very pragmatic grounds with increasing acceptance by policy elites at home and abroad. Although doubts as to their efficacy were present, it was a new design internalized by policy elites then in power to make the world work more effectively to achieve both security and human welfare through peaceful, constructive engagement.

The World Court in the Hague continued its work, now as the International Court of Justice (ICJ), but law was not enough and the newly constructed world order brought the realities of politics back into policy deliberations. The "lesson" from the inter-war period internalized by policy elites was that peace through law alone had proven to be insufficient. *Collective security* or international law enforcement against states committing aggression, which had been the cornerstone of the unsuccessful League of Nations experience, was retained, but was augmented now by individual and *collective defense* arrangements—recognizing the power of alliances and coalitions of states.

The mid-to-late 1940s was a period of substantially greater international institutionalization. In planning for the post-war years, American policy elites brought their more recent domestic policy experiences to the task. Forged in the depth of economic depression in the 1930s, the Roosevelt administration's New Deal was an approach to domestic welfare that relied on expanding institutionally the government role and capacity in the economy. Conduct of war against Germany, Italy, Japan, and their allies also required greater governmental institutionalization in the War and Navy Departments and the private-sector defense industries that supported them. In both the economy and defense before and during the war, governmental institutions were playing an enormous, historically unprecedented role in the American experience.

By 1947 the Truman administration and members of Congress had reorganized substantially the US national security effort—creating a National Security Council (NSC) and Central Intelligence Agency (CIA), a Department of Defense (DoD), the Air Force as a new service department, and a Joint Chiefs of Staff (JCS). Over the next two years, State Department and DoD officials also became key players along with their counterparts abroad in constructing both an Organization of American States (OAS) in 1948, to succeed the earlier Pan-American Union, and a North Atlantic Treaty Organization (NATO) in 1949, both organizations performing collective-defense tasks allowed by Articles 51 and 52 of the UN Charter in addition to non-military forms of peaceful engagement.

Taking the long view, liberal-internationalist elites began to see growth in the institutional elements of worldwide international or global society as well as more than trebling the number of states in the post-colonial and later the post-Soviet periods. Although states and the human agents acting for them remained primary, they also came together in international organizations connecting with people in the growing corporate and nongovernmental organization sectors. Regimes composed of agreed rules of conduct among states on particular socioeconomic issues typically were accompanied by construction of multilateral institutions—the stuff of at least partial global governance.

Ideas and material factors influenced thinking in both the political and economic domains in which these governmental and nongovernmental agents operate. What American policymakers had been constructing in collaboration with their counterparts abroad of similar mind was a new, decidedly liberal, world order within an essentially global society. The vision was one in which material capabilities mattered along with liberal values and behavioral norms. American officials worked with counterparts in other countries to institutionalize the new order globally.

Given the US position in the global distribution of economic and military might, American officials clearly understood the new order as advantageous to the United States. Global governance still took a back seat to the sovereign claims made by American policymakers and those of other states, but routinized and institutionalized peaceful engagement had become prominent as the mode by which much of the day-to-day business of state and non-state actors was to be conducted by their respective agents. Even when US policy elites by the 1980s and 1990s had lost the degree of enthusiasm exhibited in the immediate post-war years for creating new international organizations or expanding the agendas of existing ones, the institutions created earlier remained in place, sustaining this multilateral edifice of institutionalized peaceful engagement.

Institutionalizing peaceful engagement in global society contributes to constancy in foreign policy, particularly when policymakers see maintaining the stability provided by the *status quo* as being in the national interest. When American policy elites recognize net gains from the present order, there is understandable, conservative resistance to upsetting the apple cart. Policymakers of great powers who see their countries as benefiting from the *status quo* are usually reluctant to change it. They tend not to be revisionists or revolutionaries bent on changing the order of things in which they see themselves as having so large a stake.[13]

Changes can occur when decisionmakers in positions of authority (or those with influence on them) exhibit an ability to think outside of the box—challenging established ways of thinking about cause and effect, altering qualitatively relations with other countries and relationships with their leaders and others in their policy elites, considering diverse options, and constructing the ways and means of conducting policy. Much as world wars have led policymakers to reconstructions of the global order, so financial crises, whether in the 1930s or now, create an opportunity that policymakers so inclined can use to re-examine existing ways of doing things. They can adapt multilateral organization structures or establish new ones to provide the degree and kind of collective global governance they understand as being in their interest to provide.

Policy elites with liberal-international or liberal-institutional orientations are more likely to effect such changes than those with more conservative, militant, or nationalist identities—the last two of these distrustful of international, much less global, collaboration schemes. The subjective and inter-subjective understandings within and across policy elites at home and shared with policy elites abroad clearly matter as present arrangements are weighed against prospective institutional alternatives. Even partial withdrawal now from established patterns of peaceful engagement comes at very high cost. The *status quo* has enormous staying power, particularly given that peaceful engagement has become increasingly institutionalized in a multilateral form truly global in scope.

Not in anyway wedded to this liberal-internationalist design, however, the nationalist, "America First" Trump administration has challenged US relations with its allies and coalition partners while being more permissive toward Russia. Whether this is a short-term deviation from the internationalist norm or the beginning of a more permanent alteration of American foreign policy remains to be seen.

## Notes

1. See the interviews of Nixon, Henry Kissinger, Winston Lord, and others in "Nixon's China Game," PBS "American Experience" documentary series.
2. Roger Fisher, Bruce M. Patton, and William L. Ury, *Getting to Yes: Negotiating Agreement Without Giving In* (New York: Penguin, 1991).
3. I am deeply appreciative for research support by the University of Denver's Office of Internationalization, the Center for China-US Cooperation, and Taiwan's Director General "Jerry" Chang in Denver, whose good offices made possible a week in Taipei in July 2016 and return visits in April 2017 and April 2019.
4. Interview, Mainland Affairs Council (MAC), April 2017.
5. KMT refers to the Kuomintang—the Nationalist Party of Chiang Kai-Shek who led the "Nationalists" to take refuge on Taiwan in 1949 upon the victory of communists led by Mao Zedong.
6. Interview with MAC, April 2017.
7. There are 13 sail points from Taiwan and 72 sail points from Mainland China for maritime shipping and five cross-Strait passenger sail points. Ibid.
8. Ibid.
9. Nicolson, *The Evolution of Diplomatic Method*, the Chichele Lectures delivered at Oxford in November 1953 (New York: Macmillan, 1954), p. 75.
10. Ibid., pp. 75-78.
11. *Novus ordo seclorum,* or "new order of the centuries [or ages]," is the phrase (apparently adapted from Virgil's reference: "*ab integro saeclorum nascitur ordo*") that appears on the obverse side of the Great Seal beneath an incomplete pyramid still under construction, yet under an enlightenment that radiates from the all-seeing eye of the Creator—the pyramid and eye clearly freemasonic symbols. Design of the seal began in 1776 with initial inputs from Franklin, Adams, and Jefferson, but was completed in 1782 by Charles Thomson, who incorporated these and other inputs in the final design.
12. "Declaration of the Three Powers," Tehran Conference, December 1, 1943.

13. This distinction between revolutionary and conservative or *status quo* powers is drawn from Henry Kissinger's classic study of the Congress of Vienna, *A World Restored* (Boston: Houghton Mifflin, 1957).

## Chapter 3

# Threatening Force, Coercive Diplomacy, and Containing Adversaries

Containment of adversaries—threatening the use of force or other negative means should they choose to do what the United States opposes—is an explicit alternative to armed intervention or warfighting. Threats of this kind whether in coercive diplomacy or deterrence relations is a form of using force even though no guns or missiles need be fired or bombs dropped. The ways and means of containment include positively cultivating allies and extending aid to them or assistance to threatened or beleaguered countries and, on the negative side of the containment coin, engaging in deterrence, coercive diplomacy or compellence, espionage, and threat or use of economic sanctions: boycotts, embargoes, and blockades. To deter is to keep an adversary from doing something; to coerce or compel is to get an adversary's policymakers to do something they otherwise would not do. These measures usually fall short of going to war, but still keep this option open should policymakers later choose armed intervention or see themselves with no viable alternative when attacked by an adversary.

For their part, covert actions straddle the line between containment and armed intervention—whether these clandestine measures are directed by intelligence officers or conducted by "special operations" military units. Policymakers may define policy toward adversaries by these essentially negative tactics alone or they may choose to pursue peaceful engagement and containment of adversaries simultaneously—one policy mode as an adjunct to the other.

Containing adversaries as an alternative to going to war with them continues to be a central part of American foreign policy. I turn for examples to the immediate post-World War II years when the policy was developed primarily for relations with the Soviet Union and other countries within its sphere of influence. It was extended to China after the victory of Mao's forces in 1949, to North Korea in the years since the 1953 truce in the war that began in 1950, to North Vietnam after French withdrawal in 1954 and Vietnam as a whole after the American withdrawal in 1975, to Cuba after 1959–61, to Iran since 1979, and to Iraq in the 1990s prior to the decision to intervene militarily in 2003. Although peaceful engagement has become more prominent in US relations with China since the 1970s and the Russian Federation since its entry on the world stage in 1992, in the minds of American policymakers containment of both China and Russia has remained an important part of their strategic calculus.

Prior to World War II, Americans and their policymakers tended to see themselves as protected geographically by the vast oceans that separated them from Europe and Asia. After all, the last time the US had had to deal with armed intervention from abroad—the War of 1812 —seemed rather remote in the minds of policymaking elites during the later-nineteenth and into the twentieth centuries. Nor after the defeat of Spain and Mexico did they feel endangered by others on the North American continent and throughout the Western hemisphere. There was no apparent policy need for containing would-be adversaries whose operations were effectively kept far from American shores. If anything, American pursuit of opportunities abroad was more threatening to other countries in the hemisphere than they were perceived as posing dangers to the United States. It took the German sinking of the Lusitania (1915) and the continuation of submarine warfare against surface ships for President Wilson to galvanize the American public and policy elites of the day to support American armed intervention in World War I.

Following the war, the United States returned to its customary position, policymakers seeing themselves yet again in splendid isolation from the political intrigues and foreign entanglements in Europe or elsewhere outside of the Western hemisphere and American overseas territories in the Pacific. Although the seeds of the containment policy were in President Roosevelt's 1937 advocacy of "quarantine" around aggressive countries as a way of keeping them at bay, the full development of containment as a formal policy would have to wait until after World War II. Indeed, after the war policymakers came to embrace in their own minds a new context for an American foreign policy deeply engaged as a great power in world affairs with an agenda that included, but went well beyond, the country's customary external focus on trade and other forms of international commerce. Given this newly established global position, policymakers now focused on threats from adversaries they sought to contain.

## POST-WORLD WAR II ORIGINS OF CONTAINMENT AS A FOREIGN-POLICY OPTION

We begin the containment story with the Potsdam summit just outside Berlin in late July and early August 1945, attended by heads of government of the newly victorious allied great powers in Europe: the United States (Truman), the Soviet Union (Stalin), and the United Kingdom (Attlee). The Potsdam summit followed up on agreements reached the preceding February at Yalta in Soviet Crimea on the Black Sea, which had been attended by the US (Roosevelt), the Soviet Union (Stalin), and the UK (Churchill).

Although strains in allied relations were readily apparent at Potsdam, they deteriorated much further in 1946 and 1947 as competitive spheres of influence gradually took form with the Soviet Union's position in Eastern Europe at odds with American, British, and French positions in the West. Taken together, the Yalta and Potsdam agreements acknowledged facts on the ground—areas taken by military force in the defeat of Germany and its allies. Following the two summits, policymakers gradually put these separate spheres firmly in place in what was becoming an East-West division of Europe.

For their part, Soviet leaders saw Europe in these decidedly geopolitical terms, establishing their position in Eastern Europe as a buffer against Germany lest the latter rise again to pose new threats. Policymakers in the United States and their counterparts in Western Europe, however, interpreted these moves as more than just "defensive" measures. Many understood and alluded to these developments merely as the resurgence of an historically grounded Russian expansionism with antecedents dating from the reign of Czar Peter the Great in the late seventeenth and early eighteenth centuries. It was a refrain commonly repeated throughout the Cold War and after as a rationale for continuing to contain Russia.

Writing in 1946 from Embassy Moscow, career diplomat George Kennan began to lay out a framework in his classified "long telegram" for curbing what these American policymakers understood as expansionist tendencies and containing the Soviet Union within its sphere of influence. The essence of his argument subsequently was published in July 1947 as an unclassified article ("The Sources of Soviet Conduct") by the Council on Foreign Relations in its flagship journal, *Foreign Affairs*. Kennan's advocacy of containment—curbing peacefully, if possible, any Soviet propensity to commit aggression and his correct prediction that contradictions in the Soviet system would, in time, lead to its demise

—profoundly influenced the course of American foreign policy during the Cold War years.

Consistent with Kennan's analysis, Winston Churchill underscored the importance of balancing Soviet power. In a March 1946 visit with President Harry Truman in the Truman's home state, Churchill spoke at Westminster College in Fulton, Missouri. In this famous speech he depicted the formation of a new post-war Soviet sphere in classic balance-of-power terms: "From Stettin in the Baltic to Trieste in the Adriatic, an iron curtain has descended across the Continent. Behind that line lie all the capitals of the ancient states of Central and Eastern Europe. Warsaw, Berlin, Prague, Vienna, Budapest, Belgrade, Bucharest, and Sofia, all these famous cities and the populations around them lie in what I must call the Soviet sphere...."

Churchill's call was for balancing actions by the United States, which he saw then as standing "at the pinnacle of world power." To avoid war he advocated both an ideational and a material or military remedy —"establishment of conditions of freedom and democracy as rapidly as possible in all countries," coupled with measures to assure military strength: "There is nothing they [the Soviets] admire so much as strength, and there is nothing for which they have less respect than for weakness, especially military weakness."

Given understandings among American policymakers about instability in Greece that could advantage the left, coupled with dangers from the Soviet Union faced directly by Turkey, in March 1947 Truman sought Congressional approval and, securing that, began giving both countries foreign aid to strengthen and keep them firmly in the Western sphere—the Truman Doctrine. In June, some three months later, the president authorized Secretary of State George C. Marshall to reveal the administration's much broader plan to transfer capital for the rebuilding of European economies torn apart by the devastation wrought by World War II. Rather than have his own name on what became the Marshall Plan, the president wisely chose to frame it using the stature and prestige the esteemed World War II general enjoyed in Congress, support that was essential to implementing these capital transfers to Europe. As Marshall put it: "The rehabilitation of the economic structure of Europe quite evidently will require a much longer time and greater effort than had been foreseen." The containment policy directed against the Soviet Union had taken concrete form.

We now take up two cases—crises over Berlin and Cuba—as prominent examples of the containment policy. Although containment as a policy toward adversaries was developed in the Cold War context, it remains part and parcel of the way American policymakers still approach present-day countries understood to be adversaries—short of going to war with them.

## THE BERLIN CASE: ECONOMIC MEASURES, COERCIVE DIPLOMACY, AND DETERRENCE

The challenge that brought conflict with the Soviet Union to a head and most clearly framed the onset of the Cold War was the decision in June 1948 by the Soviet leadership under Stalin to deny access by road or rail to Berlin, the capital city of defeated Germany, then under joint occupation by the Big Four victorious allies—the United States, United Kingdom, France, and the Soviet Union. It was seen in the West as a clear violation of agreements worked out in meetings that had begun among the US, UK, and the Soviet Union in London in 1943, which later were extended to include France.

Although Berlin was located well within the Soviet zone of occupation, it was a city divided into four sectors—one for each ally, with rights of access by land and air for the US, UK, and France from their separate zones of occupation carved out of the Western parts of the defeated Germany. Parallel occupation arrangements were established in Austria with joint occupation of Vienna that, like Berlin, was also located in the Soviet zone of occupation. Although the Soviet leadership challenged the

Western position in Berlin, they did not extend this military challenge to Vienna, where the occupation continued until 1955.

Choosing if possible to avoid war, but wishing to force the reversal of this Soviet action in Berlin and thus contain the Soviet Union within its agreed jurisdiction, Truman and his advisers were creative—thinking outside the box—demanding the blockade be lifted, but insisting on continuation of full access through three agreed air "corridors" that had been established to link logistically the American, British, and French zones of occupation in the western parts of Germany with their sectors in Berlin.

A positive economic measure, the sustained airlift of food, fuel, and other supplies to people in the western sectors of Berlin that began on June 24 saved the city from complete Soviet takeover. Although the Soviet leaders could have used force to preclude air access, they were deterred or dissuaded from doing so lest this have led to war with their erstwhile allies. The blockade finally was lifted on May 12, 1949—an early success of the new containment policy!

These events and the fear they provoked in the minds of policymakers in Western Europe also contributed to the consensus leading to the formation of NATO as a collective-defense organization (or alliance) permitted under Article 51 of the UN Charter. US policymakers understood NATO primarily as facilitating containment of the Soviet Union and countries within its newly established sphere of influence in Eastern Europe, but many European policymakers also saw the organization as helping to contain Germany. As one British diplomat, Lord Ismay, put it rather undiplomatically, NATO was initiated not only to keep the Americans "in"—committing them tangibly to European security—but also to keep the Soviets "out" and the Germans "down," lest Germany rise yet again to threaten European countries!

Tensions remained high after resolution of this first Berlin crisis, which was followed a decade later by Soviet Premier Nikita Khrushchev's November 1958 demand that the Western allies prepare to withdraw from the city within six months. Negotiations resulted in lifting the deadline, but lest the Soviets decide to re-impose a blockade or take other military action against them, contingency plans were worked out among the US, British, and French policymakers. Institutionalized within a separate, combined staff in its own headquarters separate from NATO, this tri-partite military arrangement dubbed with the code name "Live Oak" was sustained for preparedness purposes throughout the rest of the Cold War. Indeed, signaling this readiness to respond militarily was part and parcel of the US and allied effort to deter the Soviets from any such repeat performance.

This did not stop policymakers in Moscow from continuing to challenge the Berlin arrangements, most notably when the Soviet leadership under Khrushchev decided to erect a barrier in August 1961 to stop East Germans from emigrating to the West. Closing off the Soviet sector from access by German citizens to or from the three Western sectors, this "Berlin Wall" did not apply to access to East Berlin by officials from the Western "allies" to the Soviet sector; nor did it preclude Soviet access to West Berlin.

As the three Western powers held to their post-war "occupation" rights—essential to preservation of their sectors of Berlin within the Western sphere of influence—over time they constructed with their Soviet counterparts a security regime of agreed rules to govern their continuing occupation of Berlin, which lasted until the end of the Cold War and the unification of Germany.

Challenged from time to time, rules constructed in this adversarial security regime[1] were institutionalized for military and other official passage across checkpoints dividing the city and connecting it with road and rail links to West Germany. Also part of the security regime were the modalities of notifying Soviet controllers in the Berlin Air Safety Center (BASC) of military flights to Berlin and agreed arrangements for guarding Hitler's Nazi Party deputy, Rudolf Hess, the remaining World War II prisoner held until his death in 1987 at Spandau Prison under the authority of the Big Four occupying powers.

Containment in Berlin thus took the form of routinizing procedures and institutionalizing these processes for day-to-day official transactions. This routinization of conflict relations amounted to peaceful engagement at the operational level among American, British, and French officers in relations with their Soviet "allied" counterparts. Invoking this image of fellow allies in the erstwhile war against Germany was the guise that permitted cordial (and even friendly) relationships to develop among controllers from the four powers represented in the BASC.

In addition to checkpoints connecting the western sectors to East Berlin, the BASC, and Spandau arrangements, the four powers also collaborated on reciprocal liaison arrangements in their respective zones of occupation (or "former" zones, as they were called after constituting the Federal Republic of Germany in 1949). The American military liaison mission in Potsdam was accredited to the Group of Soviet Forces headquarters there. The Soviets also maintained a liaison mission in Frankfurt accredited to US Army Headquarters in Heidelberg. Similar reciprocal arrangements were maintained by the Soviets with the British and French in their former occupation zones respectively in the northwest and southwest areas of Germany.

It was as if post-World War II occupation had never ended as the four powers retained residual rights in their "former" zones of occupation. Beyond any communications value among the parties (as in attending to illnesses or breakdowns of Western troop trains to and from Berlin), liaison missions proved to be important intelligence-gathering posts for all parties—an "open secret" sustained throughout the Cold War. Despite these agreements, there was considerable tension among the parties. Western military personnel in Potsdam were closely watched by the Soviets and subject to rough treatment and other forms of harassment, particularly in times of heightened tensions.

## DETERRENCE AND COERCIVE DIPLOMACY IN THE CUBAN MISSILE CRISIS

In 1962 the USSR secretly deployed intermediate-range ballistic missiles (IRBMs) in Cuba—a dramatic surprise when discovered by the Kennedy administration. I review this case as an example of coercive diplomacy or compellence against a backdrop of nuclear deterrence relations between the two superpowers. Indeed, the 13-day crisis (October 16–28, 1962) was marked by direct confrontation between the US and USSR. Subsequent studies of the crisis underscore the importance of the subjective and the inter-subjective, psychological and social-psychological factors in the making of foreign policy. It was not just a sterile, rational-analytic process of identifying objectives, weighing alternatives, and selecting the option or set of options expected to produce the optimal outcome.[2] As a practical matter, no foreign policy case is cut and dried. Instrumental rationality takes one only so far in understanding how decisions are reached.

The US certainly wanted and tried to compel the Soviets in October 1962 to remove from Cuba their missiles and aircraft capable of delivering a nuclear attack on the United States. At the same time, the Kennedy administration clearly wanted to avoid even low-level armed conflict with the USSR, which they feared could escalate easily to the use of nuclear weapons.

Finally, President Kennedy wanted to keep his administration together, mindful as well that Democratic Party prospects could be affected adversely in the forthcoming November elections. Bruised politically by earlier failure in the abortive attempt by US-backed Cubans to invade the island at the Bay of Pigs shortly after taking office in April 1961—an effort to overthrow Castro and his communist regime—and the subsequent relatively poor showing in a Vienna summit with Khrushchev in June of that year, Kennedy was also well aware that political adversaries at home would take him to task were he perceived as indecisive (or, worse, submissive) in dealing with this threat to American security.

Threats are constructions—interpretations or inferences drawn particularly from changing circumstances. Few disputed at the time that Soviet SS-4 IRBMs and IL-28 medium bombers capable of carrying nuclear weapons to targets in the US constituted a new and dangerous threat, particularly given the proximity of Cuba, some 90 miles south of Florida. Across policy elites one found consensus on this point and agreement that something needed to be done about it. It was a threat that could not be ignored (or so it seemed).

Later the US came to live with Soviet nuclear-armed submarines offshore on both the Atlantic and Pacific coasts and the Caribbean in locations much closer to major American cities and other targets than were the missiles deployed in Cuba in 1962. At that time, however, the threat posed by Soviet missiles in Cuba was a new one with seemingly ominous implications. Again, subjectivity matters, as policymakers tend to find threatening those new military developments that have not yet been accepted as part of the strategic landscape. Only later were the presence of submarine-launched ballistic missiles (SLBMs) in addition to intercontinental ballistic missiles (ICBMs) and long-range bombers taken as on-going, proximate threats accepted by both sides as defining the *status quo*.

The action finally taken to coerce the USSR to withdraw the missiles was a naval blockade against Soviet ships heading to Cuba, coupled with diplomatic measures at the UN, the Organization of American States, among NATO allies, and bilaterally with the Soviet Union. Had the blockade and diplomacy failed to secure removal of the missiles, invasion was still an option available to the president.

Some of Kennedy's advisers—notably UN Ambassador Adlai Stevenson supported by Undersecretary of State George Ball—advocated labeling the blockade a "quarantine," thus invoking the Roosevelt precedent as a way of containing aggressive countries. Calling it a *quarantine* instead of a *blockade* was a play on words, of course, the former seemingly less provocative rhetorically than the latter. That using such language was a way of reducing the likelihood of war met with strenuous objection by former Secretary of State Dean Acheson, who reasoned that the Soviet decisionmakers would see through the disguise—in his view a "quarantine" being every bit an act of war as a blockade.

Even as they related to each other, exchanging their different understandings, all of Kennedy's advisers were well aware that communications—inter-subjective exchanges with their Soviet counterparts—were what mattered most. Notwithstanding tactical differences among themselves, all were well aware of the high stakes in this contest, made more difficult by the inability to communicate in real time with Khrushchev and other principals in the Soviet camp. Much was left to conjecture as to what the other side was up to and how they would react to any American or Soviet actions then under consideration.

In the absence of direct contacts, decisionmakers turned to surrogates. Llewelyn Thompson, the US Ambassador to the Soviet Union, offered his interpretations of Khrushchev's actions and likely reactions. Comments made to Kennedy and other officials in a visit by Soviet Foreign Secretary Andrei Gromyko and Ambassador Anatoly Dobrynin were unpacked in detail. Journalist John Scali's conversations with Alexander Forman, a KGB agent at the Soviet Embassy, became part of the process, as did comments made by Khrushchev to William E. Knox, an American businessman who happened to be in Moscow at the time. When communiqués were received from Moscow they were subjected to detailed content analysis, parsing words and phrases in an attempt to infer correctly both surface and sub-textual meanings within messages being transmitted back and forth between Washington and Moscow.

Notwithstanding time, fatigue, worry, and other pressures on decisionmakers, cooler heads prevailed in a relatively slow, methodical process of crisis management. At least in the early stages of discussion, naysayers on the US policy-making team were not silenced but were able to exchange their views openly and freely. Only after the president made the decision to impose a blockade did closure begin to occur, particularly when the emphasis changed from exploring options to developing consensus among policymakers to support their implementation of the policy. The players avoided becoming victims of groupthink[3]—the mindless condition in which members of the group impose psychological or other costs on any naysayers who dare to challenge the commonly accepted "wisdom" or consensus accepted by the larger group.

Subjectivity mattered substantively in Soviet constructions of American threats, as it also did in the development of American understandings of the Soviet challenge. Perceptions and understandings of individuals as well as the social-psychological aspects of group dynamics among policymakers mattered in both tacit and explicit, inter-subjective exchanges on the nature of threats and the feasibility of alternative options for dealing with them. Organizational processes and bureaucratic politics set the decisionmaking context within which policymakers on each side related to each other as well as to their counterparts abroad.

US "Jupiter" IRBMs long deployed in Turkey within striking distance of Soviet targets were understood by policymakers in Moscow as comparable to the Soviet deployments of missiles in Cuba, particularly given their close range or relatively short flight time to targets. Quite apart from strategic gain for the Soviets from forward-basing of nuclear weapons in Cuba was fear that the Kennedy administration would once again try to invade the island (as had happened at the Bay of Pigs in 1961) and overthrow the Soviet-backed Castro regime.

Consistent with this understanding, leaders in the Kremlin gave their commanders in Cuba the authority to use tactical nuclear weapons to blunt any surprise invasion by American forces without first having to contact Moscow—an acknowledgment of the Kremlin's poor command communications capabilities at the time. Release of nuclear use authority to field commanders was a piece of information not known to the Kennedy administration. Had Kennedy opted for the invasion option as his military advisers advocated, the crisis may well have become a nuclear one.

Fortunately, caution on the administration's side had been induced by fears of Soviet counter-moves, if not in the Caribbean then in Berlin or elsewhere. Had the Soviet military command in Havana opted for use of tactical nuclear weapons to blunt an American invasion, the crisis might well have escalated out of control as each military action seemingly was matched by military counter-moves. In practice, the overall mutual-deterrence posture between the Soviet Union and the United States was internalized by policymakers in both Moscow and Washington, inducing greater caution on both sides than might otherwise have been the case.

To keep from coming so close to the brink of nuclear warfare, poli-cymakers in succeeding decades decidedly avoided direct conflict with each other. Although policymakers in the two countries frequently found themselves at odds as they supported their counterparts in diverse "client" states around the world, conflicts tended to be contained between or among these surrogates. Bilateral agreements between the United States and the Soviet Union that came from resolution of the 1962 crisis also became institutionalized as norms to govern future conduct, making unacceptable any future nuclear deployments in Cuba throughout the Cold War and after.

The agreements were reciprocal. The Soviets were precluded from deploying nuclear weaponry in Cuba. For its part, the United States had withdrawn its by then obsolete "Jupiter" IRBMs from Turkey as part of the crisis settlement, agreeing never again to deploy nuclear warheads on surface-to-surface missiles there. Policymakers on both sides were prone from time to time to test the limits of the agreements—the Soviets not seeing them as extending to ships or submarines putting into Cuban ports, the United States insisting that a blanket prohibition including submarines applied. For their part, US decisionmakers did not consider the nuclear warhead prohibition as extending to US fighter aircraft based in Turkey, although observance of the ban on deploying offensive, nuclear-armed missiles there remained intact.

Finally, incentive was found by policymakers in both Washington and Moscow to pursue arms control—peaceful engagement on military matters a way of reducing tensions and reducing the likelihood of war between the two. Two important agreements were reached in 1963: one establishing a hot-line between Washington and Moscow to facilitate direct communications in any future crises and the other a ban on further nuclear testing either in the atmosphere or at sea, the UK joining in the latter prohibition. These early agreements were updated and expanded in the years that followed, incorporating improved telecommunications technologies in the former and establishing limits or prohibitions on underground testing in the latter.

On norms or agreed rules of conduct coming from the Cuban missile crisis itself, US decisionmakers did not seriously consider deploying to Turkey either the slower, air-breathing, ground-launched cruise missiles (GLCMs), much less the shorter flight time-to-target Pershing ballistic missiles, as part of NATO's response in the late 1970s and early 1980s to Soviet SS-11 IRBM missile deployments in the western USSR. Even though its geographic location to the south of the USSR would have provided an ideal location for NATO missile deployments from a strictly military point of view, Turkey remained effectively off-limits due to the 1962 agreements that had defused the Cuban missile crisis.

## CONTAINMENT: DEFENDING THE STATUS QUO USING TACTICS SHORT OF WAR

Commitment to containment through deterrence or coercive diplomacy does not preclude its being combined with economic inducements and other positive forms of peaceful engagement. As an approach to dealing with adversaries that falls short of armed intervention or going to war, containment is defensive of the *status quo*. In practice, however, the tactics or ways and means of containment are often offensive in character. One can try to deter an adversary's policymakers from taking certain actions by threatening military response, seeking to dissuade them from continuing to pursue a present policy course, or even attempting to coerce or compel them to take yet a different course of action. Aside from diplomatic communications, military moves, and covert actions, policymakers may choose to threaten or impose such economic sanctions as tariffs, boycotts or embargoes, perhaps enforced by naval blockade or other military actions on land or in the air. The more they emphasize the military option, of course, the closer policymakers come to crossing the line into armed conflict.

By George Kennan's own admission "the word 'containment,' of course, was not new" as a concept when he introduced it as a policy option in 1946.[4] Roosevelt's advocacy of "quarantine" was framed in effect as containing aggressive countries. To Kennan's credit, it was the renewed emphasis and development he and others gave the concept that made it the cornerstone of American grand strategy for the Cold War. The aim quite prophetically was "to force upon the Kremlin a far greater degree of moderation and circumspection . . . and in this way to promote tendencies which must eventually find their outlet in either the breakup or the gradual mellowing of Soviet power."[5]

Starting with the premise stated in his then classified "long telegram" from Embassy Moscow in 1946 that the USSR was "a political force committed fanatically to the belief that with [the] US there can be no permanent *modus vivendi*," Kennan advocated a "realistic and matter-of-fact basis" for "dealings with [the] Russians." Noting that the "Soviets are still by far the weaker force," he called for maintaining "sufficient force" and "readiness to use it" as the best means for not having actually to go to war.

*Si vis pacem, para bellum*—if you wish peace, prepare for war (and, as a consequence, adversaries will be dissuaded from taking that path). At the same time, Kennan advocated setting forth "for other nations a much more positive and constructive picture of the sort of world we would like to see," relying on our "courage and self-confidence to cling to our own methods and conceptions of human society." An imperative in this effort to Kennan was to "see that our public is educated to the realities of [the] Russian situation."

Kennan developed his argument further in response to a request from Secretary of Defense James Forrestal, which later was published in July 1947 in *Foreign Affairs*. Noting that the Soviet Union's "political action is a fluid stream which moves constantly, wherever it is permitted to move, toward a given goal," Kennan observed also that "the Kremlin has no compunction about retreating in the face of superior forces." He reasoned that when the Soviet Union "finds unassailable barriers in its path, it accepts these philosophically and accommodates itself to them." Accordingly, his diplomatic prescription was that "the main element of any United States policy toward the Soviet Union must be that of long-term, patient but firm and vigilant containment of Russian expansive tendencies." Containing the Soviet Union was to be achieved "by the adroit and vigilant application of counter-force at a series of constantly shifting geographical and political points, corresponding to the shifts and maneuvers of Soviet policy."

Although others in the Truman, Eisenhower, and subsequent administrations tended to understand the containment strategy in largely military terms to include reliance on defensive alliances, to Kennan containment was by no means a purely military response to deter or dissuade the course of Soviet conduct. It was instead a strategy that incorporated the military along with diplomatic, economic, and informational aspects. Notwithstanding times when the Soviet Union, the United States, and their respective allies came close to going to war, whether over Berlin in 1947 or Cuba in 1962, the containment policy contributed substantially to maintaining the peace—keeping the US–Soviet conflict a "cold" (rather than hot) one.

Deterrence relations intended to contain the Soviet Union were very much part of the Cuban missile crisis. Fears on both sides that armed conflict could escalate to nuclear exchange induced a degree of caution among policymakers in both countries. A massive nuclear arsenal had been assembled during the preceding Truman and Eisenhower years to augment non-nuclear (or general-purpose) forces. Soviet leaders had done the same.

If the Soviet Union and its Warsaw Pact allies were not deterred from aggression against the West by the strength and readiness of American and allied forces, then United States policymakers retained the option of using nuclear weapons to blunt such attacks. Even if attacked only by conventional forces, US policymakers claimed the right to respond with first use of nuclear weapons, particularly since the Soviet Union and its Warsaw Pact allies enjoyed a decided numerical advantage in units, equipment, and personnel compared to what the US and NATO allies had deployed in Europe.

Understandings by policy elites about nuclear weapons capabilities had become an important component in the making and implementation of Cold War foreign policy. As Eisenhower's Secretary of State, John Foster Dulles, put it: "We need allies and collective security. Our purpose is to make these relations more effective, less costly. . . . Local defenses must be reinforced by the further deterrent of massive retaliatory power. . . ."[6] In time the strategic discourse shifted away from this massive-retaliation doctrine to the Kennedy administration's embrace of "flexible response" across a wide range of conventional and nuclear options. By 1967, flexible response had become institutionalized multilaterally as doctrine within the NATO alliance.

The stability of deterrence relations—keeping both countries from going to war—is a highly inter-subjective enterprise that on both sides depends on policymaker perceptions and understandings of threats, relative capabilities to carry out such threats, and the credibility of their will to do so when provoked. Adding further complexity to these calculations is extension of the deterrence "umbrella" to cover allies that, if attacked, will provoke an American response that includes possible first-use of nuclear weapons. During the Cold War, arms control negotiations—a form of peaceful engagement with adversaries—also became part of the larger strategic effort to stabilize deterrence relations and thus avoid war.

Reagan administration policymakers took a brief detour away from nuclear deterrence by threat of punishment to deterrence by denial—an effort to build robust strategic defenses to complement already substantial strategic offenses and both nuclear and non-nuclear, general-purpose forces deployed primarily in Europe and East Asia. Advocates pointed to Soviet military literature on nuclear warfighting and questioned why strategists in the United States should avoid this discourse. Credible nuclear war-fighting capabilities, it was said, would allow the United States to win or at least "prevail" in a nuclear war, thus denying the Soviet Union or any other adversary a credible opportunity to attain objectives by that means. Choice of words like win or prevail in this nuclear-battlefield context obscured the awful realities of war at this level —"thinking about the unthinkable," as one strategist earlier had put it.[7]

This change in articulated strategic doctrine, accompanied as it was by public rhetoric against the "evil empire," discussion of developing "hard-target kill capabilities" enhanced by increasing accuracy of American offensive weapons systems, and plans for weaponizing space (albeit for defensive purposes), induced substantial concern if not outright fear among Soviet policymakers that the US would use its technological edge to undermine both their Red Army and Strategic Rocket Force capabilities. The response by Soviet military leaders was the serious consideration they apparently gave to moving to a launch-on-warning posture, rather than waiting for an attack to be verified prior to retaliating in kind. It was an extraordinarily dangerous time indeed.

The action–reaction, strategic-nuclear arms race in this period appears also to have had a positive, albeit unexpected, outcome for American policymakers. The enormous technological and economic challenge of maintaining their position vis-à-vis the United States led Soviet leaders to allocate resources disproportionately to the defense sector, gradually undermining the country's economic base and financial standing. Change was in the offing as the party leadership under Mikhail Gorbachev implemented policies of greater openness (*glasnost*) and reorganization of the governmental bureaucracy (*perestroika*) at home, reaching out personally to President Ronald Reagan and other leaders in the West.

These were the catalysts that set in motion unforeseen and unintended consequences: the end of the Cold War beginning in 1989 with the dismantling of the Soviet sphere of influence in Eastern Europe as leaders and the populace there asserted their independence. It is not as if policymakers can control the effects of policies they make. This was followed by the subsequent demise of the Soviet Union itself, transformed after an abortive coup in August 1991 by the Red Army. The newly independent former Soviet republics emerged formally on January 1, 1992, alongside a territorially truncated Russian Federation. The doors were now open in the post-Cold War period to enhanced peaceful engagement between the United States and Russia even as the containment policy remained firmly in place.

## DETERRENCE AND COERCIVE DIPLOMACY IN AMERICAN FOREIGN POLICY

Willingness to use force in anger is central to both deterrence of an adversary and the use of coercive diplomacy. Credibility of the threat to go to war depends upon the understanding of an adversary's policymakers that the willingness to go to war is genuine—not merely a bluff, just blowing smoke. The development of deterrence theory, sometimes represented as the product of both the perceived capability to use force and the credibility of threats to do so, became a major preoccupation of policymakers, military leaders and their staffs, civilian academics and policy-research specialists throughout the Cold War. Much ink was spilled on deterrence as a "passive" use of force—threats in which aircraft and missiles were targeted on adversaries and kept in a high state of readiness but not actually launched.

Although the term was new, *deterrence* was by no means a new phenomenon. The idea of dissuading an enemy from resorting to war by maintaining military strength—again, *si vis pacem, para bellum*—had been well established in the annals of military history in the West at least since ancient Greco-Roman times. Its logic was always quite clear. What country's decisionmakers (or those of alliance partners) would want to take on a militarily superior adversary? Whatever objective or objectives they might seek by going to war would be denied by military defeat. This was dissuasion or deterrence by denial in its classic form. The capabilities conveyed by armies and defenses of the superior party were made clear to any and all adversaries.

Prior to the nuclear age deterrence had not been very effective in preventing wars. The option of going to war was always very present. Using force to serve national objectives enjoyed substantial legitimacy in a world of power against power in seemingly endless conflict during both war and peace—the balance of power always elusive. Although American policymakers in the nineteenth and early twentieth centuries generally followed the Washingtonian prescription to avoid entanglement in European political struggles and alliance politics, they did contest European power and might when extended to the Western hemisphere. US decisionmakers were not deterred or otherwise dissuaded from going to war with the UK in 1812, Mexico in 1846, and Spain in 1898. Nor were they dissuaded in 1823 from issuing the Monroe Doctrine, which closed off from further European colonization what was becoming an increasingly American sphere of influence.

In the Cuban missile crisis, policymakers on both sides understood the danger of escalating the conflict beyond a war of words in coercive diplomacy as American policymakers tried to compel their Soviet counterparts to remove offensive missiles and nuclear weapons from Cuba. It was coercive diplomacy—"a form of crisis bargaining."[8] Combining persuasion, coercion, and accommodation as modalities of action, adversarial parties communicate with each other—signaling, bargaining, and negotiating. In the typical coercive-diplomacy scenario, the coercing party specifies demands, the urgency by which compliance is expected, and the kind of punishment that will be imposed in the event of non-compliance (the figurative "stick")—all of which also may be accompanied by positive inducements, benefits or side-payments of one kind or another.

"Shows of force" or "gunboat diplomacy" as forms of coercive diplomacy are, of course, not new in the American experience. Merely sending ships to a region or offshore from a particular country is a way policymakers can bring pressure on their counterparts abroad. Although ships can fire or aircraft carriers can fly their aircraft provocatively, going even to this level is usually unnecessary for achieving the goals that have been set. When successful, coercive diplomacy of this kind is persuasive enough to get the other party to back off or comply with demands without firing a shot. On the other hand, small or minor skirmishes still short of full-scale war may occur, such actions still considered part of coercive diplomacy.

Secretary of State (retired General) Alexander Haig (previously Supreme Allied and US Commander in Europe) and those of similar mind within the Reagan administration used coercive diplomacy in the Mediterranean in August 1981 to counter offshore territorial claims to the Gulf of Sidra by Libyan leader Muammar Qaddafi's regime. In order to demonstrate by use that the Gulf of Sidra is in international waters—not a Libyan territorial sea, as Qaddafi claimed—American leaders sent two US Navy aircraft carrier task groups there in full light of day to conduct live missile exercises. This was "gunboat" or coercive diplomacy at its best (or worst). Libyan leaders responded by scrambling MiG fighter aircraft; US Navy F-14 fighter pilots promptly shooting two of them down.

The US Navy routinely challenges what US leaders consider encroachments by coastal countries on international waters as in Russian claims on the Black Sea beyond the agreed 12-mile limit. Even allies are not exempt as US leaders authorize US Navy ships to pass regularly through disputed waters claimed by Canada and other countries in the Arctic north. The difference between the very forceful Gulf of Sidra example and routinely maintaining claims to navigation rights—merely sailing ships through what US leaders consider international waters, whether disputed or not—is the degree to which a show of force is brought to bear. Coercive diplomacy as a matter of policy choice can be moderated or made more strident based on policymaker assessments of the circumstances before them.

Sending ships around the world to affirm rights of navigation was customary practice by the Royal Navy in earlier centuries—a policy emulated by American administrations from the time of Theodore Roosevelt when, as president, he directed a naval build-up. Indeed, naval strategist Alfred Thayer Mahan used the Royal Navy as a model for a US Navy then assuming an expanded, global role. The "Great White Fleet," as it was called, sailed around the world in a global demonstration of America's new seapower—a country finally to be taken seriously abroad.

Whatever their other preferences or the directions they advocated, this Rooseveltian emphasis on global power projection not just by the Navy but also by ground and later air forces remained central to the thinking of policy elites in power through World War I and in the years since World War II when US intelligence activities also expanded worldwide to include collection from space platforms. In tandem with military and paramilitary capabilities used to contain adversaries, decisionmakers also have relied on shared understandings by elites at home and abroad of US economic prowess so essential to global power projection.

American foreign policy elites have tended to see value in the importance of the Rooseveltian "big stick," their differences being mainly on how it should be wielded toward adversaries. Liberal internationalists generally prefer constructive or peaceful engagement combined with containment before resorting to warfare. Conservative internationalists tend to be more comfortable with containment and the use of force but are willing to engage adversaries when persuaded such a path can be fruitful. Militant internationalists are the most skeptical of constructive engagement with adversaries and the most prone to rely primarily on containment or armed intervention as modes of power projection for dealing with those they see as enemies.

## Notes

1. For further details, see my "Berlin and Conflict Management with the USSR," *Orbis*, Vol. 28, No. 3 (Fall 1984): 575–91. The article is based on field research conducted in Berlin and Potsdam between 1981 and 1983.

2. Graham Allison, *Essence of Decision: Explaining the Cuban Missile Crisis*, 2nd ed. (New York: Longman, 1971, 1999). See also his "The Cuban Missile Crisis: Lessons for U.S. Foreign Policy Today," *Foreign Affairs*, Vol. 91, No. 4 (July/August 2012): 11-16.

3. Irving L. Janis, *Victims of Groupthink* (Boston: Houghton Mifflin, 1972).

4. Kennan, "Containment Then and Now," *Foreign Affairs*, Vol. 65, No. 4 (Spring 1987), p. 885.

5. "The Sources of Soviet Conduct," which Kennan drafted in December 1946, published anonymously in *Foreign Affairs*, July 1947.

6. *State Department Bulletin*, January 25, 1954.

7. Herman Kahn, *Thinking about the Unthinkable* (New York: Horizon Press, 1950, 1962) and *On Thermonuclear War* (Princeton, NJ: Princeton University Press, 1960).

8. Alexander George, *Forceful Persuasion: Coercive Diplomacy as an Alternative to War* (Washington, DC: United States Institute of Peace Press, 1991), p. 68.

CHAPTER 4

# USING FORCE— ARMED INTERVENTION AND WARFARE

The American republic was founded in the crucible of warfare against the British Crown. The American experience in the centuries since then is replete with examples of armed intervention or using force against adversaries. Armed intervention was a means for American expansionism in the nineteenth century and defending commercial interests in the early twentieth century (see chapter 6). A constant in this historical record is readiness to use force, going to war as deemed necessary to defend the interests or objectives set by policy elites. US presidents and the policymakers who surround them generally exhibit little reluctance to use force when they calculate that doing so is necessary or serves their understanding of American interests or national objectives.

Preferences for peace frequently appear in official rhetoric—an aspiration no doubt genuinely understood in most cases as more desirable than paying the awful price in blood and treasure in going to war. The voices of those in attentive publics or the general public who renounce the use of force as a matter of principle are difficult to hear among much louder voices generally found in policy-elite circles. Indeed, military readiness and the use of force to serve national purposes enjoy substantial legitimacy among American policy elites, whether for containment using deterrence or coercive diplomacy discussed in chapter 3, or for armed intervention and warfare, which I take up here. As noted in the previous chapter, policy elites differ primarily on when and how to wield the Rooseveltian "big stick," neoconservatives or militant internationalists the most prone to see the advantages of using force and the most skeptical of prospects for peaceful or constructive engagement with adversaries.

Using force in interstate war or in other armed interventions is fraught with high human and material costs. Nevertheless, given the human security and other national interests or objectives they see at stake, policymakers since the eighteenth century have been willing to use force in particular contingencies. As indicated in tables 3 (wars) and 4 (other armed interventions), the use of force has very much been part of the American experience.

## Table 3. American wars.

**French and Indian War** (1754–63)
**War of Independence** (1776–1781, peace Treaty of Paris in 1783)
**Barbary Wars**: North Africa: Tunis, Algeria, Tripoli (1801–1805 and 1815)
**War of 1812** (1812–15)
**Mexican-American War** (1846–48)
**Civil War** or **War Between the States** (1860–1865)
**Spanish-American War** (1898)
**World War I** (1914-18, the US participation 1917–1918)
**World War II** (1939-45, the US participation 1941–1945)
**Korean War** (1950–1953, a peace treaty not agreed)
**Vietnam War** (1956-75, US participation formalized by 1964 Tonkin Gulf
    Resolution)
**Gulf War** or **First Iraq War** (1990–1991)
**Afghanistan War** (2001–)
**Second Iraq War** (2003–2011)

As in the late nineteenth and early twentieth centuries, the entire post-World War II period has been marked by frequent armed interventions. To answer why the use of force, I explore understandings in the heads of most policymakers on the factors that lead them to engage the country in wars or armed interventions. Prior understandings internalized by decisionmakers color the interpretations they make and the actions they decide in relation to the use of force.

When understandings decisionmakers hold that using force or going to war is in the national interest or serves particular objectives, there are relatively few inhibitions or constraints against taking such actions. What is a *threat* (and how serious it is) or *opportunity* (and how viable or worthwhile it is to pursue) is a subjective call informed by current perceptions and prior understandings held by individual decisionmakers who also interact with each other as they render advice or make authoritative choices. The benefits or costs of one alternative or another are highly subjective calculations.

Those with authority to advise or make foreign policy choices construct the decisionmaking context. It may be "rational choice" among alternatives but subjectively filtered through both present and prior understandings decisionmakers hold of what is at hand. Given this subjectivity, *who* is deciding matters. It is not rationality in the abstract apart from those engaged in what are essentially subjective and inter-subjective processes. Sometimes the decision to intervene militarily seems unavoidable or, as Kenneth Waltz put it: "The balance of power is not so much imposed by statesmen on events as it is imposed by events on statesmen."[1]

## Table 4a. Armed interventions abroad by the United States.

Afghanistan 1998 (missile attack on Islamist sites), 2001
Albania      1997 (evacuation of US and other foreigners)
Angola       1976-92
Argentina    1833, 1852-53, 1890
Bolivia      1986
Bosnia       1993-95
Cambodia     1969-75
Chile        1891
China        1843, 1859, 1866, 1894-95 (Sino-Japanese War),
             1898-1900 (Boxer Rebellion), 1911-41(various), 1946-49
Colombia     1870, 1895, 2003 (support government's anti-drug efforts)
Croatia      1995
Cuba         1898-1902, 1906-09, 1912, 1917-33, 1961 (Bay of Pigs invasion),
             1962 (naval blockade)
Dominican
  Republic   1903-04, 1914, 1916-24, 1965-66
Egypt        1882 (British Egypt), 1956
El Salvador  1932, 1981-92
Falkland
(Malvinas)
Islands      1831
Fiji         1840-41, 1858
France       1798-1800 (Undeclared Naval Warfare),
             1806-10 (against French shipping in Caribbean)
Germany      1948
Greece       1827 (marines invade islands of Argentiere, Miconi and Andross), 1947-49
Grenada      1983-84
Guam         1898, 1903
Guatemala    1920, 1966-67, 1983-89
Haiti        1888, 1891, 1914-34, 1959, 1991, 1994-96, 2004-05
Hawaii       1874, 1893
Honduras     1903, 1907, 1911, 1912, 1919, 1924-25, 1983-90
Iran         1946, 1980 (failed hostage rescue), 1984 (2 Iranian military aircraft shot down),
             1987-88 (US military actions supporting Iraq in war with Iran)
Iraq         1991-2003 (no fly zone, air strikes, navy-enforced sanctions), 2014-
Ivory Coast  1843
Japan        1854, 1863, 1864, 1868

Source: Adapted from Global Policy Forum data.
Note: This is a partial list. The focus here is on international uses of force. For this reason, excluded from this list are dark chapters in the American experience—the use of force against native-American tribes and to quell slave revolts by African-Americans. Covert actions (espionage) are not included here unless special forces or other military units were involved.

## Table 4b. Armed interventions abroad by the United States (Cont.)

| | |
|---|---|
| Korea | 1871, 1894-96 (during Sino-Japanese War), 1904-05 |
| Laos | 1962, 1965-73 (bombing campaign) |
| Lebanon | 1958, 1982-84 |
| Liberia | 1990, 1997, 2003 |
| Libya | 1981 (Libyan aircraft shot down), 1986 (air strikes), 1989 (Libyan aircraft shot down), 2011 |
| Macedonia | 2001 |
| Marquesa Island | 1813 (seizure and establishment of first US naval base in Pacific) |
| Mexico | 1836, 1842, 1859-60 and 1861 (Cortina Wars), 1876, 1913, 1914-18, 1923 |
| Midway Island | 1867 |
| Nicaragua | 1850, 1853, 1854, 1857, 1867, 1894, 1896, 1898, 1899, 1907, 1910, 1912-33, 1981-90 |
| Pakistan | 2005- |
| Panama | 1856, 1860, 1865, 1866, 1873, 1885, 1895, 1901-14, 1918-20, 1925, 1958, 1964, 1989-90 |
| Paraguay | 1859 |
| Peru | 1835-36 |
| Philippines | 1898-1910, 1989 (air cover to support government in coup attempt), 2002 (anti-insurgent actions) |
| Portugal | 1860 (west Africa colony) |
| Puerto Rico | 1898 |
| Russia | 1918-22 (Russian Civil War) |
| Samoa | 1841, 1885, 1888, 1889, 1898-99 (Samoa becomes US territory) |
| Somalia | 1992-94, 2006- |
| Spain | 1806 (Spanish Mexico),1810, 1812, 1814(taking of Spanish west Florida, east Florida, and Pensacola, respectively), 1816-19 (attacks on remaining Spanish positions, Spain finally ceding east Florida), 1822-25 (marine landings in Cuba and Puerto Rico) |
| Sudan | 1998 (attack on alleged chemical weapons plant) |
| Sumatra | 1832, 1838 |
| Taiwan (Formosa) | 1867 |
| Syria | 2008, 2014- |
| Turkey | 1849, 1922 |
| Uruguay | 1855, 1868 |
| Vietnam | 1960-64 (military advisors and special forces), war: 1965-75 |
| Yemen | 2002 (strikes on al Qaeda), 2009 |
| Yugoslavia | 1919, 1946, 1992-94, 1999 (air strikes) |
| Zaire (Congo) | 1996-97 |

Source: Adapted from Global Policy Forum data.
Note: This is a partial list. The focus here is on international uses of force. For this reason, excluded from this list are dark chapters in the American experience—the use of force against native-American tribes and to quell slave revolts by African-Americans. Covert actions (espionage) are not included here unless special forces or other military units were involved.

American presidents often find themselves in this reactive mode as, for example, when the Royal Navy challenged American independence in the run up to the War of 1812 (Madison), the South attacked Fort Sumter in 1860 (Lincoln), what appeared to be (or was made to appear as) an attack in Havana Harbor by Spain on the USS Maine in 1898 (McKinley),[2] sinking of the *Lusitania* in World War I (Wilson), bombing of Pearl Harbor and elsewhere by the Japanese in December 1941 (Roosevelt), 1950 attack by North Korea across the 38th parallel (Truman), perceived attack in 1964 by North Vietnam against US Navy ships in the Gulf of Tonkin (Johnson),[3] Iraq's invasion of Kuwait in 1990 (George H.W. Bush), and the attack by *al Qaeda* on September 11, 2001 (George W. Bush).

A review of these cases reveals a number of criteria present to a greater or lesser degree in the thinking of presidents and their advisers. They typically construct objectives in relation to what they see as the national interest, some saying, more restrictively, that force should only be used if core values or *vital* national interests are at stake. Consensus—much less unanimity—on such subjective considerations is often very elusive.

## THE WORLD WARS

George Washington's counsel in his farewell address—drafted by Madison and Hamilton—to avoid foreign entanglements kept the US out of European wars. During the nineteenth and into the twentieth centuries, however, policymakers did not apply the Washingtonian prescription to Latin America. Apart from the few remaining colonies in the Western Hemisphere retained by Britain, France, and the Netherlands, the Monroe Doctrine effectively had carved out Mexico, Central America, the Caribbean, and South America as a US sphere of influence.

The Spanish-American War turned US attention to East Asia and the Pacific, but apart from trade and investment relations Europe remained outside of American military thinking. The US naval build-up that began in earnest under Theodore Roosevelt followed the British Royal Navy model. Aspirations to play a larger global role were clearly present.

The Wilson administration that took office in 1913 finally brought the US into the war against Germany by a congressional declaration on April 2, 1917. The fighting had dragged on with much bloodshed since the outbreak of the Great War in August 1914. The German sinking of ships in the North Atlantic focused administration sights on the war and America's prospective participation in it. Opposition for any such involvement remained strong until Germany turned in 1917 to unrestricted submarine warfare against US and other merchant shipping upon which Britain depended. American policymakers were also angered by the "Zimmerman Telegram" that had been intercepted by British intelligence—Germany pledging to help Mexico regain territories lost to the United States in the Mexican War (1848).

The American contribution on the western front did not arrive in substantial numbers until 1918, but it was a welcome relief to war-weary allied soldiers. Some four million Americans were mobilized; by mid-1918 more than two million troops deployed in Europe—some 10,000 arriving daily in France when the war ended on November 11, 1918. Compared to the Russians (more than nine million dead), French (more than six million), and British (more than three million), US deaths were relatively light at almost 117,000 (due to combat or the 1918 influenza epidemic), some 204,000 wounded.

Following the war, the US returned to its nationalist position. Although Wilson had been an architect of the post-war, liberal-internationalist order centered on the League of Nations, the US Senate failed to ratify the Covenant of the League. Even commercial relations with European and other countries became unglued with passage of the Hawley-Smoot Tariff Act (1930, Hoover) and devaluing the dollar by raising the price of gold (1934, Roosevelt)—nationalist campaigns intended to promote exports and diminish imports. The result was just the opposite as the Great

Depression dragged on—drastic reduction in the volume of international trade and investment.

War clouds formed with the rise of Germany in alliance with Austria in Europe, the expansion of Japan in East Asia and the Pacific, and a new arms race that pitted major powers in fierce competition as they built up military arsenals. The German Reich, its sphere of influence in central Europe, allied with the Japanese Empire. The same Great War western allies—Britain, France, Russia (now the Soviet Union)—opposed German aggression that began with attack on Poland on September 1, 1939, the United States joining after the attack by Japan on Pearl Harbor and other US territories on December 7, 1941. For its part, China also joined the western allies in the war against Japan.

US military casualties in World War II included 416,800 deaths and 671,278 wounded. Heavy as these were, they were comparable to the British (383,600 military, 450,700 total including civilians killed) and French (217,600 military, 567,600 total), but decidedly lighter than the other European great powers sustained— Germany (5.5 million military, 6.6–8.6 million total) and the Soviet Union the heaviest losses (more than 8.8–10.7 million military, 24 million total).[4]

Not surprisingly, the devastation of World War II on top of the massive losses in World War I a quarter of a century earlier renewed the search for a new world order that would avoid yet another round of global warfare. Indeed, a more recent historical construction sees the world wars as really one great or world war (1914–1945) with an armistice or cessation of armed conflict between 1918 and 1939.

Departure from the Washingtonian prescription did "entangle" the United States not only in European but also East Asian and Pacific balance-of-power politics. The post-war understanding promoted by policy elites was that the United States no longer could find security in withdrawal to its nationalist or continental position separated by oceans from Europe and East Asia. Transportation, communications, and military technologies no longer made this possible. Like it or not, the

United States was part of the world—internationalism having displaced the Washington nationalist preference.

Given its relative power position, the US became a principal architect of the new order—its core defined by the United Nations organization and its system or multilateral networks of globally and regionally focused agencies and affiliates. Although disputes with adversaries, allies, and others still would occur, international mechanisms now existed to manage, if not resolve, these differences. Both bilateral and multilateral diplomacy remained on center stage.

Through the UN Charter, the United States and its World War II allies were instrumental in not just restoring the League of Nations collective *security* concept (the international law-enforcement mechanism under the Security Council) but also recognizing the role that alliances (collective *defense*) might play in maintaining security globally and regionally. For more than seven decades this internationalism remained the primary coin of the order whether one were liberal, conservative, or militant internationalist. Inauguration of President Trump in January 2017 posed a substantial challenge to this internationalism. "Make America Great Again" (MAGA) and "America First" signalled a return to nationalist foundations deeply rooted in the American historical experience. In his 2020 presidential campaign the slogan became "Keep America Great!"— the rhetorical focus on nationalism firmly in place.

## The Korean War

What began as a "police action" under the Security Council in response to invasion on June 25, 1950, of South Korea by North Korea across the 38th parallel remains an unresolved conflict some seven decades later. In a January 1950 address to the US National Press Club, Secretary of State Dean Acheson had described the US strategic or "defense perimeter" as protecting Japan, the Ryukyus, and the Philippines. Failure to include South Korea within the perimeter was interpreted at the time by critics of the Truman administration as having given North Korean leader Kim il-sung and his Soviet ally a "green light" to invade the south.

As always, things are usually more complex than they may first appear. Post-Cold War access to documents indicates that Kim had been planning since 1948 to unify Korea forcibly.[5] Nevertheless, the timing of the invasion likely was due in part to misunderstandings of American intent or resolve. After gaining Stalin's reluctant concurrence, Kim ordered North Korean forces south. They quickly drove back South Korean and US forces, the latter establishing a territorial base around the southern coastal city of Pusan—the so-called Pusan Perimeter. Right or wrong, the perceptions, understandings, and other subjective considerations of decisionmakers matter substantially.

The invasion marked a failure of the two-state solution on the Korean peninsula established in 1948 between a Soviet-supported socialist state under Kim in the north and an American-supported, market-oriented regime under Syngman Rhee in the south. The US took the lead role in organizing and executing the response by some 21 UN members.

Making a major diplomatic blunder, the Soviet ambassador famously stormed out of a Security Council meeting. While he was out, the US orchestrated an authorizing resolution which, given his absence, the Soviet ambassador was unable to veto. North Korea was branded the aggressor and thus subject to international law enforcement—collective security arrangements spelled out in Chapter Seven of the UN Charter, particularly Article 42.

General Douglas MacArthur led the counter-offensive on September 15th with amphibious landings of UN (mostly US) forces at Inchon on the Korean west coast just south of the 38th parallel. UN forces quickly pushed the North Koreans back, approaching the Yalu River border with China. MacArthur met privately with President Truman on Wake Island in mid-October to brief him on progress in the war effort.

At the same time, Chinese leaders under Mao were concerned about both the impending collapse of the North Korean communist regime and the threat that US-led forces under MacArthur might take the war to China. In an effort to save the day, the response was a major invasion in October 1950 by Chinese forces that pushed UN forces out of North Korea by December.

Differences between MacArthur and Truman—the latter concerned that MacArthur wanted unnecessarily to provoke China militarily, thus expanding the scope of the war. The general's public statements that had not been cleared in Washington contributed to the quarrel. Finally, the president exercised his authority as commander-in-chief and relieved General MacArthur of his command on April 11, 1951.

Command was transferred to General Matthew Ridgway who had been serving under MacArthur. There was much back-and-forth fighting with heavy casualties during the more than two years that ensued after the change of command before an armistice finally was signed on July 27, 1953, at Panmunjom (the Truce Village) just above the 38th parallel. In the absence of a peace treaty, the Korean War technically has not ended—both sides remaining fully armed and alert lest attack by one or the other occur.

## The Vietnam War

As with other European powers, the French imperial reach extended south to Africa, west to the Americas, and east to Asia and the Pacific. In many respects Vietnam was a prized possession for the rich culture of its peoples, its verdant seacoasts, lush rice-growing deltas, and mountain splendors—Saigon then referred to as the French pearl of the Orient. Much as local persons in business or government elite circles elsewhere in the French colonies selectively could become French citizens, many Vietnamese did so as well. Indeed, these francophone Vietnamese adopted the French language in daily use, identifying with the French language and most with Roman Catholicism as well as French cuisine and culture (music, literature, and the arts).

Under Nazi influence and confronted in Southeast Asia by Japanese military force, in 1940 the Vichy government in France succumbed to Japanese military presence in Indochina, albeit with the French administration to remain in place. This effectively set the stage for the nationalist, anticolonial insurgency organized by Ho Chi Minh (1890–1969) and initially directed against the Japanese and their Vichy-French collaborators. The nationalist Chinese released Ho from prison, which allowed him and his cohort to organize the Viet Minh. Ho's efforts thus received Chinese and other Western allied support to include the US Office of Strategic Services (OSS)—the World War II predecessor of the CIA.

Given the Japanese defeat and withdrawal from Vietnam in 1945 and his Viet Minh organization now in place, Ho turned his attention entirely to the French who were bent on reestablishing their control. For Ho and others in his cohort, the Japanese occupation in World War II presented an opportunity to take a strong position against all outside powers who would exercise hegemony over the Vietnamese. Anti-Japanese sentiments were generalized against all foreigners to include the French and, later, the Americans. After the defeat of Japan, the French effort to return to the *status quo ante* thus was fraught with difficulty. Though their stay was short, the Japanese had indeed challenged whatever legitimacy French colonialism had in Vietnamese society. At the end of the day, neither the Japanese nor the French were welcome.

Ho's declaration of Vietnamese independence marking the birth of the Democratic Republic of Vietnam in 1945 drew from the Franco-American legacy—that "all men are created equal" and that the Vietnamese people have "the right to life, the right to be free, and the right to achieve happiness." Having lived, traveled, and worked in France, the United Kingdom, and the United States as a young man, the declaration also reflected Ho's intimate familiarity with the West. Identifying with the left in France, he also traveled to the Soviet Union, China, and elsewhere pursuing political activities that defined his communist commitments.

In 1945, reflecting their weakened position at the time, the French initially agreed to an autonomous Vietnamese state within the French Union. They subsequently reversed this position, which led the Viet Minh finally to declare war on the French Union in 1946. Following Mao's victory over the Chinese nationalists in 1949, Ho successfully garnered support from Beijing—actions that also received Soviet blessings.

The essential elements of a successful insurgency were present: (1) *grievances* against governing authorities upon which *domestic support* was mustered; (2) *leadership* with its *organizational structure* in place, informed and motivated by a widely accepted *ideology*; and (3) *external support*, if needed, to tilt the balance against governing forces. With external support in place, the Viet Minh expanded their numbers, attacked French forces, and ultimately brought them to a disastrous defeat in 1954 at Dien Bien Phu in the northern part of Vietnam.

Key to achieving this and subsequent victories was the thinking of Ho's principal military strategist, Võ Nguyên Giáp. Quite simply, the American understanding was that Ho was a communist, not a national leader upon whom the United States could rely. Some in the State Department may have seen Ho as "the Thomas Jefferson of Indochina," but this was by no means the consensus view in Washington. True, the United States had accommodated Josip Broz Tito in Yugoslavia as a communist leader independent of Stalin and thus operating outside of the Soviet orbit. But that was in Europe beginning in the late 1940s. In the American mind of the 1950s and 1960s, by contrast, Southeast Asia lay in China's shadow and thus was decidedly different.

Besides, reflecting US history, the American self-image was as an anticolonial power that had established its independence from Britain in the late eighteenth century, tested briefly in the War of 1812. From the American perspective, this was reason enough not to aid the French substantially in their re-colonization effort any more than it actively had supported British efforts to sustain its empire following World War II— India an early and significant loss to the British.

For their part, Britain, France, and other imperial powers allied with the United States in NATO saw the American position through decidedly similar lenses. For them, it was not so much an anticolonial sentiment in America as it was a US effort to displace them to the American advantage. To many French and British observers, American anti-colonialism was merely an American cloak to cover the assertion of American power and position in their place. In this regard, Article 6 of the North Atlantic Charter (1949) excluded areas outside of the North Atlantic area, thus denying any American obligation to imperial restoration or maintenance of European hegemony. The only exception was Algeria, then considered by Paris not a colony but an integral part of France.

France's military defeat at Dien Bien Phu in 1954 resulted in the French ouster from the colony as a whole. Ho's communists now controlled the north, the fate of the whole of Vietnam not yet decided. In Geneva talks, the United States assumed a prominent role in guaranteeing nation-wide elections to be held in 1956 to decide the political outcome for a unified country. As it became clear in the United States that Ho Chi Minh and his fellow communists would prevail, the elections never were held.

Instead, the United States effectively replaced the French as guarantors of a noncommunist south. Ho and his followers remained committed to their vision. As Ho put it in 1956: "The reunification of the whole nation is the lifeline of all our people. Great unity is the force that's bound to win."[6] By the 1960s, Ho and his followers remained in both the north and the south (the Viet Cong). They extended their organizational efforts throughout the country, the strongest bases of support found among peasants in the countryside. As was the case in places as diverse as China and Yugoslavia, Vietnamese nationalism was strengthened by the mere presence of foreigners seen by them as occupying the country through links with a puppet regime in the south that depended upon American support.

From the US perspective, what many saw as a civil war had become a matter of North Vietnam invading the South. This certainly was the argument set forth again and again by then Secretary of State Dean Rusk. That the American-supported regime in South Vietnam requested US military assistance gave the legal basis for American military intervention. To say it was a civil war would have removed this legal fig leaf used by Washington to justify the US intervention.

Quite apart from legal niceties, however, American decisionmakers at the time were driven by their anticommunist understandings. Failing to contain the Soviets and, in Southeast Asia, the Chinese, was adverse to US national security interests as they understood them. Defending a "democratic" regime in the Republic of Vietnam (RVN) against invasion by the communist Democratic Republic of Vietnam (DRV) became the expressed purpose of the American intervention.

From 35,000 troops (mainly advisors and Special Forces) present in 1965, numbers quickly rose by 1968 to some 550,000.[7] The conscription that facilitated this surge in numbers gradually eroded the American domestic support base for the US effort, particularly when casualties mounted. Evening news programs that reported killed-in-action (KIA) levels on the order of 300 or more per week and even larger wounded-in-action (WIA) statistics galvanized opposition to the war.

The course of the war had shifted from just anti-guerrilla actions to use of American main force units to drive the North Vietnamese Army (NVA) and Viet Cong from any territorial positions they held. Air force and navy aviation units undertook a substantial effort to bomb and thus interdict the daily flow of supplies under jungle cover from North to South along the so-called Ho Chi Minh trail that connected North Vietnam to the South via Laos.

In any insurgency, the "outsider" is at a severe disadvantage. Insurgents cultivate domestic sources, articulating their grievances and committing themselves to changing the *status quo*. Ideologies frame the issues insurgent leaders and their organizations take on. Depicting those they are against as "outsiders" or "enemies" of the people focuses the energies of the insurgents and their domestic supporters. Organized, well-led, and focused insurgencies tend to attract external support from those seeing gains to be had from insurgent victories over incumbent authorities in a particular society. So it was in Vietnam where Ho and his cohort secured both Chinese and Soviet assistance.

The US defeat in Vietnam was due to a number of factors. As with the French, the insurgents successfully painted the United States as an outsider meddling in Vietnamese domestic matters, wreaking great destruction of life and property. Collateral death and destruction from bombing campaigns against targets on the Ho Chi Minh trail and in both North and South Vietnam—whatever their military value—strengthened popular support in the countryside for the insurgents.

Reflections in Washington on insurgency in the early 1960s had produced a persuasive but false analogy to British success against communist insurgents in Malaya (1948–1954). The British had successfully separated the insurgents from the population as a whole, effectively denying them the popular support base they needed. The same, it was thought, could be done in Vietnam. What was overlooked in this narrative was that in the Vietnamese case, notwithstanding regional and demographic differences, all major players were ethnically Vietnamese.

By contrast, in multiethnic Malaya (with Malay, Chinese, and Indian populations) the communist insurgents were predominantly Chinese operating with support from China. Not all Chinese in Malaya were communists or communist sympathizers, of course, but most of the insurgents were of Chinese identity. The majority population was Malay, while the Chinese as well as north and south Indian populations were distinct minorities. British success, then, was achieved by isolating the insurgents—turning the non-Chinese majority of the country against them. The situation in Vietnam, on the other hand, was decidedly different. Although non-Vietnamese minorities were present, it was a country in which armed forces from the North and Viet Cong insurgents in the South shared in common a Vietnamese identity not as easily split ethnically into contending camps.

From a military perspective, destroying war-making capability and unseating the regime in Hanoi required a ground invasion of North Vietnam supported by air force, marine, and navy aviation units. Both the Johnson and Nixon administrations ruled out this option, concerned as they were that doing so might prompt intervention by China or the Soviet Union, thus dramatically expanding the military and political stakes.

Restricting military options in the north to airstrikes and limiting those to targets away from the port of Haiphong or elsewhere one might find Soviet ships or other Soviet or Chinese presence, the war became one of attrition. Casualty counts mounted on both sides. Matters came to a head during the dry season in the February 1968 Lunar New Year or "Tet" offensive launched by the North Vietnamese and Viet Cong against American positions in South Vietnam. They attacked again in May at the end of the winter dry season but before the summer monsoon rains, mud, and flooding made any follow-on offensive more difficult.

Casualties on both sides were high. When the dry season returned in late fall and the winter and early spring months, the Americans expected follow-on offensives. In fact, North Vietnamese and Viet Cong losses in the two offensives were far greater than the Americans and their South Vietnamese ally realized. The expected follow-on offensives did not occur after all, but the damage to the American position had already occurred, albeit on a very different, domestic front.

Support for the war had begun to wane even before the Tet offensive. Tired of the war and the several hundred American soldiers, sailors, and airmen killed or wounded every week,[8] the US antiwar movement grew even stronger. Drafting young men at eighteen and older picked up speed. Vulnerable to the draft, both undergraduate and graduate students —the men, usually supported by their significant others—tended to see themselves potentially as cannon fodder on Vietnamese battlefields. They took action both on and off campus.

Anti-war protests grew in intensity. Indicative of this malaise and the damage done to his administration, President Johnson announced in March 1968 he would not seek reelection. The Democratic Party in disarray and effectively divided, Republican former Vice President Richard Nixon won the election with a plurality—just 42% of the popular vote!

Indeed, candidate Nixon had claimed to have a secret plan for ending the war but, in fact, continued the struggle and, in 1970, extended the war to Cambodia. The army finally got its way, clearing sanctuaries in the "Parrot's Beak"—the Cambodian salient extending into Vietnam like an arrow pointing at Saigon (or so it was portrayed)—and elsewhere in the Cambodia-Vietnam border area. The action provoked a domestic response well beyond what had occurred previously. In one tragic incident on May 4, 1970, Ohio National Guardsmen fired upon students at Kent State University who were protesting the US invasion of Cambodia. Four students were killed and nine wounded.

In a division of labor, the air force and navy depicted the Ho Chi Minh trail as a series of segments or "route packages"—each service responsible for destroying trucks carrying supplies or making different parts of the trail impassable. The burden was entirely upon airpower during the winter dry season, monsoon rains in the summer months substantially slowing the north-to-south movement of supplies.

Inter-service rivalry took a new form with the competition between the air force and navy, each claiming an edge over the other. Hyperbole reigned. Air force intelligence claimed that operations had interdicted 85 percent of supplies on the trail going to the northern part of South Vietnam—a tactical zone referred to as I (pronounced "eye") Corps, 100 percent going to points further south (tactical zones labeled II, III, and IV Corps)!

For its part, the army long wanted to deny sanctuary in Cambodia to the North Vietnamese and Viet Cong. During the last days of the Johnson administration, a senior CIA official was dispatched to Saigon for consultations with military officers only to learn that reports of supplies coming from Cambodia into Vietnam were scarce and of questionable reliability. Quite apart from dubious intelligence reports to sustain the case, the military reasoning was that interdiction by air had been so successful that supplies going to insurgents operating in South Vietnam had to be coming from somewhere. Hence, in briefings Cambodia became the "back door" to Vietnam. The Johnson team was not persuaded, but the Nixon administration that assumed office early in 1969 ultimately made the decision to extend the war to Cambodia in what became the war's major turning point.

Misjudgments based on faulty intelligence (or particular interpretations intended to influence policymakers) were only too commonplace. Enemy casualties were routinely overstated—as many as 2000 or more enemy allegedly killed each week, six or seven times weekly US losses! Such statistics suggested that the United States and its Vietnamese and other allies were winning (or at least holding their own in) the war. Misrepresentation or omissions occurred not just at the strategic but also at the tactical level. Perhaps varying in degree, overstating enemy losses also has occurred in the Iraq and Afghanistan campaigns.

Contributing to domestic malaise in the United States were two incidents in 1968 and 1969: My Lai (some 100 miles south of Da Nang) and "Hamburger Hill" (in the A Shau Valley near the Laos border). The former was the site of the March 16, 1968 mass murder of some 300–500 villagers by American soldiers. On May 10–20, 1969, frontal assaults were made against North Vietnamese positions with no particular military or other strategic value worth the blood price paid by American soldiers. For example, assault on a location labeled Hill No. 937 caused massive casualties on both sides, earning it the tragic name "Hamburger" Hill. The conflict in Vietnam had become a war of attrition in which numbers killed apparently mattered more to officials than destroying or weakening the enemy's war-making capability which, following Clausewitz,[9] should have been the military focus.

Particularly troubling to the American public and the Congress were such decisions to commit troops in this war of attrition—taking enemy positions at great human cost and then abandoning them. Infamous among these ventures, Hamburger Hill was by no means unique. US losses were 72 killed and 372 wounded, the North Vietnamese allegedly losing more than 600.

Adding fuel to the domestic anti-war movement, the My Lai massacre was finally disclosed to the press ten months into the Nixon administration (November 1969). To say the least, the just-war concept of sparing non-combatants seemed an abstraction, except for the few soldiers who tried to shield these civilians. Somehow the Clausewitzian understanding of war had been lost—that the way to win any battle (or an entire war for that matter) was to destroy or substantially weaken the enemy's war-making capability. By this, Clausewitz did not mean body counts (as if the contest could be settled quantitatively by counting which side had lost more soldiers either absolutely or proportionally).

Invading the north, thus disrupting military command-and-control and destroying war-making capability on the ground, was understandably precluded by fear of Chinese or Soviet intervention that would have expanded the war substantially. The invasion option was just too dangerous. On the other hand, right-wing advocates were likely correct that taking invasion off the table and limiting attacks to air strikes made the war unwinnable. If so, to fight unwinnable wars is a strategic mistake. It also contradicts a basic just-war tenet that going to war must have some chance of success.

Many contended then (as they do now) that such a war should never have been undertaken in the first place. Even if invasion of the north had been pursued, there was no assurance that popular support for the American-backed regime in Saigon could have trumped that enjoyed by the North Vietnamese and their Viet Cong cohorts in the south in what was a nationalist struggle in which the "outsider" is inherently in a deficit position. Failure by senior policymakers to understand this was catastrophic for the soldiers, sailors, airmen, marines, and others who lost their lives or were wounded in the conflict, not to mention the national treasure misallocated to an unwinnable war.

The Nixon administration eventually adopted a "Vietnamization" policy —reducing the American ground combat presence and relying on the South Vietnamese Army to assume the lead role. This failed ultimately with the fall of Saigon to North Vietnamese forces on April 30, 1975. Just as the shift to local (South Vietnamese) forces failed, this localizing of the conflict again failed in Iraq three and a half decades later.

## ARMED INTERVENTIONS IN IRAQ AND AFGHANISTAN

We turn first to neoconservative, militant understandings in action —interventions in Afghanistan (2002) and Iraq (2003). Although his administration invoked the term *conservative*, this adjective—implying a very careful, cautious, often slow-moving change from the *status quo*— by no means characterized President George W. Bush's foreign policy.

The label *neoconservative* applied to the policy elite that came to positions of power in 2001 was also a misnomer that obscured commitment to fundamental change in the course of American foreign policy—advocating pre-emptive use of force against adversaries such as Iraq, moving away from arms control by abrogating the ABM Treaty and "unsigning" the Comprehensive Test Ban Treaty, and avoiding further institutionalization of multilateralism in commitments to the International Criminal Court and the Kyoto Protocol on carbon emissions intended to curb global climate change. On a rhetorical level at least, the administration was truly "revolutionary" in its ambition not only to defeat terrorism following the September 11, 2001 attacks by *al-Qaeda* in New York and Washington but also to transform authoritarian regimes, particularly those in the Middle East, where both oil and commitments to Israel seem always to be part of the equation.

Going to war in Afghanistan in 2002 with the backing of NATO allies in a multilateral coalition was indeed a robust response to the Taliban regime in Kabul—reactionary forces that had given safe harbor to *al-Qaeda*. The presidential response to the September 11, 2001 attacks by *al-Qaeda* was directed not just against the Taliban and *al-Qaeda* but also more broadly against all groups and the states backing them that resort to terrorism as a means to advance their agendas. Anti-Zionist, anti-Israeli sentiment among these groups aside, an even deeper grievance in their minds lay with their opposition to American and other Western promoters of globalization—liberal values that threaten traditional Islamic cultures in the Middle East and South and Southeast Asia. Adding fuel to these reactionary fires was Western pressure for liberalization of social policy in even conservative regimes, coupled with increasing American, British, and other European military presence in the region.

Reading their public, self-justificatory statements in the years both before and after the attacks, it is not hard to identify motives held by *al-Qaeda* leaders for attacking the United States and other regimes seen as serving their own interests in coalition with American policy elites. Particularly offensive to the leadership of *al-Qaeda* and others of like mind who supported them was the presence at the time of American military bases in Saudi Arabia—home to Islamic sacred shrines in Mecca and Medina—or elsewhere in the Gulf.

Given these grievances, the choice of 9/11 targets was not arbitrary: the World Trade Center symbolized increasingly globalized, liberal capitalism in which the United States is the dominant player and the Pentagon the military instrument used to advance American interests worldwide. Had they been successful in attacking the Capitol or the White House, *al-Qaeda* operatives would have struck a blow to the political center of the globalization project, the command centers for the use of military force, and the support base for the state of Israel.

Successful regime change effected by armed intervention against the Taliban in Afghanistan began with air attacks in October 2001, followed by a ground invasion and defeat of the Taliban by mid-November, and installation of an interim government in December. Given these successes gained by intervening militarily in Afghanistan, there were increasing calls within the neoconservative policy elite for similarly decisive action in Baghdad, drawing support from Iraqi expatriates also committed to overthrowing Saddam Hussein's regime.

Armed intervention without immediate cause for going to war made the decision to invade Iraq in March 2003 more problematic than the earlier invasion of Afghanistan, which had a much clearer and widely accepted *casus belli*: complicity by the Taliban in giving aid to *al-Qaeda*— a secure base for its operatives to use. Given this complicity by the Afghan regime, it had been relatively easy for the Bush administration to establish legitimacy internationally for armed intervention and to assemble multilateral participation by NATO alliance members and other coalition partners. The same was not true in the lead-up to war with Iraq.

In many respects the armed intervention in Afghanistan in 2001 was similar to going to war a decade earlier against Iraq after its invasion of Kuwait. Both campaigns were directed against perpetrators of attacks and conducted multilaterally under the legal authority of the UN Security Council. Liberating Kuwait as well as dissuading or deterring Iraq from executing any plans to attack Saudi Arabia or other Gulf states were the objectives pursued by President George H.W. Bush and other policymakers in 1991. Denying sanctuary to *al-Qaeda* given by the Taliban regime in Afghanistan defined the purpose sought by the American leadership under President George W. Bush in 2001 and 2002.

By contrast to these two cases, going to war with Iraq in 2003 lacked the international legitimacy that comes from responding under UN auspices defensively and multilaterally to an attack—acts of war perpetrated by others. Regime change in Baghdad remained a core objective but intervening for this purpose required further justification—or so thought the secretary of state and others in the administration and on Capitol Hill. On the other hand, the pro-war coalition that ultimately proved decisive in persuading the president to go to war included the vice president and secretary of defense, supported by neoconservatives holding important civilian positions in the Department of Defense (DoD).[10]

That bureaucrats can try to block or slow the implementation of new policies with which they may disagree has been well established, but there was no such opposition or bureaucratic inertia evident in the defense secretary's offices. Although not widely reported, in addition to the administration's political appointees, career civil servants sympathetic to neoconservative ideas—some put in their positions during the Reagan–Bush administrations—formed an important bureaucratic base, particularly in the Office of the Secretary of Defense (OSD), which facilitated policy implementation. Those elsewhere in DoD who registered opposing views, notably in the Department of the Army, were removed from their positions,[11] thus sending a clear and unambiguous signal to any who would stand in the way of what had become a solidary administration and DoD policy position.

Much to the dismay of the vice president and secretary of defense, who feared policy reversal, the national security adviser, Condoleezza Rice, did use her position of influence with the president to arrange a private dinner with his secretary of state—affording the senior cabinet officer an opportunity to express his reservations before the president finalized his decision to invade. Notwithstanding his best efforts, Secretary of State Powell proved unpersuasive and lost this eleventh-hour political battle on the Potomac to the Cheney–Rumsfeld coalition. Having had his say, he complied with the decision and subsequently defended the administration's position in the UN Security Council.

Search for a viable *casus belli* had become the policy-maker challenge in the weeks prior to invading Iraq. On what ground could regime change through invasion be legitimated? As insiders later admitted, the one justification upon which consensus could be built was armed intervention to forestall Iraqi acquisition or use of weapons of mass destruction—chemical, biological, or nuclear. Going well beyond disarmament of a state thought to possess (or that might come to possess) weapons of mass destruction, the decision to intervene was accompanied by an aspiration articulated by President Bush and others to establish in Iraq a democratic regime as a new liberal model for other Middle East countries to emulate.

As with most actions, the intervention served multiple purposes or had multiple effects—some intended, some not. We cannot know with certainty, of course, the relative priority or even all of the motives in the heads of policymakers that drove the decision to invade. Whatever the actual motives or stated purposes might be, we at least can estimate beforehand and assess afterward the diverse outcomes that flow from any such decision. In the Iraqi case, removing Saddam Hussein's regime not only allowed what turned out to be a fruitless search for weapons of mass destruction but also settled old scores.

Looming prominently were important gains to be realized from the invasion—indeed, in the eyes of many, the real reasons for invading were very strategic: Israel and oil. Regime change certainly removed Iraq, for a time at least, as one of Israel's potent enemies. Of course, an unintended consequence was that this also advantaged Iranian policymakers, now free from the Iraqi threat to turn greater attention to their own campaign against Israel and to exercise increased influence in the Gulf as well.

Removing Iraq as a near-and-present danger to Israel thus was a mixed blessing since doing so also removed a significant regional threat to Iranian leaders previously posed by Saddam Hussein's regime in Baghdad. Be that as it may, the invasion did establish strategic bases in Iraq and expansion of others in the region that could be used to defend American oil and other interests. To many observers, particularly those wearing realist lenses, this was the decisive rationale for intervention, albeit under a dual cover: the search for weapons of mass destruction and the promotion of American liberalism, trying to use the intended democratic transition in Iraq as a model for all of Araby!

## ARMED INTERVENTION, SOVEREIGNTY, AND INTERNATIONAL LAW

Understandings of international law or the rule of law matter when policymakers internalize them as guides to the making and implementation of foreign policy. Otherwise, laws stand as abstractions (or distractions) "out there" and do not enter the decisionmaking policy space unless others push them "in here." Certainly the decision to invade Iraq was not the first (nor likely will it be the last) time legal constraints were perceived as contrary to objectives seen as serving the national interest.

Consistent with past practices, US decisionmakers did turn successfully to the UN and NATO to secure backing for the invasion of Afghanistan in 2002, which unseated the Taliban regime in Kabul that had given sanctuary to *al-Qaeda*. The story was decidedly different, however, when it came to mustering international support for invading Iraq on the premise that the regime in Baghdad was acquiring weapons of mass destruction (WMD). Notwithstanding an extraordinary effort by the secretary of state, the director of the CIA, and other officials to make the case for invading Iraq on these grounds, UN Security Council members passed resolutions limited only to condemning violations of earlier Security Council resolutions and warning that multilateralism and security-oriented alliances unspecified actions might be taken in the absence of Iraqi compliance.

Led by President Bush and British Prime Minister Tony Blair, policymakers from the United States and the United Kingdom coalesced, albeit not without substantial reservations, particularly on the British side. The July 2002 "Downing Street" documents of a meeting of the prime minister and other British officials, leaked to the London *Sunday Times* on May 1, 2005, give us an interpretive understanding of their American policymaking counterparts. The memo prepared for the meeting complained that "the US Government's military planning for action against Iraq . . . lacks a political framework. In particular, little thought has been given to creating the political conditions for military action, or the aftermath and how to shape it." The British identified the aim of US military planning as simply "the removal of Saddam Hussein's regime, followed by elimination of Iraqi WMD."

There was concern, however, that "a post-war occupation of Iraq could lead to a protracted and costly nation-building exercise," particularly since "the US military plans are virtually silent on this point." Most interesting is the reflection on the relative lack of interest by American policymakers on the constraining effect of international law:

> US views of international law vary from that of the UK and the international community. Regime change *per se* is not a proper basis for military action under international law. But regime change could result from action that is otherwise lawful. We would regard the use of force against Iraq, or any other state, as lawful if exercised in the right of individual or collective self-defence, if carried out to avert an overwhelming humanitarian catastrophe, or authorised by the UN Security Council.[12]

At the meeting on July 23, 2002, Sir Richard Dearlove, the head of British secret intelligence (MI6), observed that in "his recent talks in Washington . . . military action was now seen as inevitable. Bush wanted to remove Saddam, through military action, justified by the conjunction of terrorism and WMD" and "the intelligence and facts were being fixed around the policy." He observed that the US National Security Council "had no patience with the UN route" and that "there was little discussion in Washington of the aftermath after military action." For his part, the foreign secretary added that "it seemed clear that Bush had made up his mind to take military action, even if the timing was not yet decided. But the case was thin."

All of this posed a direct challenge to the corpus of international law, particularly that relating to sovereignty and armed intervention. Although senior policymakers in the Bush administration may have cared less than their British counterparts about these legal considerations, securing British cooperation as a coalition partner did lead the US to take them more seriously than they otherwise likely would have felt obliged to do. What the British wanted was UN authorization for the intervention, a position also finding support by policymakers in the US Department of State.

A broad interpretation of the self-defense exception as authorizing pre-emptive intervention was revolutionary in its implications. Critics in other policy elites and attentive publics abroad expressed concern that continuation of a US propensity to intervene unilaterally undermined any residual constraining influence that sovereignty retained. The concern was that the precedent set would become common practice not just by great powers but also by other states engaged in regional conflicts.

From this point of view, extending the self-defense exception well beyond its customary interpretation to include a generalized right to pre-empt could have destabilizing consequences adverse to a conservative interest in sustaining the existing order of international relations. To both liberal-internationalist and conservative-internationalist policy elites, changing established norms to establish a virtually unfettered right of pre-emptive intervention is fraught with problems. The status quo in which US policymakers and those of other great powers have so vested an interest is put in jeopardy when resort to armed intervention becomes commonplace.

Calculations of what is in the national interest (not to mention vital interest) of the United States vary substantially as different administrations in Washington formulate their foreign-policy objectives. Human rights and humanitarian objectives, whether understood as part of national interest or not, have also influenced American foreign-policy choices from time to time. There is also an identifiable ideational motive for some interventions, such as spreading liberal thought or democracy as its political form. In chapter 6, I identify a strong historical propensity in American foreign policy to use force not only for defense of the homeland but also to intervene militarily or otherwise in diverse contingencies motivated by one or another of these aims.

## CRITERIA FOR INTERVENING (OR NOT INTERVENING)

Threats and opportunities are constructions in the minds of decision-makers. They do not all agree on these subjective calculations or on the weight or utility to be placed on diverse criteria for deciding to use force. The criteria that decisionmakers tend to consider to a greater or lesser degree, depending on who is participating in (or influencing) the decisionmaking process, are listed below. Their rank order in importance often varies significantly among members of the decisionmaking group. Thus, these eight criteria in table 5 are by no means a rank-ordered list.

What matters for our purposes—explaining the making and implementation of American foreign policy—is not norms, legal principles, and organizational frameworks on rights to intervene and established modes of conduct abstractly "out there," but rather the extent to which these factors are internalized by the policymakers and fellow members of the policy elites of which they are a part. The ideas they have and the subjective judgments about interests and other purposes they make are what drive American foreign policy in general and, in particular, the propensity to use force in armed interventions and the warfare that results when met by armed resistance or attack.

## Table 5a. Decisionmaking criteria for armed intervention.

1. *objectives in relation to calculations of national interest*: Next to defining the meaning of national security, nothing is more subjective than understandings of what is or is not in the national interest—not to mention specifying *core* or *vital interests*

2. *expected cost in lives and treasure*: Difficult to estimate, the more typical error is underestimating both human and financial costs

3. *likelihood of winning* (or risk of losing or not attaining objectives): Dangers in confronting other great powers and the complexity of trying to counter insurgencies effectively have made expectations of "winning" difficult to estimate

4. *legal and moral bases for armed intervention*: How much stock a given president and advisers put in the prohibition against intervening in the domestic affairs of another sovereign state affects the range of options they select. Nevertheless, certain legal exceptions may allow armed intervention: if (a) the legitimate government of a state invites the intervention, (b) the United Nations Security Council authorizes it under Article 42 of the UN Charter in efforts to maintain or restore international peace and security, (c) an alliance like NATO, consistent with Article 51 of the UN Charter, authorizes it under Article 5 of the North Atlantic Treaty for collective-defense purposes, (d) a legal claim of a national right only to rescue citizens caught in harm's way due to natural disasters or political unrest, and (e) a customary international claim to intervene for human rights, as in stopping genocide.

Notes: With respect to item 4(e), treaties and conventions on human rights do not provide a legal basis for armed intervention unless these abuses are threatening inter-national peace and security, thus an Article 42 (chapter 7) basis under the UN Charter. On the other hand, some argue that a right to intervene for humanitarian or human rights purposes is a construction that is emerging in customary international law. The more states intervene for such purposes, the stronger is the argument that a customary international law basis obtains.

## Table 5b. Decisionmaking criteria for armed intervention (Cont.).

5. *readiness of military forces for deployment*: Are military forces ready for deployment in sufficient numbers to carry out assigned tasks? Even if they are technically *ready*, have they been taxed by prior deployments that continued to call for sacrifices that undermine morale so important to combat effectiveness? Is public and congressional support substantial enough to warrant calling up for overseas deployment reserve forces or committing Air and Army National Guard units to augment active duty forces? For major contingencies, is there public and congressional support for activating the selective service system, reinstituting the draft?

6. *support from allies or coalition partners*: Going it alone means imposing the entire human and financial cost of the intervention on the American citizenry. By contrast, enlisting allies and coalition partners not only shares costs, but also tends to legitimate an intervention as having international support—a multilateral action, not just an American, unilateral event.

7. *expected net effect on the human condition*: Often difficult to estimate accurately, armed interventions gain in legitimacy when the net effect is expected to be positive. By contrast, when the net effect on the country and its people (as well as the sacrifices made by the intervening party) are judged to be negative, the proposed intervention may not be warranted.

8. *degree of public support for armed intervention*: This factor may become the most important if the intervention is to be sustained over a long period of time—measured in years, not just months or days.

## NOTES

1. Kenneth N. Waltz, *Man, the State and War.* (New York: Columbia University Press, 1959), p. 209.

2. In fact, explosion of a steam engine below decks—not action taken by the Spaniards—was the cause of the sinking of the Maine.

3. North Vietnamese torpedo boats were accused of firing upon the destroyer *USS Maddox* on August 2, 1964 when, in fact, the *Maddox* had fired warning shots against the boats first, thus provoking the North Vietnamese response. The report of a second incident on August 4th apparently did not occur.

4. The WWII National Museum, New Orleans.

5. James J. Matray, "Dean Acheson's Press Club Speech Reexamined" in *The Journal of Conflict Studies*, Vol. XXII, No. 2 (Spring 2002).

6. Ho Chi Minh Museum, Ho Chi Minh City (Saigon), April 4, 2015.

7. Under Eisenhower there were some 600 advisers, and 16,000 under Kennedy.

8. Average US killed in action (KIA) in 1968 was 278 per week. The average number of draft notices was 30,000 per month. Source: Dan Caldwell, Pepperdine University.

9. The reference is to the renowned Prussian strategist, Baron Carl von Clausewitz (1780-1831) who argued that to win any battle, much less a war, the effort should be to destroy or substantially weaken the enemy's warmaking capability. He makes this claim repeatedly in *On War*, various editions.

10. Agreement on policy sealed by a three-decade close friendship between Vice President Richard Cheney and Secretary of Defense Donald Rumsfeld constituted the core group, supported by DoD Deputy Secretary Paul Wolfowitz (generally recognized at the time as the intellectual leader for many neoconservatives), Undersecretary for Policy Douglas Feith, Assistant Secretary for Intelligence Stephen Cambone, and certain members of the Defense Advisory Board, notably Richard Perle.

11. The secretary of defense forced the resignation of the secretary of the army and the way was cleared for the chief of staff of the army to retire. Both left over disagreement with Secretary Rumsfeld and Deputy Secretary Wolfowitz on the size of forces needed to invade and occupy Iraq—

the latter opting for a much smaller commitment of forces than the army leadership thought necessary.
12. "Downing Street" documents, July 2002.

# PART II

# FOREIGN POLICY AND THE AMERICAN EXPERIENCE

# CHAPTER 5

# INTERPRETIVE UNDERSTANDINGS AND AMERICAN EXCEPTIONALISM

Foreign policy was no strange subject matter to the policy elites that constituted the American republic in the 1780s. Cultivation of French ties had been decisive in defeating British forces in the American Revolution—ties that had been developed by Benjamin Franklin as the American envoy in France (1776–85), successfully securing that country's support for the revolutionaries. The importance of foreign affairs to both security and commerce did not have to be introduced, but had been part of the normative fabric internalized by leaders and policy elites since the earliest colonial days. Britain's relations in foreign policy with France, the Netherlands, and Spain on matters of war, peace, and commerce were central to the security and wellbeing of the colonies in America.

It is from historical experience—the interpretations that gain legitimacy and become the commonly accepted "wisdoms" drawn from the past —that we can observe the construction of norms over long stretches of time. When internalized by policy elites, these shared meanings and value orientations decidedly affect the way they think and act on policy questions. Commonly accepted meanings and orientations become institutionalized as established norms that also account for continuities in policies over long spans of time. I turn briefly to the colonial experience to find the roots of norms and orientations that became internalized by policymakers, influencing the ways they think and the means they employ in the making and implementation of foreign policy.

## THE EIGHTEENTH-CENTURY ROOTS OF PRESENT-DAY UNDERSTANDINGS

Openness to commerce, coupled with militancy toward adversaries abroad, are recurrent themes deeply set in the American experience. The British Crown told its subjects going to the New World to "build and fortify" their settlements "for their better safeguard and defence." Security mattered. For this purpose the Jamestown settlers were to equip themselves with "armour, weapon[s], ordnance, powder, victuals, and all other things necessary for the said plantations and for their use and defence."[1]

Relations with states "in league or amity with us" allowed England to reach out for external support for its settlers, telling foreign governments to take action against those who would "rob or spoil by sea or by land or do any act of unjust and unlawful hostility to any the subjects of us." With respect to the native population, the objective was "in time" to bring indigenous peoples "to humane civility and to a settled and quiet government" while, at the same time, making the colony free of any foreign influence. It was, after all, an English colony with rights to defend itself—a declaration addressed explicitly "to all Christian kings, princes and estates" (i.e., France, Holland, Spain, Portugal, and any other European state).

English subjects settling in Plymouth expressed similar concern in the Mayflower Compact (1620) that their security should be found in the unity of common defense for their "better Ordering and Preservation." This formed the principal reason to "covenant and combine" themselves together into "a civil Body Politik." Security was to be found in unity, a view held by settlers and their leaders at both Jamestown and Plymouth. It was a civil society constructed by the settlers, albeit remaining loyal to their Stuart king, James I. This early understanding of security through the unity offered by social covenant foreshadowed justifications offered more than a century and a half later for union among 13 colonies as they declared their independence and later constituted themselves under the Articles of Confederation (1783) and then the US Constitution (1789).

Settlers throughout the colonial period perceived threats from the indigenous, native-American populations they were displacing as well as from Spain to the south and France to the north and west. Along with commercial advantage, security of the English colonies was also a motivation for forcing the Netherlands in 1674 to cede their New Amsterdam colony as part of a broader settlement of Anglo-Dutch wars in Europe. No longer would colonies in New England be separated physically from English colonies to the south. New York connected the colonial union, which not surprisingly the British later saw as strategically vital to retaining their position during the American Revolutionary War (1776–81).

Tribes allied with the French against British colonial interests were the enemy in the French and Indian War (1754–63), the North American theater in the Seven Years' War that resulted in cession to Britain of the frontier south of the Great Lakes and east of the Mississippi River. This was the war in which George Washington, then in his 20s, had fought in British forces, establishing his identity as a military man. He would in time become linked to the military wing of a revolutionary elite opposed to the Crown, leading an armed insurgency against Britain and its Royal Army. Benjamin Franklin, John Adams, and Thomas Jefferson were among those prominent in the insurgency's political wing.

In our recounting of historical events that led to the establishment of an American republic we sometimes pass over too quickly the internalization of English norms by colonial elites. After all, they were subjects of the Crown until finally establishing their new identities as Americans. Normative constructions in Britain mattered to elites in the American colonies. To the leadership of the American Revolution, this was not some foreign, "English" history. It was their history. In this regard, the legitimacy of rebellion against the Crown for what were seen as infringements on the rights of subjects was already well established.

Early precedent was set demanding rights and other concessions from the Crown in the Magna Carta (1215). Much later was the English civil war in the 1640s (execution of Stuart King Charles I in 1649), followed by a turbulent period that concluded in 1689 with proclamation of the English Bill of Rights and accession by William and Mary to the throne upon invitation of parliament. These successful challenges to monarchical authority contributed to making rebellion legitimate in the minds of an American revolutionary policy elite well-steeped in this history. Indeed, by the end of the seventeenth century sovereignty in Britain and the colonies no longer rested in the Crown alone, but rather with the "king in parliament," as the new constitutional arrangement would come to be called.

Franklin's diplomacy in Paris had secured French intervention on the American revolutionary side, which proved decisive in the military defeat of British forces at Yorktown in 1781. The Treaty of Paris negotiated in 1783 with the British by Franklin, John Adams, and John Jay declared that the former colonies were now "free sovereign and independent states." Foreign policy obviously mattered. Worthy of further historical study were the networks Franklin used to secure this success. Then, as now, networks connect or crosscut policy elites at home and abroad. Franklin's success was due not to some convergence of abstract factors "out there," but rather to the personal and interpersonal connections he established and the subjective understandings and inter-subjective exchanges he cultivated "in here" within and across policy elites.[2]

How to replace the king-in-parliament formula remained the central political problem faced by the new republicans who framed the Articles of Confederation and their "amendment" just six years later in the form of an entirely new US Constitution. The distribution of powers between king and parliament was a project still under construction in Britain, although the players really had no idea at the time the direction this evolution would take in the centuries to follow.

Notwithstanding these events that elevated parliamentary authority, kings were still important, particularly in foreign affairs. It was this understanding that motivated Alexander Hamilton in 1787 at the constitutional convention in Philadelphia to advocate lifetime tenure for an elected president (as if he were king) and a similarly constituted lifetime senate (like the British House of Lords)—those serving in these positions on good conduct and removable only for cause.

Although Hamilton's more extreme position was not accepted, it did reflect thinking across policy elites that a separate, strong executive was an essential part of constitutional arrangements. It was their understandings of the late eighteenth-century British or "Georgian" model at the time of monarchical authority still prominent in foreign affairs that influenced their decision to opt for a stronger presidency in relation to the Congress than otherwise might have been their choice. In this regard, the US Supreme Court has seen the Crown's late eighteenth-century primacy in British foreign affairs being passed to the federal government as a unit (not to the states in their separate capacities), the American presidency assuming in the United States the prominent position it has relative to the legislature in foreign affairs previously exercised by the Crown.[3]

This idea of a presidency, particularly strong in foreign affairs, was central to thinking within the Federalist Party. One hears an echo of this sentiment among policy elites and attentive publics associated with the present-day Federalist Society—a name that evokes memory of this position on executive primacy held by members of the erstwhile Federalist Party in the eighteenth and early nineteenth centuries.

Although George Washington was not formally a partisan, a strong presidency in foreign affairs was consistent with the understanding he shared with Federalists, who included his presidential successor John Adams, Alexander Hamilton, and—perhaps most importantly on constitutional issues—John Marshall. As Supreme Court Chief Justice, Marshall later affirmed the federal government's supremacy in both interstate and international commerce.[4] Given the constitutional treaty-making power in which the executive has the lead role and the presidential position as commander-in-chief of the armed forces, important foundations were in place for expanding presidential power in foreign policy over the next two centuries.

Congress remained an important influence in foreign policy through its right by a majority vote of both houses to appropriate money for all federal expenditures and to declare war, as well as the concurrence by two-thirds of its senators in treaty ratification and confirmation by a simple majority on diplomatic and other presidential appointments. Nevertheless, on foreign policy and national security matters the balance of power and authority between the branches was still clearly tipped to the executive side.

The contrasting Jeffersonian view that put primacy with the people and their representatives in the Congress was more domestically focused. His own diplomatic experience as Minister to France (1785–89) and as Secretary of State (1789–93) in Washington's first term contributed to his understanding of the role the executive plays in foreign policy. Jefferson was to apply this in his own administration by sending naval forces in 1801 to pursue pirates in the Mediterranean that had been interfering with American commerce and to engage in negotiations with France for purchasing the Louisiana territory west of the Mississippi River in 1803.

## EARLY CONSTRUCTIONS OF PRECEDENTS AND NORMS TO GUIDE FOREIGN POLICY

Precedents set in Washington's administration, it being the first presidency of the new Constitutional republic, were the bases of important norms that became institutionalized with the passage of time. Secretary of War Henry Knox accompanied President Washington to the Senate in August 1789 for an advisory on treaties made with native-American tribes. Instead of conducting a debate in his presence, the matter was referred to committee. That was the last time Washington or any president since has appeared in person on treaty matters. Washington and all of his successors have met the constitutional requirement to seek the "advice and consent" of the Senate on the ratification of treaties by formal, written exchanges and the work of their staffs.

The French Revolution well underway and the British at war with France, Washington sent John Jay to negotiate with the British, seeking to broaden the American diplomatic outreach, settle remaining post-Revolutionary War issues, and achieve commercial and other objectives. The resulting Treaty of London in 1794 (or "Jay Treaty") got the British to remove their residual military forces from the northwest territories south of Canada, delineate the US border with British Canada, send war debts to arbitration, and open trade with Britain and its colonies, albeit with limits on US cotton exports. Washington and his treasury secretary, Alexander Hamilton, strongly endorsed the treaty and secured the necessary two-thirds vote in the Senate—a chamber dominated at the time by the more anglophile Federalist Party members in the north, who also had important commercial interests at stake.

The restriction on cotton exports was particularly onerous to southern interests represented by the more francophile Jeffersonians in the Democratic-Republican Party (predecessor of the Democratic Party) then dominant in the House under the leadership of James Madison, Jefferson's protégé, who opposed the treaty. Thomas Jefferson himself was no longer Washington's secretary of state, having returned to private life in 1793. Even though it had no constitutionally defined role in the treaty-ratification process, the House of Representatives had to decide whether to fund its provisions. In a 51–48 vote (Madison among the nays), the House finally chose not to use its appropriations power to block compliance with treaty obligations. It was an extraordinarily important precedent.

Beyond such precedents, Washington's farewell address was also a summary of prescriptive norms for the new republic. Their repetition in speeches and documentary references over the coming centuries effectively wove these shared understandings into a foreign-policy fabric or tapestry used selectively to justify or legitimate policy choices made in different times and circumstances than Washington ever could have imagined. In his own time, however, he recognized how important unity of the 13 states was to national security at home and in the conduct of foreign policy abroad. He worried, as had John Jay and Alexander Hamilton in the first nine Federalist Papers, that different northern, southern, and western interests could divide the country and lead to a break-up of the union into competing coalitions or alliances that would be less able to resist foreign encroachments they feared emanating from both Britain and Spain.

Supporters of peaceful-engagement policies toward other countries find a basis for their position in Washington's prescriptions in the farewell address to "observe good faith and justice towards all nations" and to "cultivate peace and harmony with all" as being in the country's "interest." He called for flexibility in the conduct of foreign policy that avoided both "permanent, inveterate antipathies against particular nations and passionate attachments for others."

Trade was a great economic opportunity for the new republic, but he urged that "in extending our commercial relations," it should "have with them as little political connection as possible." Washington was concerned lest "foreign intrigue" or "the impostures of pretended patriotism" lead the country astray. The country need not in any event "entangle our peace and prosperity in the toils of European ambition, rivalship, interest, humor or caprice." Accordingly, the US was "to steer clear of permanent alliances with any portion of the foreign world," relying only on "temporary alliances for extraordinary emergencies."

Policy elites opposing entry of the United States in World Wars I and II saw themselves as true to the Washingtonian norm of avoiding the balance-of-power entanglements of European politics. Even the departure from neutrality in World War I—a "temporary" alliance—was abandoned quickly after the war as the Wilson administration sought, albeit unsuccessfully, to displace balance-of-power politics with a legally grounded collective security system within a League of Nations.

Ratification of the League Covenant failed, particularly given Republican opposition to Article X, which they saw as entangling the United States unnecessarily not only by committing the country "to respect and preserve as against external aggression the territorial integrity and existing political independence of all Members of the League," but also potentially by committing it to remedies the League's "Council shall advise."

The emergency leading to temporary alliance having passed with victory in the war against the Central Powers (the German, Austrian, and Turkish empires), opposing policy elites with their power grounded in the US Senate moved the country back to its Washingtonian moorings of non-involvement or neutrality in relation to European great-power politics. For his part, even Democratic President Franklin Roosevelt, who took office in 1933, included this sentiment in his oratory as late as 1940, explicitly referencing Washington and pledging to stay out of World War II.

Only after World War II and the onset of the Cold War was the Washingtonian non-involvement principle finally broken. The isolationist form neutrality took in the inter-war period of the 1920s and 1930s was replaced by a new internationalism. Nevertheless, the old non-involvement principle was by no means entirely dead. West European policy elites during the Cold War, fearful of their own security and mindful that the Americans were latecomers to the two world wars, openly worried that the United States might withdraw yet again, leaving them to face the Soviet and Warsaw Pact threats by themselves.

In the decades following World War II most American policy elites acknowledged the importance of involvement abroad, but they differed as to how deep any of these commitments should be. Moreover, after every foreign-policy defeat or disappointment (as in Vietnam) nationalist voices could be heard calling for a return to the domestic, minimizing foreign entanglements—a turning inward, nationalist line to which the Trump administration subscribed.

## THE MORALISM OF EXCEPTIONALISM

Values deeply embedded in American culture and held across the society are also internalized by members of policy elites. In turn, they influence not only the way they see and understand the world but also the way they choose to act. Moral principles one finds in both religious and secular sources as guides to conduct quickly become subsumed by moralism —the moral-laden discourse we frequently find among presidents and policymakers within their administrations that reflects their thinking or provides justification for the policy choices they make.

Shared meanings or modes of thinking in a particular policy elite can have enormous impact on the course foreign policy takes when members of this elite come to power and assume authoritative positions in government. Even from the outside we can see their influence in individual capacities and in both international and nongovernmental organizations. Personal and organizational networks crisscross the public and private policy spaces and link these participants directly or indirectly to foreign policymakers in government—linkages that extend abroad in truly global patterns of influence. These policy elites establish relationships with their governmental and nongovernmental counterparts in other countries, setting in motion patterns of reciprocal influence that may modify or sustain prior understandings, meanings, and other ideas that influence policy choice.

In 1630, a decade after Puritans landed at Plymouth in New England, Governor John Winthrop wrote a journal entry revealing his view of the colony's standing with God: "We entered into covenant with Him for this work. We have taken out a commission. The Lord hath given us leave to draw our own articles. . . . We have hereupon besought Him of favor and blessing" and "we shall find that the God of Israel is among us. . . . For we must consider that *we shall be as a city upon a hill* [emphasis added]. The eyes of all people are upon us." Good conduct compliant with this godly covenant will make "light brake [sic] forth as the morning"—"light spring out in darkness." [5]

It is a sermon that has had a long shelf life, invoked not only by John Adams and Abraham Lincoln, among others in the eighteenth and nineteenth centuries but also by recent presidents to convey this long-established idea of American exceptionalism. Using metaphors capturing the essence of this "exceptional" national self-image, Ronald Reagan, then governor of California, asserted an oft-quoted, classical-liberal claim to righteousness: "America is a shining city upon a hill whose beacon light guides freedom-loving people everywhere." His apparent belief that God inspired the American construction is clear: "You can call it mysticism if you want to, but I have always believed that there was some divine plan that placed this great continent between two oceans to be sought out by those who were possessed of an abiding love of freedom and a special kind of courage."[6]

Reagan's farewell address to the nation as president carried the same God-inspired, liberal sentiment:

> I've spoken of the shining city all my political life, but I don't know if I ever quite communicated what I saw when I said it. But in my mind it was a tall proud city built on rocks stronger than oceans, wind-swept, God-blessed, and teeming with people of all kinds living in harmony and peace, a city with free ports that hummed with commerce and creativity, and if there had to be city walls,

the walls had doors and the doors were open to anyone with the will and the heart to get here. That's how I saw it and see it still.[7]

Ronald Reagan's immediate successor, George Herbert Walker Bush, expanded upon the metaphor, noting while campaigning for the presidency in 1988 that "the city on the hill shined so bright it became 'a thousand points of light.'"[8] For his part, Bill Clinton incorporated Winthrop's perspective by acknowledging a "new covenant"[9] that gave America an important, scriptural basis for pursuing a progressive agenda in both domestic and world affairs.

Following attacks by al-Qaeda on September 11, 2001, George W. Bush observed: "America was targeted for attack because we're the brightest beacon for freedom and opportunity in the world." He added that "no one will keep that light from shining." The reaction was certainly consistent with the religious understanding he had expressed in his presidential campaign in 2000: "Our nation is chosen by God and commissioned by history to be a model to the world."

Seeing themselves as different from people in other countries, Americans are prone to interpret waves of immigration since the founding of the republic as evidence that coming to the US is what people out there would do if only they had the chance. Not that immigrants have always been treated kindly. Far from it. No, the typical American view is that the first-generation newcomers must earn their way to citizenship and accept this distinctive American "way of life." Only their children born on American soil can enjoy a free ride on the citizenship conveyed to them by law in civil society.

American exceptionalism[10] is an understanding internalized knowingly or unknowingly—an historically grounded, shared meaning that affects the way many Americans (including policy elites) think about the world and their privileged place in it. It was, after all, a new republic designed by the architects of the US Constitution. Visiting the United States in 1831 as a young man still in his 20s,[11] Frenchman Alexis de Tocqueville observed how this sense of exceptionalism had already become well established among the masses of the public.

Exceptionalism is a highly subjective, national self-image that in the American case quickly takes a moralizing turn. "God bless America" is not only a common refrain in presidential and other political speeches, but also an anthem that prays God "to guide" the country "through the night with a light from above." Quite apart from how others in foreign lands might see and understand them, Americans like to see themselves as morally superior. It is as if God had singled out the country and its inhabitants as the model republic for the rest of the world to emulate. The sentiment found explicit expression in the nineteenth-century doctrine of manifest destiny that was used to legitimate American expansionist policies on the North American continent, construct a US sphere of influence in Latin America, and export American liberal-republican understandings.

There is a fine line between benign beliefs in ethnocentric constructions embedded in the lenses policymakers wear to interpret the world around them and, by contrast, the stereotypes that mislead, erroneously portray, or falsely represent people in a particular society. Our purpose here is neither to confirm nor refute the empirical validity of such claims but only to identify them as belief patterns held by many about themselves and about others in different societies. What matters is the extent to which these claims about oneself or about others are internalized by policymakers, thus influencing the foreign-policy choices they make.

Notions of superiority are not uniquely American, of course. There is a universality in the ethnocentrism embedded in different national cultures and internalized to a greater or lesser degree by policymakers residing in these societies. Thus, given their national prominence in philosophy, literature, architecture, fine arts, music, and even cuisine, the French in Tocqueville's time, as now, tend, it is often said, to see themselves as culturally superior.

If this identification of notions of superiority as belief patterns held by individuals within and across policymaking elites is correct, the allusion to cultural, not moral, superiority does differentiate claims made in the French and American ethnocentric variants. It is the moral claim in the American case that accounts for the sense that the country has been singled out for exceptional purposes, whether expressed in religious or secular terms. Put another way, this moralism, sometimes even expressed in self-righteous form, is at the root of American exceptionalism.

In some societies ethnocentrism takes positional form. From imperial days to the present, the legacy of more than five millennia of written history has made China in the Chinese understanding the "Middle Kingdom" at the world's center. People come to court China. The country need not venture too far from the Middle Kingdom to make its way in the world. Thus, as discussed in chapter 2, it was President Nixon who sent his national security advisor and other diplomats to venture forth prior to his own state visit to China in 1972—not the Chinese who reached out and came first to the United States.

For their part, Islamic countries that combine religious understandings with matters of state see this connection between the spiritual and the temporal as morally and practically superior to the secular conduct of politics—the separation of church and state prominent in the United States and non-Islamic, Western societies. The larger point is that beyond these few examples, we find ethnocentric notions of superiority as commonplace in the twenty-first century as in the past. One can find particular, culturally informed, ethnocentric understandings throughout the world, but it is the uniquely American brand that interests us here.

## THE IDEOLOGICAL CORE OF AMERICAN EXCEPTIONALISM

Liberalism is the ideological core of American exceptionalism. Often held with the intensity of religious fervor, at its roots American liberalism is republican, reflecting deep commitment to the idea that representative democracy and secular values elevate the individual and allow broad political, economic, and social freedoms. The idea of spreading this American democratic thought globally is not new in the American experience. Taking ideas with European origins and planting them in the New World as a greenhouse in which they could grow and mature for export abroad is central to an American vision of the country's origin, place, and role in the world. It is a perspective one finds not only expressed in patriotic terms but also is a belief carried to a greater or lesser degree by those who make and implement American foreign policy. Although these policymakers in their professional sophistication may try to minimize expression of this ideological component, it still seems always to be present.

Indeed, spreading liberal values with which Americans virtually all agree has been a recurrent theme in US foreign policy since the eighteenth-century founding of the republic. Subject to the rule of law, individuals enjoy broad civil liberties. They are free to express their thoughts and gather with others for political or other purposes, to engage economically in all forms of commerce, and to travel anywhere in the country and throughout the world. Why shouldn't the rest of the world conform to this model? To make the world over in this liberal, essentially ethnocentric image is a recurrent theme in American foreign policy.

That Americans do not always see themselves as ideological is indicative of just how ideological they are. The tenets of liberalism—the secular religion that defines its politics across the political spectrum—are part of national beliefs. Monuments to liberty and to Washington, Jefferson, Lincoln, and other national figures stand as secular temples in the national capital and in other cities. From childhood Americans hear and read stories with morals they internalize about the founding of the republic, the framing of the US Constitution, and establishing a uniquely American way of life. This is the stuff of ideology carried into adult life and reflected across policy elites and in the mass public.

American liberalism contains both socially liberal and socially conservative variants. Social liberals or "progressives" differentiate themselves from social conservatives, who are more prone to "classical liberal" values that in principle minimize or reduce the role of government. Social liberals or progressives are more prone to see government in its public works as extending a "hand up" to individuals to help them help themselves. The social conservative, by contrast, prefers to leave such matters almost entirely to individuals, turning for remedies to the private sector rather than to government. In practice, of course, both turn to government when they see it as in their interest to do so. Quite apart from what they may do, the rhetoric they use continues to reflect this difference of view on the proper role of government. Differences aside, social liberals and conservatives do converge on the importance of individuals—what they say and do—which defines their commitment to an essentially liberal ideology.

It was Franklin Roosevelt's New Deal that effectively transformed popular usage of the word *liberal* to what I refer to here as social-liberal or "progressive" understandings. Rather than a *laissez-faire* approach to the market and social questions of the day, governmental institutions were constructed and given a decisive role to play. This faith in government institutions needed in the Great Depression and World War II carried over into constructing the new post-war international order in which US decisionmakers played so leading a role.

Just as in domestic society, where federal and state agencies had been called upon to play instrumental roles in dealing with socioeconomic and military-security challenges, this approach also gained legitimacy for addressing international issues. Policymakers had internalized the value of institutional approaches by governments to problems in civil society. Creation of a United Nations organization and UN system of affiliated international organizations, which had substantial legitimacy abroad where governmental and institutional approaches to societal questions were already well established, now found a receptive audience at home. Successes in the New Deal and World War II contributed to a perception of the efficacy of this newly found reliance on governmental institutions not only in the public understanding, but also in the minds of policymakers at that time.

Early signs of a gradual loss of faith in governmental institutions to deal with socioeconomic matters became apparent in the 1960s and 1970s. That government was the problem and not the preferred solution became the new article of ideological faith among social conservatives in the 1980s. Promoted in particular by the Reagan administration, this condemnation of governmental activism continued on a rhetorical level throughout the rest of the twentieth and into the twenty-first centuries. Quite apart from rhetoric, however, domestic reliance on the state continued to grow particularly in the military-industrial but also in non-defense sectors of economy and society.

The impact of this ideational shift ironically was realized in practice less at home than in US foreign policy. Policy elites in power, reflecting public distrust of governmental approaches, put relatively less emphasis on international organizations than in earlier decades. Institutionalized multilateralism continued in security-oriented alliances like NATO and in the routines of well-established institutions like the UN and its system of international organizations. Gone for the most part, however, was the earlier enthusiasm for institutional approaches to issues on the global agenda.

Although some growth in international organizations did take place, as in the opening in 1994 of a World Trade Organization (WTO) to replace the earlier General Agreement on Tariffs and Trade (GATT) framework, American policymakers tended to be very selective in their endorsements of multilateral approaches to problems, often working to curb or curtail the agendas of existing organizations. It was more of a "cherry-picking" approach to multilateralism—choosing it on a case-by-case basis when understood by policymakers as serving their particular national interests—

rather than being based on some generalized preference for dealing with issues multilaterally in institutional settings.

Varying substantially over the decades since World War II, these different understandings on government and institutional efficacy within and among policy elites and internalized by the policymakers themselves have influenced the way US policymakers conduct foreign policy in general and, in particular, how they approach international organizations. In the redefined American preference, issues previously on the agendas of multilateral institutions were to be left as much as possible to the private, nongovernmental sector both at home and abroad. Even the creation of the WTO gained acceptance among policy elites to the extent that it was understood as advancing free trade and other globalization goals beneficial to corporate and other private-sector, economic-liberal understandings of national interest. By contrast, attempts institutionally to deal multilaterally with the global environment and international crime proved far more difficult to advance.

As discussed in chapter 1, the Trump administration that took office in 2017 has pursued an "America First" foreign policy, clearly less committed either to advancing liberal values globally or to engaging multilaterally, whether through global institutions or diplomatic efforts. Put another way, the administration has walked away from the commitment to a rule-based liberal order constructed by both Republican and Democratic administrations in the post-World War II period. Notwithstanding these variations on institutional and multilateral preferences, however, we still observe a high degree of constancy in the American style of liberalism that continues to focus on individual civil rights and liberties domestically, putting decidedly less emphasis on the communitarian and economic-egalitarian values one finds more commonly in European and other liberal societies.

In the American understanding, globalization is liberalism on a global scale. The canons of a global civil society take three normative forms, thus guaranteeing through the rule of law individual rights: (1) to express their ideas freely in any form of communication, which now includes the Internet, social media networks, and other forms of telecommunications with truly global reach; (2) to be free to travel or move not just within one's home country but also across national borders anywhere in the world; and (3) to enjoy economic freedom to use one's resources to produce for market, buy and sell (import and export), and invest at home or abroad (reaping rewards from these transactions or suffering losses, as may be the case).

These three components constitute the ideological essence of the globalization project. The best of worlds from this admittedly ethnocentric perspective is one that duplicates America's own priorities: civil liberties as well as the social and commercial activities in which Americans customarily and openly engage within and across the 50 American states. Not that Americans are alone in holding these preferences. Others are found primarily in the First-World, advanced-industrial and post-industrial states and societies that subscribe to similar liberal values, albeit differing among them on the role government should play in the marketplace and in advancing egalitarian and communitarian values.

## THE PURITAN QUEST AGAINST THE FORCES OF DARKNESS

It is strong national, liberal-republican, moralist ethnocentrism that continues to influence American thought patterns in the making and implementation of the country's foreign policy. Americans tend to see themselves as carrying a moral torch, bringing light to the world. Lipset calls it "Protestant-inspired moralism" and comments that "Americans must define their role in a conflict as being on God's side against Satan —for morality against evil."[12] This was as much a part of President George W. Bush's framing of the post-9/11 problematique: the necessity of defeating what he called an "axis of evil" constituted at the time by Iraq, Iran, and North Korea.

Staking diabolical forces or figures through the heart is part of the puritanical heritage deeply set in the American culture. Although making specific references to evil may have propaganda value and serve manipulative purposes as policy elites try to garner public support for policies, there is also a sense that such moralist views oftentimes are in fact understandings held to a greater or lesser degree by the leaders themselves. Presidents and other policy spokespersons are often so persuasive in using such moralist language that they are perceived as speaking quite genuinely, which in fact may be the case.

The genre of moral quests to be met in foreign policy was clear in President Reagan's characterization of the Soviet Union in the 1980s as an "evil empire." For his part, President Eisenhower's Secretary of State, John Foster Dulles, argued in the 1950s that countries had a moral obligation to take a stand against communism. How could Sweden or other neutral or nonaligned countries really be neutral in this global challenge to the forces of good? To be so was no more than an accommodation of evil forces.[13]

In the same moralist vein, Franklin Roosevelt's war message (1941) declared Japan's "unprovoked and dastardly attack" a "day of infamy," calling for "the American people in their righteous might" to commit themselves to achieving "absolute victory" over the Japanese empire. Such moralism was also central to Woodrow Wilson's war message (1917) almost a quarter-century earlier. To Wilson it was a "war to end all wars" and to establish "a universal dominion of right." He underscored that "our motive will not be revenge . . . , but only the vindication of right." Indeed, "the world must be made safe for democracy," and to achieve this end "we shall conduct our operations as belligerents . . . [and] observe with proud punctilio the principles of right and of fair play we profess to be fighting for."

Moralism on Wilson's part[14] was famously present in the post-war negotiations leading to the League of Nations Covenant. British diplomat Harold Nicolson "observed him with interest, admiration and anxiety, and became convinced that he regarded himself, not as a world statesman, but as a prophet designated to bring light to a dark world." In this regard, Nicolson commented that Wilson was an "idealist" and "possessed, moreover, the gift of giving to commonplace ideas the resonance and authority of biblical sentences." For the president "the Balance of Power was now for ever discredited," having, in his words, put in its place "the reign of law, based upon the consent of the governed and sustained by the organized opinion of mankind."[15]

Wilson also came under the microscope of British economist John Maynard Keynes, then in his mid-30s, who observed the president directly at the same Paris negotiations in 1919:

> The President was like a Nonconformist minister, perhaps a Presbyterian. His thought and his temperament were essentially theological, not intellectual, with all the strength and the weakness of that manner of thought, feeling, and expression. It is a type of which there are not now in England or Scotland such magnificent specimens as formerly.[16]

To Keynes' satiric and critical eye, Wilson's approach, though short in substantive value, was not lacking in moralist tone:

> The President's Programme for the world, as set forth in his speeches and his Notes, had displayed a spirit and a purpose so admirable. . . . It was commonly believed at the commencement of the Paris Conference that the President had thought out, with the aid of a large body of advisers, a comprehensive scheme not only for the League of Nations but [also] for the mbodiment of the Fourteen Points in an actual Treaty of Peace.

> But in fact the President had thought out nothing; when it came to practice, his ideas were nebulous and incomplete. He had no plan, no scheme, no constructive ideas whatever for clothing with the flesh of life the commandments which he had thundered from the White House. He could have preached a sermon on any of them or have addressed a stately prayer to the Almighty for their

fulfilment, but he could not frame their concrete application to the actual state of Europe.[17]

Keynes tells us that the president's resolute commitment to principle embedded in the moral platform he had constructed made him inflexible in the normal give-and-take in diplomatic negotiations in which "the President stood for stubbornness and a refusal of conciliations."[18]

Moralism among policy elites is shared within the larger American society from which they come. When Americans in attentive publics and particularly the society as a whole become aware that the country's actual conduct in the "back alleys of the world"[19] may not always measure up to moral ideals that are so central to the national self-image, they prefer to see such untoward conduct as an aberration—something subject to corrective action, thus bringing the country back on track.

Thus, it is agencies gone awry that engage in assassination as a matter of policy or it is a few "bad apples" that torture detainees in wartime prisons set up at Abu Ghraib in Iraq, Bagram in Afghanistan, Guantánamo in Cuba, or elsewhere. These are commonly understood as errors by a few, subject to correction when discovered by others, and to punishment, for having damaged the national reputation by their untoward conduct. Even when such practices are understood as not just the province of a few, but rather intended policy, justification for such moral departures is often cast in the same Manichean, light versus dark, moralistic tones. In this self-justificatory, moralist understanding, to survive or make one's way in a world prone to evil conveys the right to do what one otherwise would not do—to act pragmatically, as necessity requires.

In a world filled metaphorically (and theologically) with darkness—one composed of many back alleys—it becomes necessary in some minds to deal pragmatically on the dark side of the reality that faces the policymaker. Vice President Cheney's secular reference to what might be necessary on the "dark side" in the post-9/11 world reflects this moralist understanding deeply set in the American historical-cultural experience. This good-versus-evil image was not unique to the vice president. Put religiously, the "righteous" have the obligation to slay the forces of evil with whatever means may be necessary.

Covert actions and "special" operations, and the agencies that conduct them, gain support from policymakers who have internalized the secular, if not religious, version of this idea that as a matter of state there may be an obligation to do or authorize things that would not pass the moral test if done in an individual, private capacity. As Max Weber put it in his lecture on "Politics as a Vocation" (1918), it is an "ethic of responsibility" that is held by the agents of the state, much as Machiavelli's Prince had to do things in the interest of security that were proscribed to others. In this formulation, common people outside of government remain governed by what Max Weber called the "ethics of ultimate ends"— a more conventional morality concerned religiously with one's own salvation that prohibits assassination, torture, going to war, theft, lying, eavesdropping, or other harmful conduct.

Not all Americans, much less all policymakers, accept this alleged right or obligation to do wrong. But some do. A few take the blind "patriotic" position that whatever the country does—right or wrong—it is the citizen's duty not to challenge authorities carrying out their national-security responsibilities. They may be prone to leave it to specialized agencies and their agents to do the dirty work on the dark side. Still others in the American public are oblivious to the whole question, perhaps not even cognitively aware of governmental conduct that does not conform to their prior expectations.[20] Finally, the many who are indignant about this mode of conduct (whether in policy elites or in the general public) are prone to see it as a "stain" harmful to the national image—a perspective that itself is often puritanical in both its construction and its articulation.

Those who accept the legitimacy of conduct on the dark side see it as an essential element of national security. Earlier in American history it may have been possible to eschew adverse conduct by the state and even to condemn it roundly when practiced by Britain or other great powers of the day, but proponents see that as a luxury relegated to the past when the US did not have the global position it now does and the responsibilities domestically and internationally that go with it. For those policymakers who think this way, the country has grown in maturity out of the protective Washingtonian guidance to avoid foreign entanglements and all that necessarily or customarily goes with power politics. It is to them a world of *Realpolitik* in which the US should play its cards wisely, whether in the light of day or on the dark side.

The Trump administration acquiesced when it became clear that the Crown Prince of Saudi Arabia's men brutally assassinated and dismembered *Washington Post* journalist, Jamal Khashoggi at the Saudi consulate in Istanbul on October 2, 2018. It was classic *Realpolitik* to overlook any culpability for the incident that might be in the hands of Mohammed bin Salman (MBS) for ordering the murder. In the absence of sufficient evidence in the public domain to prove "beyond a reasonable doubt" that MBS had ordered the murder, it was convenient for the president and secretary of state to avoid challenging the Saudi government. After all, US national interest in maintaining good relations with the Saudi kingdom —as understood by the administration—trumped any concern with moral or legal accountability.

In a similar way, the administration continued to support Saudi actions in Yemen—the president vetoing an April 2019 bipartisan resolution against continuing US support for the Saudi war, which passed 247-175 in the Democratic-controlled House and 54-46 in a Republican-controlled Senate. Moral concerns with any US culpability for war crimes and human suffering in Yemen were set aside as contrary to calculations of US national interest. Given strategic considerations related to oil, the balance of power in the Gulf vis-à-vis Iran, and business interests, the administration refused to compromise its support for its Saudi partner. President Trump made his position clear: "This resolution is an unnecessary, dangerous attempt to weaken my constitutional authorities, endangering the lives of American citizens and brave service members, both today and in the future."

On a brighter side, the idea that America is not only exceptional but also has a special role to play in the world is memorialized in the national monuments that capture this shared meaning. Since the founding of the republic, this prominent self-understanding of the country's exceptional role has driven US policymakers to extend illumination to others, spreading the word as secular (sometimes even religious) missionaries with an oft-repeated sermon calling for more democracy and building new republics in America's own "enlightened" image. Seen from this perspective, strident advocacy in 2003 by President Bush of democracy being best not only for Iraq but also for the Middle East as a whole, though noteworthy, was not particularly novel or unique in the American experience.

When we probe the religious foundations of American moralism, we find Manichaean understandings discussed above, the city of God versus the city of man in Augustinian thought,[21] good versus evil, and the essential depravity of humankind in Calvinist thought.[22] This religio-cultural, essentially Protestant, tradition[23] defines the moralism of American exceptionalism. The language of Madison and Hamilton on human depravity survives in twenty-first-century American understandings. As Madison put it so eloquently:

> The history of almost all the great councils and consultations held among mankind for reconciling their discordant opinions, assuaging their mutual jealousies, and adjusting their respective interests, is a history of factions, contentions, and disappointments, and may be classed among the most dark and degraded pictures which display the infirmities and depravities of the human character. If, in a few scattered instances, a brighter aspect is presented, they serve only as exceptions to admonish us of the general truth; and by their lustre to darken the gloom of the adverse prospect to which they are contrasted.[24]

If only men were angels, as Madison and Hamilton tell us in Federalist Paper No. 51! Still, this negativism is offset by a certain idealism: that the earthly city embodied in the American republic ultimately will prevail —the shining city on the hill.

## INTERNALIZED UNDERSTANDINGS AND POLICY CHOICE

Policy choice, then, is not just a coldly rational calculus in which gains and losses are weighed in the abstract, choosing the alternatives that maximize gain or minimize loss in particular contingencies. Although such "instrumental rationality" exercised by policymakers takes us part way, the path quickly becomes a dead end if we do not also take into account the ideas, shared meanings, and understandings policymakers develop, refine, and amend in inter-subjective exchanges with others. Instrumental rationality, defined as finding the optimal ways and means to maximize gains or minimize losses in the pursuit of objectives. may be trumped in some circumstances by a "value rationality" reflected in concern for national honor, duty, or commitment to a cause or promises made with little attention paid to material benefits or costs. Finally, the "bureaucratic rationality" of making and implementing policy that conforms with established ways of doing things may hold sway.[25]

As we seek to make the world and foreign policy within it more intelligible, interpretive understandings of material and ideational factors are what matter—not these factors *per se*, as if they were entities unto themselves. No, material or ideational factors "out there" do not really have an existence separate from us as causal factors in the theories we formulate about how the world works. It is the integration or synthesis of our understandings of international and domestic factors with those emanating from our consciousness as human beings that allows us to cut across individual, group, societal, and system levels of analysis "out there" to bring these understandings within ourselves.

Such an approach gives us grounds for hope that human beings can construct the ways and means of improving the human condition. Things need not stay the way they are. Unfortunately, this approach is also a ground for despair as human beings in power may share meanings leading them to pursue policies that take us in the opposite direction. Because policy elites are fellow human beings, we can find within them the seeds of enlightened policies that also serve their understandings of interest while allowing other players to reap benefits as well. They can learn to advance ideas grounded in interest that foster a rising tide that, as President Kennedy observed, raises all boats, not just my boat or the boats of those with like mind, but also the boats of others not so inclined. It can be positive sum, everyone having something to gain (or less to lose), albeit typically in different amounts.

On the other hand, we can bring more negative interpretive meanings to the table. Distrust, dislike, fear, and the like, lead us to see the decision space in zero-sum terms with one side's gains coming out of the other side's hide. Perhaps that in general is the way a particular decisionmaker or policy elite may see the world. It is the logic that underlay the Trump presidency's commitment to a short-term transactional calculus of gains and losses in making foreign policy deals. How long, after all, is one to take beneficence to the world only to suffer wounds for so doing? No good deed goes unpunished as others seek to take advantage. "Not even worth communicating with them," some are prone to conclude. We know what motivates them and the adverse criteria that inform their decisions and actions. It is a self-fulfilling prophecy, of course, as distrustful agents act in ways injurious toward others, suffering the same in return.

However policy elites see the world "out there," American exceptionalism nevertheless remains a core belief shared by most that profoundly influences the making and implementation of both domestic and foreign policy. It is a statement of how Americans tend to see themselves. Wrapped in patriotic understandings, it is shielded from critical scrutiny. It is not really subject to debate, particularly by those who see the unique American role in the world as an article of faith. The president and other officials wear flag pins or other patriotic symbols to signify their commitment to the country. Internalized to a greater or lesser degree by policy elites in and out of power, American exceptionalism remains a significant ideational influence on how policymakers knowingly or unknowingly tend to think and act.

Indeed, this exceptionalism is captured strikingly in the symbolic architectures of the capital city—the union in the lady of liberty that sits atop the Capitol dome with the "father" of the republic standing across the mall in the Washington monument, which together gave birth to the new republic that Americans see as an inspiring light to the world. The symbolism suggests influence of freemasonic iconography drawn from Egyptian mythology—the femininity of Isis (Lady Liberty) atop the capitol dome joined with the masculinity of Osiris (the phallic monument to Washington—"father" of the country), and the overarching spiritualty of the sun god Ra (the sun rising in the East, transiting the sky by day before setting in the West).

It was the new order of the ages (*novus ordo seclorum*) accompanied by the approving eye of the Creator (*annuit coeptis*—the year of the eye) that one finds inscribed on the Great Seal of the United States approved by the political leadership of the new republic in 1782. Flanked by the White House and the liberal light of the Jefferson Memorial, the sun rises dutifully in the east over the Capitol, its light passing in the course of the day over the Washington Monument, the White House, the Jefferson and other memorials, before setting in the west over the Lincoln Memorial, which symbolizes the preservation of the union.

This exceptional symbolism captures the beginning and the sustaining continuity of an idea—shared understandings not only on how the world should be organized but also what secular republican values should drive it. It is the memorialization of American exceptionalism that is captured in the architecture of the national capital.

## NOTES

1. Quotations are from the Virginia Charters (1606 and 1608).
2. Well-established in Pennsylvania freemasonry, Franklin cultivated French liberals (to include his newly found friend, Voltaire) in the Masonic *Loge des Neuf Soeurs* in Paris—a network with links to the French court essential to securing his diplomatic victory.
3. *United States v. Curtiss-Wright* (1936).
4. *Gibbons v. Ogden* (1824).
5. John Winthrop, "A Model of Christian Charity." The Manichaean light-dark contrast is found in John 1:4–5, 3:19–21; Matthew 5:14–16; and Revelation 21:23–6. John Milton also saw England as "holding up, as from a Hill, the new Lampe of saving light to all Christendome [sic]...." C.A. Patrides (ed.), *John Milton: Selected Prose* (Columbia, MO: University of Missouri Press, 1985, 1986), p. 81
6. "The Shining City upon a Hill" speech, January 25, 1974.
7. "Farewell Address to the Nation," January 11, 1989.
8. "I have spoken of a thousand points of light, of all the community organizations that are spread like stars throughout the Nation, doing good." Inaugural Address, January 20, 1989.
9. Acceptance speech, Democratic Party Convention, New York, July 16, 1992.
10. Seymour Martin Lipset, *American Exceptionalism* (New York: W.W. Norton, 1996).
11. Lipset refers to the American republic's "organizing principles and founding political institutions" as being in Tocqueville's view "exceptional, qualitatively different from those of other Western nations" (ibid., p. 13). Tocqueville (1805–59) published his observations in *Democracy in America* (1835). As his trip in 1831 indicated, he was clearly linked to American policy elites of the day. Among the leaders he met during his tour in the United States were President Jackson and Texans Sam Houston and Stephen Austin—fellow freemasons, which may account for the degree of access a Frenchman just 26 years of age could have to these prominent figures.
12. Lipset, pp. 19–20.
13. Townsend Hoopes, *The Devil and John Foster Dulles* (Boston: Little Brown, 1973).

14. Alexander L. George and Juliette L. George, *Woodrow Wilson and Colonel House: A Personality Study* (New York: John Day Co., 1956, and Mineola, NY: Dover Publications, 1964).

15. Harold Nicolson, *The Evolution of Diplomatic Method*, the Chichele Lectures, Oxford University, November 1953 (New York: Macmillan, 1954), pp. 84–7.

16. John Maynard Keynes, "The Council of Four, Paris, 1919," *Essays in Biography* (New York: Norton, 1951, 1963), p. 21.

17. Ibid., pp. 21–2.

18. Ibid., p. 31.

19. Questioning the legitimacy of assassination as a tactic in US foreign policy, the author asked former Secretary of State Dean Rusk about this practice during a seminar the secretary held in 1975 at the University of California, Berkeley. Referring broadly to what goes on in the "back alleys of the world," Rusk invoked a pragmatic rationale for dealing realistically with the world as he saw it. The auhor being just 30 at the time, Rusk answered politely but paternalistically about realities in the world that in his mind he knew so well.

20. On a failure to perceive what one does not expect to see, Leon Festinger, *A Theory of Cognitive Dissonance* (Stanford, CA: Stanford University Press, 1957).

21. St. Augustine, *The City of God*, trans. Gerald G. Walsh et al., ed. Vernon J. Bourke (Garden City, NY: Doubleday, 1958).

22. Total depravity is one of five points of orthodox Calvinism—unconditional election, limited atonement, irresistible grace, and perseverance being the other four. Duane Edward Spencer, *TULIP: The Five Points of Calvinism in the Light of Scripture* (Grand Rapids, MI: Baker Book House, 1979).

23. The Platonist–Augustinian tradition inspired Luther, Calvin, and other Protestant writers, differentiated them from the thinking in Aristotle and Aquinas more influential in Roman Catholicism. God's will is more determining in the rescue of human beings from the darkness in the former; good works by human beings exercising free will matter in the latter.

24. *Federalist Paper* No. 37. Hamilton refers to "the ordinary depravity of human nature"—the Calvinist theological understanding of "total depravity" as defining the human condition. *Federalist Paper* No. 78

25. Instrumental rationality (*Zweckrationalität*), the weighing of gains and losses—the common understanding of the term *rational*; value rational-

ity (*Wertrationalität*), the commitment to cause exhibited by the person willing to take risks and make sacrifices; and bureaucratic rationality in the routines and procedures that can make organizations function efficiently. Max Weber, *Economy and Society*, 2 vols., Guenther Roth and Claus Wittich, trans. and eds. (Berkeley, CA: University of California Press, 1978), pp. 24–6, 33, 36–7, 41, 154, 217 *et passim*.

## CHAPTER 6

# INTERVENTION AND EXPANSIONISM

We look back in time, exploring the thinking within policy elites that helps us account for the continuities we observe in more than 235 years of American foreign policy since the end of the Revolutionary War. In this review of intervention and expansionist foreign policy, I find recurrent themes that to varying degrees either unite or divide policymaking elites: (1) expansionism by purchase or conquest in the nineteenth century that served some, though not all, elite understandings of American interest; (2) moralist perspectives of God-given mission for some (and secular commitment by others) to promote liberal republicanism at home and abroad; (3) pursuit of gains to be found in international commerce —divisions on trade and protectionism among policy elites based on different understandings of regional or economic interests; and (4) a willingness to threaten or use force to serve commercial, security, or other understandings of interest—"war-hawk-"style militancy in some, but by no means all, policymaking elites.

In the increasingly globalized world economy and politics of the twenty-first century, expansionism no longer takes the same territorial form it once did. Policymakers understand that maintenance of the country's global capital position and continued access to resources now require a global presence by the corporate and financial sector that links these firms to their counterparts in other countries.

Armed intervention and warfare also have been and remain a large part of the American foreign-policy experience. (See chapter 4.) Naval, ground, and air forces operate both from home and from overseas bases that sustain the American interests or purposes policymakers identify. The agenda is substantial: dealing with threats from states, terrorist and criminal groups, maintaining security essential to commerce, and responding to environmental challenges, disasters, and other humanitarian needs.

## NINETEENTH-CENTURY WARS AND TERRITORIAL EXPANSIONISM

As minister to France while the US Constitution was being written in Philadelphia, Thomas Jefferson had worked closely with networked, anti-monarchical, republicans on the eve of the French Revolution. As with Franklin who represented US interests in France during the Revolutionary War, Jefferson cultivated members of French liberal elites —Lafayette Condorcet, and other freemasons.[1] Export of liberal ideology that also expanded US hemispheric influence was also apparent in the construction of new republics in the American image throughout Latin America. Beginning in the 1820s, this trend continued throughout the nineteenth century.

For most of the century, however, armed interventions by US military forces took place in contiguous territories—Florida, Texas, and Mexico— all part of continental expansion. One exception was intervention against the Barbary pirates in North Africa (1801–04) for disrupting trade by commercial interests in the Mediterranean. With Jefferson no longer wishing to pay tribute for protecting American merchant ships subject to pirate attacks in waters off the North African or Barbary coast (as the Adams administration had advocated), naval warfare began in 1801. Jefferson sent several warships to the region, and a number of naval battles ensued. Following a decisive marine landing,[2] peace was finally restored by agreement with the Pasha of Tripoli in 1805.

Another exception occurred when the US took sides in 1891 on behalf of the Chilean president in a civil conflict against forces tied to the Chilean legislature (incidents that included intercepting a commercial ship carrying arms to the legislative side and a riot in Valparaiso in which several American sailors were killed, wounded, or imprisoned by local authorities). Two years later the US intervened on the republican side against the monarchy in Honolulu, Hawaii. Annexation as a US territory occurred five years later (1898). In that same year war with Spain during the McKinley administration produced engagements that extended well beyond American soil to Cuba, Puerto Rico, and the Philippines.

By contrast, the foreign policy of the early republic in the last two decades of the eighteenth century was decidedly less ambitious. Notwith-standing their success in the Revolutionary War against the British, the Federalists became resolute in their avoidance of future conflicts, if at all possible. Certainly this was the tone of Washington's farewell address (1796), which warned against entanglements in European conflicts.[3]

The republic needed time to grow financially and militarily stronger if it were to hold its own against the great powers of the day. Concerned to allow the new republic a chance to survive in a hostile world, Washington and the Federalists who supported him sought to avoid warfare that would put the country unnecessarily at risk. They were also still smarting from the high costs of the Revolutionary War that, due to Hamilton's influence, were finally accepted as national debt. The Federalist, Hamiltonian position clearly served the capital or financial interests in New York and elsewhere in the northeast.

The Jeffersonian purchase of Louisiana from the cash-strapped French in 1803 was a peaceful form of territorial expansion, but resort to the use of force accounted for most of the acquisitions that followed. Although territorial expansion is customarily represented in American histories as a domestic issue, these land acquisitions were in fact part of a foreign policy that in the 1800s brought the US into armed conflict or negotiations with foreign powers: (1) war with Spain over Florida in 1818, which was purchased the following year and, in 1898, over Cuba and Puerto Rico, also extending by treaty US territorial control in the Pacific to Guam and the Philippines; (2) negotiations with the UK in 1817 setting the boundary between Canada and the US on the Great Lakes (extending it to the Louisiana territorial line the following year) and in the Pacific northwest in 1846; (3) war with Mexico from 1846 to 1848 (after the US annexed Texas in 1845), the peace treaty ceding territory from Texas to California—the southern border of Arizona and New Mexico expanded further in 1867 by purchase of additional land (the Gadsden Purchase); (4) negotiations with Russia over the purchase of Alaska in 1867; and (5) naval and military support for a successful coup against the Hawaiian monarchy in 1893, followed by annexation of the islands in 1898.

If for security and financial reasons the Federalists had become the "peace" party, in the first decade of the nineteenth century the Jeffersonian Democratic-Republicans were labeled by their opponents as pro-war. Jefferson's foray against the Barbary pirates and Madison's war against Britain in 1812 established the foreign-policy identity of the new Democratic-Republican Party and the standing of the party's southern and rural-west "war hawks" (John C. Calhoun of South Carolina, Henry Clay of Kentucky, and others)—a policy elite advocating a more militant posture toward Britain. They opposed concessions made to the British in the 1794 Jay Treaty as an unnecessary tilt in favor of their former colonial master.

Preoccupation by Britain in the early nineteenth century with continental foes bolstered the position of these American "war hawks": that the US need not fret about taking on the great power of the United Kingdom in 1812. American policymakers reasoned that their grievances constituted collectively a legitimate *casus belli* against Britain that included: restrictions the latter had imposed on US trade with France, then at war with Britain; conscription on the high seas of American sailors into the Royal Navy; and support American policymakers claimed Britain was giving to Indian tribes against American settlements on the western frontier.

Opposed to the "war hawk" line were Virginians John Randolph, James Madison, and other moderates, who constituted a separate, competing policy elite within the same Democratic-Republican Party. This anti-war policy elite also had subscribers in Federalist elite circles in the northeast that opposed any hostilities that might upset trade and other forms of commerce. Notwithstanding this cross-party, cross-elite coalition, the war hawks eventually prevailed.

The War of 1812—really a sideshow of the Napoleonic wars in Europe—was the outcome that occurred ironically in Madison's presidency, notwithstanding his earlier opposition to "war-hawk" posturing. Federalists continued to oppose what they now called "Mr. Madison's" war. For their part, British policymakers were by no means dissuaded from taking on the Americans in what the latter called a second war of independence, which militarily turned out to be a closer call than Madison and others in the policy elite then in power wished to acknowledge. Nevertheless, fortune turned out to be on the American side in a war the president earlier had sought to avoid.

Following defeat of the British, expansion of the country south and westward became a key issue in American foreign policy. As president, Tennessee "westerner" Andrew Jackson, a veteran of the American Revolutionary War, had a commitment to expansionism that followed from his earlier experiences as commander of military campaigns against native American populations on the frontier and later his decisive victory in 1815 over the British in the Battle of New Orleans. Four years after the war, Jackson's forces turned south and took Florida from Spain. Not only was the ouster of Spain accomplished but also the removal of a sanctuary for British agents to organize or support native populations against American settlers.

Recurrent militancy toward the adversarial "other" was accompanied by shared beliefs that the US had a God-given mission or "manifest destiny" to be the dominant player throughout the hemisphere, creating republics in its own image and likeness and spreading the country's liberal ideas. Although the label manifest destiny did not come into use until 1845, the sentiment was apparent even in the earliest days of the new republic—some seeing it as akin to religious duty, others being more content to see it through more secular lenses simply as advantageous to American interests.

Jackson's taking of Florida from Spain in 1819 was an early marker of an anti-Iberian policy initiated by President James Monroe and pursued by subsequent administrations throughout the nineteenth century. Monroe and his secretary of state, John Quincy Adams, not only accepted the Florida land grab but also turned foreign-policy attention south of the border where national liberation movements were forming new Latin American republics.

Rapprochement with Britain after the War of 1812 was already established by the 1820s when this wave of successful independence movements throughout the Western Hemisphere struck against Spain and Portugal. In the wake of these successes, Monroe set forth his doctrine in 1823 that declared the Western Hemisphere closed to further colonization while leaving British, French, and Dutch colonial holdings in place.

Enforcement of so sweeping a doctrine depended upon assistance by the British Royal Navy as the US Navy was still more of a coastguard than a blue-water force substantial enough to defend what American policymakers saw as the country's interests on the high seas. Indeed, at the time American and British policymakers shared this anti-Iberian understanding of their interests: keeping Spain and Portugal from returning to reoccupy their former colonies in the Western Hemisphere.

In the carefully crafted statement of his doctrine in 1823, Monroe reached out explicitly to his "brethren" to the south (South American liberators Simón Bolívar, José de San Martín, Bernardo O'Higgins, and others), giving them some assurance that their fledgling republics would be protected from any further efforts by Europeans to colonize (or recolonize) them. Monroe himself a freemason, the word *brethren* can be taken as a generic reference in his doctrine to fellow republican leaders or to the fact that these leaders were freemasonic "brothers" committed to anti-colonial, republican, or liberal values.

New lands to the west were viewed by the Jackson presidency (1829–37) as a place to send native-American tribes, clearing them from eastern lands. Two Supreme Court decisions that put Jackson and Chief Justice John Marshall at loggerheads also had constitutional implications related to foreign policy. In *Cherokee Nation v. Georgia* (1831), Indian tribes were defined not as foreign entities but rather as domestic "dependent nations" under federal jurisdiction. Thus "treaties" made with the tribes did not have the same binding character in law as treaties with sovereign states but since Indian affairs were a domestic, federal concern, states did not have the legal right to interfere in these matters.

The point was made decisively in *Worcester v. Georgia* (1832) when the Marshall Court ruled that Georgia's removal laws that forced Indians from their lands were unconstitutional and thus null and void. Jackson's infamous retort was quite simply: "Mr. Marshall has made his decision, now let him enforce it!" Native Americans were removed to western lands acquired through a foreign policy of conquest or purchase. The federal government thus refused to stop the actions Georgia took against the tribes.

From Democratic-Republican, Jeffersonian roots, Jackson's populist agenda (that also favored agricultural interests in the south and west) became the basis of a reorganized, essentially new Democratic Party. Those in the party's policy elite favoring a stronger role for Congress, tariffs to protect northern commercial interests, and government participation in developing the west bolted from the party, becoming the core of the new anti-Jackson or Whig Party that formed in 1833 after his election to a second term.

Expansionists took their cues in the 1830s and 1840s from Presidents Martin Van Buren, James K. Polk, and other Jackson Democrats. Van Buren had been Jackson's secretary of state in the first term and vice president in the second term, and was to become president in his own right between 1837 and 1841. Succeeding Jackson in the presidency, Van Buren maintained the anti-tariff, free-trade policies that made imported goods cheaper to the import-dependent south, which ran against Whig-supported protectionist policies favored by manufacturing and other capital interests in the northeast.

The annexation of Texas in 1845, the Oregon treaty of 1846 with Britain, which finally defined the northwest US–Canadian border, and victory in the Mexican War led by General Zachary Taylor (1846–48) marked substantial expansion of the American republic, its leadership seizing territories west of the Mississippi all the way to the Pacific coast. The loss of Mexican territory to the United States in the Treaty of Guadalupe Hidalgo (1848) was staggering—all of present-day California, Nevada, Utah, most of Arizona, and western parts of Wyoming, Colorado, and New Mexico.

It is little wonder, then, that Mexican General Santa Anna's forces made so desperate an attempt to hold the line against the expansionist American foreign policy pursued under the self-justificatory mantle of manifest destiny—God's will indeed! To facilitate railroad access to California, the Gadsden "purchase" (authorized in 1853 with consent of the Senate by President Franklin Pierce) added almost 30,000 square miles to the southern borders of present-day Arizona and New Mexico.

Transcontinental expansion—manifest destiny—was now complete. In this westward march, policy elites committed to this goal had prevailed over Whigs and others who opposed them or, at least, tried to slow them down. Whig policy-elite leaders—such notables as Daniel Webster (New

Hampshire), Henry Clay (Kentucky), and William Henry Harrison (Ohio) —were not in favor of this Jacksonian brand of expansionism, which they also thought could upset the balance in Congress between the anti-slavery north and west and slave-owning states in the south and west.

Drawn heavily from old Whig Party ranks (Abraham Lincoln himself having earlier been a Whig), the new Republican Party was formed in 1856, with Lincoln winning the White House as a Republican in the1860 election. The major foreign policy issue during the Civil War that followed was keeping Britain—given its cotton trade and other interests—from recognizing or otherwise aiding the southern claim to legitimacy as the Confederate States of America (CSA).

To the North it was a civil war, to the South a "war between the states" (USA and CSA). The stakes were too high for southerners to concede—major concerns being potential dominance by a northern and western Republican coalition, the ending of its slave-based economy if abolitionists had their way, and the potential transformation of southern society as a whole. After the Union victory at Gettysburg (1863), however, British policymakers saw that the tide had turned decisively in the Union's favor, any thought of their intervention on the South's side subsequently abandoned.

Flushed with victory in the Civil War (1865), Republicans altered their earlier stance and became in effect the new expansionist party. Put in partisan terms, in the civil war Republicans in the north had defeated the Democrats, then a predominantly southern party. Given elimination of slavery, Republicans no longer had to deal with the slave-versus-free state issue, which had prompted their and earlier Whig attempts to stop or slow the expansionist process. The great American west was now open for settlement and commercial development all the way to the Pacific Ocean. Policy elites saw great business opportunities that went well beyond the search for precious metals spawned by the discovery of gold in California in 1849.

Pursuit of commercial interests in Asia and the Pacific was already well underway even before the Civil War: Commodore Perry's forceful opening of Japan to American trade began with an initial naval visit in 1853 during the Millard Fillmore administration. Upon returning in 1854 with a more powerful fleet in the Franklin Pierce administration, he reached agreement with Japanese authorities that allowed entry to US traders. It was an early harbinger of the use of force—in this case naval capabilities—to advance American commercial interests in Asian ports.

After establishing bases of operations in Hawaii and the Philippines in the 1890s, policymakers in the William McKinley administration pursued an "open door" policy with China, with Secretary of State John Hay seeking in 1899 "assurances from the other interested powers" of non-interference in American commercial trade with the Chinese. In an even more explicit statement the following year, Hay asserted that US policy was to "safeguard for the world the principle of equal and impartial trade with all parts of the Chinese Empire."[4]

Territorial expansion remained a core issue in American foreign policy throughout the nineteenth century. Immediately after the Civil War, President Andrew Johnson's administration (with the notable influence of Secretary of State William Seward) purchased Alaska from Russia. Yet another expansionist wave began toward the end of the century led by policy elites tied to two presidents: William McKinley (Ohio Republican, 1897–1901) and Theodore Roosevelt (New York Republican, 1901–1909). Roosevelt had been McKinley's assistant secretary of the Navy, orchestrating preparations that led to war with Spain in 1898. Not content merely to stay in Washington, Roosevelt joined the war effort and earned accolades for his service as a colonel leading the Army's "Rough Riders" in Cuba, notably to victory in the Battle of San Juan Hill.

The build-up to war with Spain in 1898 was accompanied by press reports designed to muster public support, which reached a crescendo with the alleged sinking by Spaniards of the battleship USS Maine.[5] Historical echoes of the earlier "war hawks" could be heard in the jingoism expressed by pro-war policy elites reaching beyond their attentive publics to the American people as a whole. In President William McKinley's administration, Assistant Secretary of the Navy Theodore Roosevelt rose to increasing prominence with his bullish approach to the forthcoming war.

Spain did not surrender its remaining positions in the New World without a fight, but it yielded territorial control ultimately to militarily superior US forces not just over Puerto Rico and Cuba but also over the Philippines as yet another prize. Although the US appeared to have a decisive advantage militarily, Spanish policymakers were neither dissuaded nor deterred from resisting American advances either in the Caribbean or the western Pacific. Again, too much was at stake merely to give up without a fight.

The expansionists thus prevailed throughout the century, also taking Hawaii[6] where military intervention in 1893 supported local republicans in their overthrow of the Hawaiian monarchy. The US annexed Hawaii as a territory in 1898, finally making it a state in 1959. Expansionist elites felt justified in these annexations even as counter-elites challenged them.[7]

A minimal use of force by the US Navy had paid off, not only securing important military bases at Pearl Harbor and elsewhere in the Hawaiian Islands to support the American position in the Pacific but also gaining commercial advantage in trade with East Asian countries. Actions abroad that brought Hawaii, the Philippines, and Cuba into the American sphere set precedents for the continued use of force and expansion of American influence overseas that we have seen in the century or more since.

## The Twentieth Century: Expansion of Commerce and the Spread of Liberal Ideas

Expansion of the American sphere continued in Latin America under Theodore Roosevelt's administration, which supported separatists seeking independence from Colombia. At odds with the government of Colombia, the separatists allowed completion by the US of a canal across the Isthmus of Panama, thus cutting 8,000 miles from the 14,000-mile maritime route around South America. Intervention in 1903 by the US Navy blocked Colombian forces from quelling a separatist revolt, which was decisive in creating Panama, a new republic willing to accept the canal.

By no means, of course, was American presence new to politics on the Isthmus of Panama. The Bidlack Treaty (1846) with Colombia gave the US rights to transit the isthmus. A railway was built across the isthmus at the time of the California gold rush (construction underway, 1849–1856). The treaty also granted rights to US military intervention to quash revolts or other social unrest in the isthmus.

Work on the canal began in 1907 and was completed in 1914. Shortened maritime distance and continued improvements in the transcontinental rail's 3,000-mile east–west journey were strategically important assets, particularly since policy elites were interested not just in reaching and integrating America's own territories but also in advancing commercial and other interests well beyond the country's territorial borders.

Military capabilities were an increasingly important core asset in the thinking of policy elites identified with McKinley and Roosevelt. However softly the United States might speak, it needed a "big stick" if it were to be taken seriously. The Rooseveltian policy elite thus made it clear that threat or use of force was a central component of American foreign policy.

As for Latin America and problems Europeans were experiencing in debt collections there, Roosevelt invoked the Monroe Doctrine's opposition to foreign military intervention in hemispheric affairs, but at the same time proclaimed an American right to intervene, particularly if necessary to preclude other countries from doing so. Dubbed the "Roosevelt Corollary" to the Monroe Doctrine (1901), this new interventionist norm went well beyond these more limited purposes as the US pursued other interests served by interventions in Cuba, the Dominican Republic, El Salvador, Haiti, Honduras, Mexico, Nicaragua, and Panama over the next three decades. Armed interventions to support US business interests in Central America and the Caribbean during the Roosevelt and Taft administrations reached a crescendo under Wilson's pro-US business, very interventionist administration (1913–1921). Indeed, Wilson ordered more armed interventions in Latin America than any other president!

Theodore Roosevelt's claim to a "right" to intervene in Latin America was still a norm in the early stages of construction. As he put it: "Chronic wrongdoing ... ultimately [may] require intervention by some civilized nation, and in the Western Hemisphere the adherence of the United States to the Monroe Doctrine may force the United States, however reluctantly, in flagrant cases of such wrongdoing or impotence, to the exercise of an international police power."[8] For its part, the US Navy invaded Veracruz in 1914 and the Army conducted cross-border operations into Mexico, pursuing bandits or insurgents like Pancho Villa, which occupied the Army's attention in 1916–1917 just prior to US entry into World War I.

These actions foreshadowed an American propensity later in the twentieth and twenty-first centuries to intervene abroad both diplomatically and militarily in the service of what policy elites in power understood as American interests, regardless of where in the world they might be. The Pan-American Union (its origins in 1889) had focused on building cooperative relations in the hemisphere, but it was not until President Franklin Roosevelt's "Good Neighbor" policy (1933) that the United States abandoned its propensity to intervene with armed force in Latin America.

The principle of non-intervention in the domestic affairs of another American republic, codified later in the Organization of American States (OAS) Charter (1948), became core to inter-American politics in the Roosevelt–Truman years. The Monroe Doctrine's tenet against further colonization (now interpreted more broadly as intrusions by any foreign power) remained in effect, but the doctrine was no longer to be used as a basis for US intervention in the domestic politics of Latin American states.

Breaking with this "good neighbor" policy that had been sustained in the Roosevelt–Truman years, the Eisenhower administration authorized the CIA to intervene in Guatemala against the left-oriented Jacobo Arbenz regime (1954) that threatened American business interests, notably United Fruit. With the Eisenhower administration's concurrence, the CIA later planned a counter-revolutionary invasion against the Castro regime in Cuba that had come to power in 1959. The succeeding Kennedy administration authorized execution of the plan on April 17, 1961, at the Bay of Pigs, which was a colossal failure.

Three months before, the Monroe Doctrine was implicitly acknowledged as still in force in Kennedy's January 20, 1961 inaugural address: "Let every . . . power know that this hemisphere intends to remain the master of its own house." These tenets were later invoked in Kennedy's response to the Soviet placement of nuclear capabilities in Cuba (October 22, 1962).

The Johnson administration subsequently intervened in Panama (1964), the Dominican Republic (1965–1966), and Guatemala (1966–1967). The Reagan–Bush years saw various military operations, sometimes coupled with CIA covert actions, in El Salvador (1981–1992), Nicaragua against the Sandinistas (1981–1990), Honduras (1982–1990), Grenada (1983–1984), Bolivia (1987), and Panama (1989). The Clinton administration intervened in Haiti (1994-1995) and the George W. Bush administration sent troops to Haiti (2004) but also supported covert actions against the Chavez regime in Venezuela.

Although direct references to the Monroe Doctrine are less frequent today, it still defines a mental frame supporting those who see the Western Hemisphere as an inherently US sphere of influence. Notwithstanding various twists and turns in interpretation, it remains an influential social construction that has enjoyed a very long shelf life both in mind and practice.

Beyond serving commercial interests through armed interventions, policymakers also actively promoted America's liberal ideology. The United States delayed entering both twentieth-century world wars and, when it did so, policymakers in Washington insisted on casting its involvement in liberal terms. In World War I, President Wilson argued for a new post-war world order to be based not on power and balance-of-power concepts and alliance understandings but rather on peace through applying international law against aggression, supported by a collective-security enforcement mechanism in the League of Nations. It was to be a war to end all wars and to make the world safe for democracy. Similarly, the rhetoric of President Franklin Roosevelt and Prime Minister Winston Churchill on the eve of World War II evoked liberal, anti-fascist principles in their Atlantic Charter (1940)—a vision that they sustained throughout the war, later incorporated in the UN Charter.

Cold War competition with the Soviet Union and other socialist countries produced exceptions to the non-intervention principle, often taking the rhetorical form of presidential "doctrines" used to justify selected interventions—in effect an effort to carve out additional exceptions allowing the US to intervene. Some interventions in this post-World War II period were clandestine actions orchestrated by the CIA, usually relying on US support for local armed forces and thus avoiding or minimizing direct use of American troops.

In covert actions the Eisenhower administration effectively changed regimes in Iran by restoring the Shah (1953) and in Guatemala by displacing the left-leaning Arbenz government (1954). US armed forces intervened in Lebanon (1958) with justification claimed in what became known as the Eisenhower Doctrine: "employment of the armed forces of the United States to secure and protect the territorial integrity and political independence of . . . nations . . . against overt armed aggression from any nation controlled by International Communism." In a similar fashion, the Kennedy administration intervened in Laos by sending special forces there (1961 and 1962) as well as in Cuba at the Bay of Pigs (1961), followed overtly in 1962 by a naval blockade of the island (see chapter 3).

Intervention in Vietnam grew during the Kennedy administration by expanding the advisory and covert role by special forces with gradual escalation to full combat achieved during the Johnson presidency, particularly during the 1965–69 period. (See chapter 4.) In the same time frame the US intervened briefly in the Dominican Republic (1965), giving rise to the Johnson Doctrine that claimed justification for intervention against what were understood to be communist threats in the Western Hemisphere "when the object is the establishment of a Communist dictatorship." Indeed, after deciding to intervene, the Johnson administration brought the matter to the OAS in Washington, securing justification there on the claim that the intervention amounted to a collective-defense effort consistent with Article 51 of the UN Charter.

The Nixon–Ford years witnessed other interventions either by US armed forces or through clandestine activities. Though it was not an armed intervention by US forces, the Nixon administration did direct the CIA to take covert action against the left-oriented regime of Chilean President Salvador Allende, which resulted in his assassination in a military coup that installed General Pinochet as president (September 11, 1973—often referred to in Santiago as the "Chilean 9/11"). In the Ford administration, US military forces were employed to counter the communist Khmer Rouge capture in the Gulf of Siam of a US commercial ship, the Mayaguez (1975). In the same year the US government did not block diplomatically or otherwise the Indonesian government's decision to invade Portuguese East Timor, which quickly became a very bloody intervention by Indonesian armed forces.

Pro-intervention and anti-intervention metaphors have often been convenient devices used by policy elites to garner support or generate opposition in both the general and attentive publics to proposals of one kind or another. Until and including the US intervention in Vietnam, for example, appeasement of Hitler at Munich in 1938 was often used explicitly as a metaphor to sustain the argument for intervention, lest appeasement of aggressors, it was said, merely whet their appetites for further aggression. Those supporting armed interventions of one sort or another often invoked "Munich" as what happens when one does not take a stand against dictators—not doing so merely whets the dictator's appetite for more aggression.

Reaction to loss of the war in Southeast Asia produced "quagmire" as an alternative metaphor to that of Munich. If Munich had been used politically to justify interventions, reference to getting "bogged down in quagmires" as in Vietnam was used metaphorically to discourage thoughts of sending US military forces abroad. Such metaphors, when accepted at face value, stand in the way of critical thinking about what is proposed by particular elites.

Nevertheless, when President Carter found his administration directly challenged by Soviet intervention in Afghanistan (1979), his administration found a way around the quagmire metaphor by working through surrogates—giving support to the anti-Soviet *mujahedeen*. A further challenge was posed by the new Khomeini regime in Iran, which also had seized power in 1979, illegally taking control of the US embassy in Tehran and imprisoning diplomats and other Americans held as hostages.

Concern about Soviet or other intervention adverse to American interests in the Gulf region led to the formulation of a new Carter Doctrine on intervention: "An attempt by any outside force to gain control of the Persian Gulf region will be regarded as an assault on the vital interests of the United States of America, and such an assault will be repelled by any means necessary, including military force." In a separate, failed effort to rescue the hostages, President Carter authorized use of special forces in a covert action in Iran (1980), a limited armed intervention.

After securing release of the hostages upon his taking office, President Reagan turned national attention back to intra-hemispheric threats posed by left-oriented elements understood to have support by the Soviet-backed Castro regime in Cuba. Supplementing overt support for the "Contras" against the Sandinistas who had come to power after defeat of the pro-US Somoza regime in Nicaragua were clandestine actions primarily under the CIA designed to build up the capabilities of this anti-Sandinista insurgency. The Reagan Doctrine asserted: "We must not break faith with those who are risking their lives—on every continent, from Afghanistan to Nicaragua—to defy Soviet-supported aggression. . . .

Support for freedom fighters is self-defense and totally consistent with the OAS and UN Charters. It is essential that the Congress continue all facets of our assistance to Central America. . . ." Consistent with this doctrine, the US also supported the El Salvador government's actions against insurgents there.

Congress was opposed to funding the Nicaraguan Contras, but the administration financed them in an off-the-books effort managed from within the National Security Council using "laundered" money from covertly authorized transfers to Iran by Israel of US-manufactured military hardware. This Iran–Contra scandal dominated headlines in the mid-to-late 1980s; however, both President Reagan and Vice-President Bush denied knowledge of these transactions as part of the "plausible-deniability" policy that effectively allowed senior decisionmakers to deny knowledge and thus accountability for any administration misdeeds committed by subordinates.

On a much smaller scale, the Reagan administration also sent US military forces to Lebanon (1982) as part of a multi-state effort to help stabilize the country, then in civil war, and to Grenada (1983) in an effort to forestall what was represented as danger from a left-wing, pro-Cuban, or communist takeover on the Caribbean island. Reagan ordered withdrawal of American forces from Lebanon in 1983 after a truck-bomb attack killed 241 US marines.

Quarrels with Libya over rights of navigation in the Gulf of Sidra off Tripoli's shores that resulted in the US shooting down of two Libyan MiG fighter aircraft in 1981 and the Libyan government's involvement in terrorist activities (including a bombing incident in West Berlin directed against American soldiers) led to US air strikes in 1986 launched by aircraft based in the UK and aboard aircraft carriers in the Mediterranean. Principal targets included the Libyan leadership and facilities used to support terrorist activities abroad. This did not in itself end Libyan state-backed terrorism in the 1980s: a bomb was placed aboard Pan American Flight 103 that exploded over Lockerbie, Scotland in 1988.

For its part, the succeeding administration of George H.W. Bush intervened successfully in Panama (1989) against the Noriega regime, seen as a threat to US interests there, which included sustaining American access to the canal. Interventions elsewhere continued apace. Content with having liberated Kuwait from Iraqi occupation (1991), the US and its coalition partners stopped short of seeking regime change in Baghdad. Leaving Iraq intact was also a bulwark against Iran—the Bush administration not wishing to disturb any further what it saw as a regional balance of power between Iraq and other Arab states vis-à-vis Iran.

Given inter-communal strife in Somalia that had resulted in starvation, deaths, and other adverse consequences, the Bush administration's final armed intervention was to send US forces there in 1992, largely for humanitarian purposes—there being little basis for seeing strategic or other value as cause of action. The Somalia contingency, however, grew well beyond intervention to rescue US and other foreign nationals endangered by domestic turbulence in a particular country—intervention for such limited purposes generally accepted under customary international law. What distinguished the Somalia case from other humanitarian interventions of more limited scope was its focus not just to rescue one's own or other foreign nationals but also to use armed force to preclude further harm to local populations.

The Somalia intervention proved to be more costly in US lives than either Bush or his successor, Bill Clinton, ever imagined. Beyond importing and distributing food, which required establishing security ashore, US forces and civil advisers soon took the first steps in what amounted to a nation-building effort that entangled them in inter-clan warfare and other complexities of Somali society. Administration critics complained of "mission creep" that went too far beyond the initial humanitarian intent to save lives and avert famine. Given these concerns and in the wake of atrocities committed against US military personnel, the Clinton administration soon withdrew American forces in 1993.

Although the Somali experience did not keep the United States from intervening in Haiti, which was torn by civil strife in 1994, Washington was more reluctant to intervene either in Central Africa (Hutu–Tutsi inter-communal bloodshed affecting Rwanda, Burundi, and Congo) or in the Balkans. These contingencies set off a national debate in the United States on the whole question of humanitarian intervention: should US forces be placed in harm's way for such purposes and, if so, under what conditions?

Opponents sought to avoid humanitarian intervention unless doing so secured not just American interests in general but also what was referred to more restrictively as the vital interests of the United States. In this more conservative or nationalist view, the US was not to be the "world's policeman." Others saw armed intervention as a morally necessary remedy for countering genocide and other human rights abuses. However persuasive or compelling, the legal argument justifying armed intervention in such circumstances did not rest on moral principles *per se*. Instead, legal justification for armed intervention was sought in the more general authority vested in the UN Security Council to authorize use of force to maintain international peace and security—applying this broad authority to contingencies in which genocide or other human rights abuses threaten international peace and security.

This UN Charter, Article 42 exception was relatively easy to satisfy in both the Central African and the Balkan cases, given the serious implications regionally for war and peace among several states in each region. The Haiti case had been more problematic, given that civil strife was, as in the Somali case, confined for the most part within its own borders. Concerning Haiti, one could raise questions about the legitimacy of a military government in Port au Prince that had overthrown a popularly elected leadership, but using this reasoning as a basis to carve out a legal exception to the non-intervention principle was more tenuous.

In practice the United States left the Central African matter to France, Belgium, and other interested European or African parties, initially leaving Balkan matters to Britain, France, Germany, Italy, and other European states. The US delayed taking action in the Balkans until 1995 when NATO air strikes began to support efforts on the ground. In the same year the US hosted negotiations among the warring parties in Dayton, Ohio, discussions that produced peace accords among the parties. NATO-backed air strikes again were used against Serbia in 1999 to counter atrocities and forced dislocation of peoples ("ethnic cleansing"), the US avoiding commitment of American ground forces until late in the campaign.

President George W. Bush and his administration wrote an entirely new chapter in an American historical experience already replete with examples of armed interventions. Claiming a right to intervene pre-emptively was reminiscent of the Roosevelt corollary to the Monroe Doctrine. Moreover, the administration's US National Security Strategy document made clear the Bush administration's commitment to maintaining American supremacy over time. It was this policy orientation that set the stage for post-9/11 interventions in Afghanistan, Iraq, later Syria, and supporting Saudi operations in Yemen.

## INTERVENTION AND ELITE UNDERSTANDINGS OF AMERICAN INTEREST

The present-day American propensity to intervene abroad is really an extension of territorial-expansion policies seeking both commercial advantage and promotion of American liberal ideology that policy elites have pursued since the earliest years of the republic. As such, the more recently identified phenomenon of "globalization" has really been a long-term construction in the US interest advanced by policy elites—making in the US image a world open to trade, investment, and other forms of commerce and one that enjoys freedom of assembly and the free movement of people and ideas. Liberalism par excellence![9]—a vision of a commercially open world also shared by many policy elites abroad, particularly those in other capital-rich countries.

It is an internationalist vision challenged directly by the nationalist Trump administration that came to office in 2017. To the extent that these liberal values need protection, the focus should be at home, not abroad. Why does the United States see itself as a world policeman? There is an over-extension of US alliance and other commitments abroad that ought not be taken for granted. Commercial agreements are subject to transactional changes that assure US gains and avoid allowing others, like China, from taking advantage of American largesse.

It is the case that defending what policymakers understand as American economic or other interests abroad no longer requires seizing territory for such purposes. American firms linked to their counterparts in global markets, the work of nongovernmental organizations abroad, the presence of embassies and consulates around the globe, monetary arrangements with Treasuries and central banks in other countries, and the operations of naval, air, and ground units from overseas bases are the present-day currency that elites have used to advance their understandings of US interests.

It is not clear whether the Trump nationalist challenge to multilateralism and the global-liberal agenda is a short-term deviation or the beginning of a permanent reversal of the internationalist track record of both Democratic and Republican administrations since World War II. Spreading liberalism and successfully embedding liberal and liberal-republican ideas abroad have seemed part-and-parcel of a multi-century, on-going globalization construction project. It is a world in which individuals are free to assemble, communicate, and travel in the conduct of their activities at home and abroad. Aside from strategic bases, policymakers have seen holding territory abroad as unnecessary in a world so constructed that it becomes merely an extension of the liberal domain found in the United States and other countries sharing this vision.

## Notes

1. On political clubs and French freemasonry, see Roger Chartier, *The Cultural Origins of the French Revolution*, trans. Lydia G. Cochrane (Durham, NC and London: Duke University Press, 1991), pp. 161–66.
2. The Marine Hymn commemorates victory, referring "to the shores of Tripoli."
3. Alexander Hamilton also urged the new republic not to become "entangled in all the pernicious labyrinths of European politics and wars." Federalist Paper No. 7 (1787).
4. Statements by Secretary of State John Hay on September 6, 1899 and July 3, 1900.
5. In fact the sinking was apparently due to a steam-engine explosion below decks.
6. An official apology to native Hawaiians signed by President Clinton acknowledges the US government role in overthrowing the Hawaiian monarchy in 1893. Stephen Kinzer, *Overthrow: America's Century of Regime Change from Hawaii to Iraq* (New York: Henry Holt/Times Books, 2006), ch. 1.
7. Although its legitimacy was questioned by the Democratic administration of Grover Cleveland, the president ultimately did not reverse the policy.
8. Annual Message to Congress, December 6, 1904.
9. On globalization as merely a form of "Americanization," see Kenneth N. Waltz, "Globalization and Governance," *PS: Political Science and Politics*, Vol. XXXII, No. 4 (December 1999): 693–700.

# PART III

# POLITICS ON THE POTOMAC

# CHAPTER 7

# PRESIDENTIAL POWER

In Richard Neustadt's now classic formulation, presidential power—the ability to persuade—has a high subjective and inter-subjective content that goes well beyond the formal constitutional allocation of (and limits to) authority.[1] Presidential power rests ultimately in the eyes and minds of members of often-contending policy elites in and out of power as well as their followers among attentive and mass publics. Popularity of a president with the general public contributes directly to the legitimacy an administration enjoys, which is also understood by policy elites in their assessments of presidential power in both domestic and foreign policy.

Neustadt identifies *professional reputation* and *popular prestige* as key factors that may vary substantially during the tenure of a particular president. Professional reputation is how policy elites understand the competency of a given president and the administration as a whole. Neustadt refers to these policy elites as "Washingtonians" whether they actually reside in Washington or elsewhere, particularly in his formulation those living on the northeastern seaboard between Washington and Boston. Theirs is an assessment of overall job performance and, for our purposes here, how well or poorly the president conducts foreign policy.

Although the general public may not focus on the details or understand the complexity of issues on domestic (much less foreign) policy agendas as well as policy elites and attentive publics do, the esteem people hold for a particular president can enhance or diminish the persuasive power of the incumbent and the administration as a whole. To Neustadt's analysis of presidential power (see figure 4), I add that popular prestige also affects professional reputation among policy elites as they take account of the president's legitimacy or standing with the people, not just his partisan base. Subjective assessment of a president's ability to communicate and persuade the general public is part and parcel of professional reputation among policy elites—Neustadt's Washingtonians.

Figure 4. Components of presidential power.

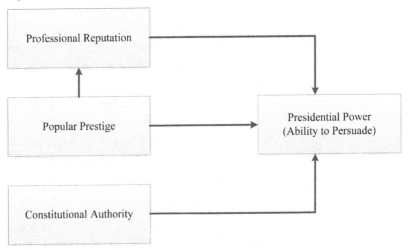

There were variations in the several terms of his presidency, but Franklin Roosevelt's high popular prestige and professional reputation during the Great Depression years and the world war that followed conveyed enormous presidential power to expand the executive's reach in both domestic and foreign policy. Few presidents since have reached, much less sustained, such heights over time. I turn to examples of how presidential power has varied within and across several administrations in relation to changes in popular prestige and professional reputation.

## THE JOHNSON, NIXON, AND FORD PRESIDENCIES

Lyndon Johnson's standing on both variables reached a high point after defeating Barry Goldwater in the 1964 presidential election—a landslide in which he garnered some 61 percent of the popular vote. He was, as a result, even better able to use his widely acknowledged professional skills on Capitol Hill not only to advance important civil rights legislation and promote his Great Society programs but also initiatives in the foreign-policy arena. High popular prestige and professional reputation gave him what he needed to respond assertively with armed intervention in both the Caribbean and Southeast Asia. Particularly given the benefit of historical hindsight, grounds for these interventions are suspect now, but at the time calls for decisive action in response to threats were widely accepted by policy elites.

US forces were deployed in April 1965 to the Dominican Republic in response to an alleged communist threat with Castro-Cuban connections. On a similar track, having persuaded Congress in 1964 to pass the Tonkin Gulf Resolution after an alleged attack by North Vietnam on US naval forces there, the administration increased dramatically American participation in the Vietnam War from about 35,000 in 1965 to some 550,000 troops by 1968. The administration managed the intervention in the Dominican Republic and quickly multilateralized it, securing formal acceptance within the Organization of American States.

Reaching the heights of his professional reputation and popular prestige in 1964 and 1965 facilitated the president's decisions to conduct these armed-intervention missions. His enhanced power to persuade made it relatively easy to overcome any domestic opposition he faced at the time. The intervention in Santo Domingo was short-lived, but the war in

Vietnam proved in time to be Johnson's undoing. The president's descent on both measures during the course of the war was truly breathtaking. His loss of persuasiveness (and thus his effectiveness) in politics on the Potomac led him finally in March 1968 to remove himself from running for re-election.

Owing to high casualties sustained in the Vietnam War—the emergence of a strong anti-war (and anti-draft) movement, peace talks in Paris with North Vietnam seemingly at an impasse,[2] and deep divides within the Democratic Party, Republican rival Richard Nixon won the White House in 1968 with just 43.4 percent of the popular vote.

A minority president in his first term, Nixon did not have the same popular prestige that Johnson had enjoyed after his landslide election four years earlier. Nevertheless, whether they agreed with him or not, the new president enjoyed a professional reputation for having expertise in foreign policy. Policy elites knew of the extensive experience in these matters he had had as member of the House (1947–50), Senate (1950–53), and vice president for two terms in the Eisenhower administration (1953–61). Since leaving office after his defeat by John Kennedy in the 1960 presidential election, Nixon as private citizen continued to focus on foreign policy.

Notwithstanding deep chasms in American society over the war, Nixon enjoyed substantial support from a Republican and southern Democratic, pro-war coalition on Capitol Hill, which allowed him to sustain the American position in Vietnam. His Nixon Doctrine articulated soon after taking office in 1969—that "we shall look to the nation directly threatened to assume the primary responsibility of providing the manpower for its defense"—was the basis for "Vietnamization" of the conflict while diplomats sought "a just peace through negotiated settlement."

The president's persuasiveness also was apparent in keeping opponents in Congress and elsewhere at bay both in the continuation and in the expansion of the Kennedy-Johnson arms control agenda on strategic armaments with the Soviet Union that began with the hotline and limited nuclear test ban agreements and continued with outer space and nuclear proliferation treaties. For its part, the Nixon administration engaged in a dramatic policy shift marked by the opening of relations with China. Both were part and parcel of peaceful engagement with adversaries detailed in chapter 2.

Nixon's landslide victory in 1972 with almost 61 percent of the vote marked a high point in his presidential power, which facilitated: (1) managing a new international monetary regime of floating exchange rates produced by his earlier decision in 1971 to unpeg the dollar from gold; (2) ending the draft and opting for an all-volunteer force as means for defusing the anti-war movement; (3) working toward reduction of American presence in Southeast Asia—his "Vietnamization" initiative; (4) taking decisive action in 1973 to halt the Egypt-Israel war in the Sinai desert west of the Suez Canal; and (5) dealing with the fallout from US support for Israel in the war—the oil-import crisis provoked when Arab petroleum-exporting countries working within OPEC cut production, doubled the price, and imposed an embargo on crude oil exports to the West.

Policy elites were divided in their assessments of how the president and his administration conducted foreign and national security policy —challenged by National Guardsmen shooting students protesting the war at Kent State in Ohio in 1970, continuing fallout from the decision to invade Cambodia in 1971, and the continuing, seemingly endless war in Southeast Asia. Resignation of Vice President Spiro Agnew on corruption charges he did not contest—receiving cash bribes while governor of Maryland (a practice that began when he was a county commissioner and continued when he was vice President)—were damaging, but few could predict the great fall in both the president's professional reputation and popular prestige that subsequently occurred.

Beyond domestic turbulence provoked by Vietnam war policy, it was political scandal that was Nixon's undoing: the break-in by administration operatives of the Democratic Party headquarters at the Watergate condominium complex during the 1972 election campaign, its cover-up, and subsequent actions by the president that brought him to the brink of impeachment on charges that included obstruction of justice. Nixon resigned in August 1974, the low-water mark in his presidential power, urged to do so by fellow Republican leaders headed by conservative Republican Senator Barry Goldwater.

Relying heavily on a positive professional reputation garnered from his earlier experience as Republican minority leader in the House of Representatives, the new president, Gerald Ford (1974–1977), held office during a difficult transition period. Although succeeding to power without election and thus lacking the concomitant popular prestige that comes from winning at the ballot box, Ford nevertheless put his stamp on foreign policy in 1975 with a doctrine of his own. The Ford Doctrine observed that "the center of political power in the United States has shifted westward" as "Pacific interests and concerns have increased." Relying on "American strength" as "basic to any stable balance of power in the Pacific," the president called for both "partnership with Japan" and "normalization of relations with the People's Republic of China"— the latter signaling continuation of Nixon's China policy.

Notwithstanding such pronouncements, these transition years were troubled ones, marked by massive inflation and unemployment, the controversial presidential pardon of Richard Nixon, defeat in Vietnam in 1975, and amnesty for those who had evaded the draft. Lacking an electoral mandate, Ford's reactions to the difficulties that confronted him undermined his professional reputation among policy elites and cost him substantial popular support as well. These adverse circumstances, although for the most part beyond the president's control, contributed to his loss in the 1976 election to Georgia's Democratic Governor James Earl ("Jimmy") Carter.

## Post-Vietnam Carter and Reagan Administrations

As state governors running for president frequently do, Carter campaigned as a force for constructive change in the Washington establishment. Informed by allegedly "fresh" thinking and new approaches to be found in the countryside, governors are portrayed as if they were still the real thing, as yet uncorrupted by special interests and customary politics on the Potomac.

By no means unique to Carter, this was the same theme found in subsequent campaigns for the presidency by both Democratic and Republican governors: Ronald Reagan in 1980 (California), Bill Clinton in 1992 (Arkansas), and George W. Bush (Texas) in 2000. It is a refrain that resonates with the moralism one always seems to find in American politics—the new president coming to Washington from the people in the countryside as a purifying force somehow to change Washington by insulating policymakers from "special interests" and others who are often portrayed as blocking or corrupting the popular will. It was the same refrain that drove Donald Trump's successful campaign in 2016 —"draining the swamp" of alleged moral corruption in Washington.

President Carter—a liberal internationalist—took advantage of the brief, several-month honeymoon that most new presidencies enjoy by setting out an ambitious agenda on human rights and arms control, the latter advancing toward an "ultimate goal" proclaimed in his inaugural address: "elimination of all nuclear weapons from this Earth." Language of a treaty with the Soviet Union limiting strategic armaments (SALT II) finally was agreed, but opposition in the Senate, mainly by Republicans and southern Democrats, kept the treaty from ratification. The Soviet invasion of Afghanistan in 1979 put the final nail in the treaty's coffin, although in practice both sides continued to view it as a binding executive agreement between the American and Soviet leaderships.

Notwithstanding foreign-policy success in completing normalization of relations with China and, in the Middle East, bringing Egyptian and Israeli leaders Anwar Sadat and Menachem Begin together in the 1979 Camp David accords, Carter's professional reputation for the conduct of foreign policy suffered among those who opposed the return of the canal zone to Panama. For Carter's opponents, the last straw was seizure by the Iranians in 1979 of US diplomats held hostage in Tehran. An abortive rescue mission and the inability of the administration to get the hostages released and settle the matter diplomatically[3] undermined Carter's professional reputation and his popular prestige, which contributed substantially to his loss of the presidency to Ronald Reagan in the 1980 election.

The stage was set for completing a major party realignment. Nixon had begun courting the South to Republican ranks, cultivating what was called a "moral" or "silent" majority attracted ideologically to Republicans. It would wait, however, until Reagan used his popular prestige and political skills to facilitate movement of southern Democrats into a newly constituted Republican Party.

By the 1990s, most southern Democrats had moved into Republican party ranks—a major realignment that ended the New Deal coalition crafted by Franklin Roosevelt that connected labor, urban interests, minorities, and intellectuals with the more conservative southern wing of the Democratic Party. For its part, the Republicans became predominantly the party of southern whites, those in rural areas, and the residual from the old Republican Party bastions in the northeast and west coast, often of more moderate or "progressive" persuasion than southern or rural Republicans.

Although opposing policy elites were critical of Reagan for his reported inattention to details and alleged somnolence at White House meetings, these criticisms were offset by his enhanced professional reputation as the "great communicator" with both policy elites and the general public. He also assembled a strong cabinet, particularly with George Shultz at State and Caspar Weinberger at Defense. His vice president, George H.W. Bush, brought with him substantial experience in foreign affairs on Capitol Hill from four years in the House of Representatives, as CIA

Director, and as ambassador to the United Nations and China, which contributed to the overall professional reputation of the Reagan-Bush administration.

Given his personal popularity and the professional reputation his administration enjoyed, Reagan had considerable license to pursue his foreign-policy objectives. Concerned with an alleged communist threat in the Caribbean and Central America and perturbed by the spread of Cuban influence in the region, the president sent American troops to the island of Grenada—a relatively short, armed intervention that stabilized the anti-Castro government there. He also directed the CIA to organize an opposition movement to counter the left-oriented Sandinista regime in Nicaragua—the "Contras."

When Congress later cut off funding for this covert action, CIA Director William Casey shifted action to the national security adviser's office in the White House. Earlier promise of trading arms to Iran in exchange for release of hostages now had a new basis for continuance. Relying on Israeli officials to effect the transfers, revenue from continuing sales to Iran were reallocated to funding the Contras—Reagan's "freedom fighters."

While underscoring publicly his commitment to the Contras and the cause they represented, the president denied knowledge of the covert action—financing US support by selling arms. As with prior presidents, Reagan (and his vice president) had been put in a position of "plausible deniability" that allowed others to take the fall in the event the action became public knowledge.[4] Nevertheless, the "Iran-Contra" scandal that ensued still damaged the professional reputation of his presidency, allowing his opponents in Congress to constrain further the president's freedom of action at least in the Western Hemisphere.

It was Reagan's interactions with his Soviet counterpart, Mikhail Gorbachev, that marked the greatest success of his administration: steps leading to the end of the Cold War and the dismantling of the Soviet Union that occurred during his successor's watch. The Reagan military build-up had indeed challenged the Soviet leadership, particularly the pursuit of both the technologically intensive Strategic Defense Initiative (dubbed "Star Wars") and robust strategic offensive weapons systems better able to penetrate Soviet airspace and with greater accuracy to take out hardened targets. All of this was accompanied by tough talk: speaking of the Soviet Union as an evil empire and advancing the idea that the United States, armed with robust strategic offense and defense, was preparing itself to prevail even in a nuclear war.

The intent was to deter Soviet leaders from undertaking any attack using conventional forces, much less a nuclear strike. The magnitude of the American effort was immense: just under 7 percent of GDP allocated to defense at the height of the Reagan build-up. Efforts to keep up with the US contributed to undermining the Soviet economic base as more and more GDP was allocated to defense, reaching levels on the order of 35–50 percent![5]

If this broad estimate is even close to the mark, it is little wonder that the Soviet economy collapsed. It also helps us understand Gorbachev's willingness to pursue arms control with the Reagan and Bush administrations. Strategic arms reductions talks (START) and other arms control negotiations on conventional forces in Europe finally resulted in important agreements: reducing substantially both nuclear and non-nuclear forces on both sides and establishing confidence- and security-building measures intended to stabilize relations in the post-Cold War period.

## THE BUSH AND CLINTON ADMINISTRATIONS

Although George H.W. Bush, elected to the presidency in 1988, did not enjoy the same degree of popular prestige as his predecessor, he had established for himself and those in his administration a strong, experience-based professional reputation even among opposing policy elites. The new president was generally recognized as one who understood well the ways and means of making and implementing foreign policy on increasingly complex issues facing any administration. Managing US policy at the end of the Cold War, which subsequently saw the demise of the Soviet Union, was indeed a formidable task.

Well established with decades of involvement in politics on the Potomac, the president surrounded himself with advisers of comparable experience and foreign-policy expertise: General Brent Scowcroft as national security adviser (the same position he had held in the Ford administration), James Baker at State, and Richard Cheney at Defense (who had been Ford's chief of staff, closely aligned with the president's secretary of defense, Donald Rumsfeld) and later as a member of Congress. These were the core political players, joined by then-Chairman of the Joint Chiefs of Staff General Colin Powell, in assembling under UN Security Council auspices a coalition of more than 40 countries to counter the Iraqi invasion of Kuwait in 1991. Success in orchestrating this multilateral response clearly enhanced the president's professional reputation among policy elites and popular prestige among the general public as well.

Push from policy elites on the political right for regime change in Iraq was strong—overthrowing Saddam Hussein's Baathist regime by extending the military campaign to Baghdad finding a receptive ear in Secretary of Defense Cheney. Backed by advice from Scowcroft, Baker, and Powell, however, the president disapproved of any plans to extend the war beyond the agreed mission to liberate Kuwait and to deter Iraqi aggression against Saudi Arabia or other Gulf states. Leaving the Iraqi Army intact was also seen by administration officials as essential to maintaining a regional power balance vis-à-vis Iran lest the latter seize an opportunity to extend its sphere at a time of Iraqi weakness.

An attempt was made nevertheless to give moral support to any uprising against Saddam's Sunni-Arab regime, whether in the northern areas of the country, heavily populated by Kurds, or in the south, where Shia-Muslim Arabs had their own set of grievances against the Iraqi leader. A *de facto* protectorate was established in the north supported by Kurdish forces on the ground and a no-fly zone enforced by Anglo-

American air forces that effectively suppressed any Iraqi government efforts to penetrate air space in the northern part of the country. No such provision was made in southern Iraq, thus posing no obstacle to repression of Shia uprisings by Saddam Hussein's regime. Though by no means intended by US officials, allowing Saddam's punitive repression of dissidents in southern Iraq to go unopposed became a matter of deep resentment among the Shia.

Notwithstanding foreign-policy successes and the enhancement of his popular prestige and professional reputation, Bush lost the 1992 election to Clinton. Contributory to his defeat was the third-party candidacy of H. Ross Perot, which not only appealed to many independents or unaffiliated voters, but also drew, on balance, more Republican voters away from Bush than Democrats from Clinton. In the "lame-duck" period following the election, President Bush still benefited from a strong professional reputation among policy elites and remained a decisive player in foreign-policy matters. Responding to humanitarian calls for relief in Somalia, the president ordered armed intervention under UN auspices in December 1992—an effort to provide security in a country torn by warfare among competing clans.

Inheriting this intervention, the new Clinton administration that took office in January eventually abandoned the effort—blamed by opposing elites both for failure of the American expedition and for having expanded the mission well beyond the original objective of providing humanitarian relief. American forces were withdrawn in 1994 and 1995. A minority president in his first term, the new president had strong support within his partisan base and among many independent voters but, like Nixon in his first term, lacked the same mandate in popular prestige that comes from winning an electoral majority.

Unlike Nixon and similar to Carter and other governors who became president without much foreign-policy experience, Clinton did not enjoy at the outset his predecessor's professional reputation among policy elites on these matters. Governors who run successfully for the presidency on a platform of not being Washingtonians ensconced in the politics of the Potomac and who also lack experience in foreign affairs face an often very steep learning curve in the first year or two of their administrations.

The two presidents were not completely unprepared. Carter had studied engineering at the Naval Academy and later served as a naval officer in the US nuclear submarine fleet. Clinton, though lacking direct foreign-policy experience, had substantial knowledge of international relations first as an undergraduate in the School of Foreign Service at Georgetown, later as a graduate student and Rhodes scholar at Oxford, and as protégé of Arkansas Senator William Fulbright, then chairman of the Foreign Relations Committee. In the first two years of his administration, criticism by policy elites of Clinton's inexperience in foreign policy gradually waned, much as it had under Carter—the professional reputations of both bolstered by their analytical acumen and their willingness to engage with the teams of experienced advisers each had assembled.

Clinton's post-Cold War foreign policy was marked by diverse responses to civil strife in the Middle East, Europe, the Caribbean, Central Africa, and Southeast Asia. The president actively supported peaceful engagement among the parties in Northern Ireland and between Israel and Palestinians, with substantial gains in the former, but enormous frustrations over setbacks in the peace process in the latter. Although the president had begun to terminate US presence in Somalia in 1994, he did not abandon his interventionist stance. Indeed, he sent American troops to Haiti that year to bring a degree of order and security to people endangered by on-going civil strife.

In Yugoslavia neither Bush nor Clinton wanted to commit troops on the ground lest the US find itself bogged down in a "quagmire"—the Vietnam-era metaphor that tended to dissuade policymakers from armed intervention abroad. President Clinton did authorize air attacks under NATO auspices, but ground operations were left to NATO allies (notably the British and French) in conjunction with UN peacekeepers. Only after negotiations mediated by the United States with the parties (now separate states in their own right) conducted in Dayton, Ohio, in 1995 was the US prepared to send troops to join peacekeeping operations.

Clinton was unwilling to intervene in the Central African Hutu–Tutsi conflict that began in 1993 in Rwanda, Burundi, and the Congo. Similarly, the president was unwilling to send US forces to East Timor in the Indonesian archipelago. With support from the Clinton administration, however, Australia took the lead in 1999 under UN auspices in East Timor, overseeing its independence from Indonesia in 2002 early in the George W. Bush administration.

The majority that assured Clinton's re-election in 1996 gave him the greater popular mandate he sought, but this would in time be undermined by scandal highlighted by his opponents on Capitol Hill. Although the president survived the trial in the Senate brought by impeachment in the House, both his popular prestige and professional reputation suffered substantial damage. Preoccupation with such matters also diverted attention from foreign-policy concerns that otherwise might have been center stage. Thus, less attention was given to diplomatic agendas on arms control, establishing an international criminal court, and protocols on climate change and other environmental issues. Even when agreements were reached, they suffered from opposition on Capitol Hill. Indeed, Clinton's presidential power—his ability to persuade—was much diminished.

## Ups and Downs: Johnson, Nixon, and George W. Bush

Three presidential cases stand out from the rest as exhibiting extreme variations in presidential power: Lyndon Johnson, Richard Nixon, and George W. Bush. Although we do not have statistical data for professional reputation among policy elites, Gallup and other polling data on public perceptions of presidential job performance do give us an indicator of popular prestige. Public assessment of Johnson's job performance was at a high of 77 percent approval soon after assuming office. Re-elected by a 61.1 percent landslide in November 1964, his Gallup poll rating was at 70 percent at the beginning of his term.

From these heights the president's job rating descended to about 40 percent by the beginning of 1968, leading the president to announce in March that he would not run for re-election. His job performance sunk to its low point of 34 percent in August 1968—the result of the impact on his presidency of a long and unpopular war in Vietnam and the domestic turmoil it produced. Johnson's power to persuade had diminished substantially compared to the capacity he had demonstrated earlier not just in foreign policy, marked by armed intervention or escalation of conflicts abroad, but also on civil rights, Medicare, and other "Great Society"domestic initiatives.

Nixon was elected in 1968 with 43.4 percent of the vote (42.7 percent going to Johnson's vice president and former Democratic Senator Hubert Humphrey and 13.5 percent to Alabama Governor George Wallace—a southern Democrat running as an American Independent). Although a minority president in terms of popular vote, Nixon's job rating reached a high of 65 percent early in his administration. After his 60.7 percent landslide victory in 1972 over Democratic Senator George McGovern, however, Nixon's job rating went into decline, due primarily to adverse response to the Watergate burglary, its cover-up, and related allegations of obstruction of justice—bottoming out at 23 percent upon resigning his office in August 1974.

For different reasons George W. Bush experienced a similar meteoric rise and fall with significant implications for his presidential power to persuade, much as both Johnson and Nixon had experienced. Elected in a close, highly contested election in 2000 (settled by a US Supreme Court decision on vote count in Florida), Bush won 271–266 in the electoral college with a minority share of 47.9 percent of the popular vote (his opponent, Clinton's vice president, Al Gore, receiving 48.4 percent). Bush's job performance scores in the 50s and low 60s rose to the 85–

89 percent range after the 9/11 attacks on the World Trade Center and the Pentagon.

Presidential power was at an historic high and contributory to decisive action in Afghanistan in 2002 and in Iraq the following year. Much as had happened to Johnson over Vietnam, however, the war in Iraq became increasingly unpopular with the passage of time. Complaints against the administration's conduct of the war, abuses of detainees including water-boarding and other forms of torture, kidnapping (or "extraordinary rendition") of suspected terrorists, secret prisons, and domestic spying were added to other domestic-policy negatives. The president's power to persuade continued to diminish, his job performance rating dipping to 25 percent toward the end of his administration.

## THE OBAMA AND TRUMP YEARS

Both the Obama and Trump administrations have had to operate in a deeply polarized, highly partisan environment. Obama left office on a high note, his Gallup rating as indicator of popular prestige at 59 percent. Although he lacked extensive experience at the federal level (just four years as Illinois US Senator, 2005–2008), he did serve on the Foreign Relations Committee, chairing its subcommittee on European Affairs. Also a member of Senate Committees on Veterans Affairs as well as Homeland Security and Government Affairs, he was intimately familiar with foreign affairs challenges during his time in the US Senate.

Obama's familiarity with domestic issues stemmed from his time as state senator (1997–2004) and service on domestically focused US Senate committees (Environment and Public Works as well as Health, Education, Labor and Pensions). All of this direct experience aside, his professional reputation grew as Washingtonians became increasingly aware of the president's keen intellect and analytic abilities. Nevertheless, he had to deal with polarized politics, particularly after Democrats lost both houses of Congress in the 2010 election. For his part, Senate Majority Leader

Mitch McConnell openly sought to make Obama a one-term president and vowed to block his legislative initiatives.

On foreign policy Obama's eight years in office were marked by restraint, which resulted in criticism from both Republicans and more hawkish Democrats. Reacting to policies pursued by the Bush-Cheney administration, Obama condemned the use of torture, extraordinary rendition, and secret prisons. Vowing within a year to close the prison at Guantánamo Bay in Cuba, Obama was blocked by Congressional unwillingness to have "terrorists" transferred to federal prisons in the United States. Although the number of prisoners remaining there was reduced substantially, Guantánamo remained open throughout his White House years, as it still does in the Trump administration.

Celebrating the potential of the "Arab Spring"—an apparent embrace of democracy by popular forces in Tunisia, Libya, Egypt and elsewhere—the Egyptian President Mubarak was imprisoned and Libyan leader Gaddafi was killed. Uprisings also occurred in other Arab states before a reaction by military and other conservative forces crushed many of those who had taken to the streets.

Most tragic was the civil war in Syria. Beyond advisers and military aid to the Kurds, Obama was reluctant to commit US forces to Syria, given his understanding of the complexity of Sunni, Shia, Alawite, Islamic State, Kurd and other factions there—not to mention Russian support for the Assad regime and Turkish concerns that Kurdish successes in Syria might strengthen separatist movements by Turkish Kurds.

Obama asserted in an August 20, 2012 press conference that use of chemical weapons by the Assad regime was a "red line" that must not be crossed—interpreted by most that doing so would provoke a US response: "We have been very clear to the Assad regime, but also to other players on the ground, that a red line for us is . . . chemical weapons moving around or being utilized. That would change my calculus. That would change my equation."

When the Assad regime crossed the red line, Obama chose not to make a military response, instead sending his Secretary of State, John Kerry, to negotiate a deal with Russia and Syria to put the latter in compliance with the Chemical Weapons Convention by eliminating its chemical weapons arsenal. Criticized by Republicans and some Democrats for not taking decisive action to deliver militarily on his red-line threat, Obama pointed to his diplomatic success. His liberal-internationalist preference for a diplomatic approach to adversarial relations was clear.

Obama continued the withdrawal of troops from Iraq begun by his predecessor as well as from Afghanistan after a brief "surge" in troop strength there. A major achievement was acting on intelligence that located Osama bin Laden, architect of al Qaeda's 9/11 (2001) attack on the World Trade Center and Pentagon. In a risky decision, Obama ordered special forces to Pakistan to apprehend or kill bin Laden. His death was a major success for the Obama administration but much was left to be done in Syria where the Islamic State set up by ISIS controlled significant territory.

A landmark achievement was multilateral negotiations with Iran on nuclear weapons, the US delegation led by Secretary of State John Kerry. The five permanent members of the UN Security Council, Germany, and the European Union negotiated with Iran and reached agreement in 2015 on a Joint Comprehensive Plan of Action (JCPOA). In return for relaxation of sanctions, Iran agreed to submit to International Atomic Energy Agency (IAEA) monitoring on both reductions in existing capabilities and severe limits over a 15-year term on developing enriched-uranium capacity that could be used for making nuclear weapons.

The great frustration for President Obama, however, was how the urgency of Middle East efforts diverted attention from his initiative to shift the focal point of US policy to Asia and the Pacific. Nevertheless, his diplomats did participate in negotiating a Trans-Pacific Partnership (TPP) agreement signed in 2016 on reducing both tariff and non-tariff trade barriers with "Pacific rim" countries. Apart from its benefit to participating countries, the TPP also was an effort to maintain US influence in the region as a counter to on-going Chinese efforts to expand its sphere of influence.

All of this changed with the inauguration of President Donald Trump in January 2017. The new president stood apart from his predecessors as having no government experience, also successfully avoiding military service during the Vietnam War. A New York real-estate developer from Queens who made his mark in Manhattan, Atlantic City (casinos), and elsewhere, Trump brought to the White House a transactional approach to foreign policy that assessed costs and benefits of deals in short-term, zero-sum competitive terms. He had not incorporated customary diplomatic and other political norms held by the establishment, which he promised during his presidential campaign to oppose—"draining the swamp" as he put it.

In office he relied almost exclusively on unwavering support from his southern and rural populist base that had elected him—an electoral college majority albeit losing the popular vote to his opponent, Hillary Clinton, by some three million votes. Well into his fourth year in office, his popular prestige (Gallup's job performance poll) always remained well under 50 percent, in a range between 35 and 46 percent. Though not measured statistically, his professional reputation was at a low ebb among Washingtonians more accustomed to presidents following customary norms while in office.

It became clear that the president's conduct was at odds with the expectations of both Bush presidents, not to mention Carter, Clinton, and Obama. An indirect indicator of this reputational deficit was the absence of a joint photographic opportunity—posing with former presidents, Republican or Democratic, that had become customary. Only at the funeral of George H. W. Bush was a photo taken of surviving presidents sitting with their wives at the service in the National Cathedral.

Following Neustadt's prediction, Trump's presidential power—the ability to persuade—was substantially reduced due to low popular prestige outside of his minority base and poor professional reputation among Washingtonians. Republican majorities in both houses of Congress in his first two years did enable passage of a massive tax cut but efforts to eliminate Obama's Affordable Care Act (ACA) and most other domestic initiatives failed passage. A Democratic House that took their seats in January 2019 was a new obstacle to his persuasive power as president. Indeed, charges of abuse of power in relation to Ukraine and obstruction of Congress were core to his impeachment in December 2019.

Nevertheless, given the constitutional authority a president has in foreign affairs, Trump was able to make major changes in US policy. As much for personal reasons—his open hostility toward his predecessor—Trump sought to reverse what most observers considered among Obama's (and Secretary of State Kerry's) principal achievements. The first to go (on the first day in office as president) was the TPP, which he said was disadvantageous economically and contrary to American economic independence. Later unilateral actions continued this "America First" approach on trade to include repudiating the North American Free Trade Agreement (NAFTA) pursued by the Bush and Clinton administrations, negotiating a new US-Canada-Mexico trade deal more favorable to the US, and imposing tariffs on selected trade partners in an effort to force their compliance with American demands.

Withdrawal from the CPOA in May 2018 reversed another landmark Obama achievement. Notwithstanding IAEA confirmation of Iranian compliance with its obligations under the agreement, Trump claimed that the CPOA was flawed and that it did not curb Iran's support for terrorist groups or other untoward behavior internationally.

Other unilateral actions in Israel's favor were taken in December 2017 (announcing that the US would move its embassy from Tel Aviv to Jerusalem), in March 2019 (US recognition of Israel's sovereignty over the Golan Heights taken from Syria in the 1967 war), and in November 2019 (accepting the legitimacy of Israeli West-bank settlements). These moves reversed US policy established in November 1967 by a unanimous vote on UN Security Council Resolution 242 that condemned territorial acquisition by war, called for Israel's military withdrawal from the territories it occupied, and sought a peace that acknowledged "the sovereignty, territorial integrity and political independence of every State in the area and their right to live in peace within secure and recognized boundaries."

Although the Carter administration's efforts (the Camp David Accords in 1978 between Israeli Prime Minister Menachem Begin and Egyptian President Anwar Sadat) resulted in normalizing Israeli-Egyptian relations, subsequent attempts by succeeding administrations failed to settle other Arab-Israeli questions to include the status of Jerusalem, Israeli holding the Golan Heights for security purposes, Israeli-Palestinian conflicts in Gaza, and Israeli settlements west of the Jordan River (west bank), territories claimed by Palestinians. Confidence buoyed by President Trump's election in 2016, Israeli Prime Minister Netanyahu's government also expanded west-bank settlements. Acting unilaterally President Trump entered he fray decidedly on Israel's side on all of these issues except for Gaza that continues to be subject to frequent Israeli military responses.

Loyal to their (and the president's base), most Republicans in both houses of Congress accepted these unilateral actions without public opposition whatever their private concerns may have been. Unlike domestic issues in which the president's power to persuade is crucial, in foreign policy presidents have much greater latitude. Except when taking the country to war when Congress may assert its Article I war and appropriations powers, presidents can make most foreign policy decisions on their own. It is helpful in implementing foreign policies, of course, when a president has persuaded members of Congress and others in government that he is pursuing a wise and sound policy.

Treaty ratification and support for executive agreements or other presidential initiatives requiring appropriation of funds do depend on the president's persuasive power. Blocking by Congress of President

Trump's efforts to secure funding for a robust border wall with Mexico in efforts to keep migrants from entering the US is an example of a president lacking the power to persuade. Given this deficit, the president used his executive authority to declare a national emergency and order funds appropriated for other defense purposes be spent instead on building the wall. In a 5-4 decision in July 2019 the Supreme Court ruled that the administration could use the money for this purpose while waiting for litigation on this issue to be resolved.

## EXECUTIVE–CONGRESSIONAL CONSTITUTIONAL AUTHORITY

This chapter began with a focus on the highly variable factors (professional reputation and popular prestige) that account for the dynamics of presidential power within and across administrations. Formal constitutional authority is the more slowly moving variable that Neustadt also identifies. As with the other components of presidential power that are highly subjective in character, constitutional authority rests on generally accepted legal understandings that come to us from the language of the Constitution, interpretations by the Supreme Court, statutes (or even treaties) that set parameters on the exercise of executive and legislative authority, precedents, and generally accepted practice over long stretches of time. Again, constitutional authority is not something "out there," but rather lies "in here" in the minds of presidents, and those presidents seek to persuade.

In the short run it often appears as if constitutional authority were a constant, changes in constitutional authority usually occurring glacially over much longer periods of time. Increasing presidential assertiveness in the exercise of war powers in the seven decades since World War II, for example, has contributed to growth in presidential authority in such matters (buttressed by Supreme Court decisions, treaties, and statutes). Before taking up this on-going executive–congressional struggle over war powers, I turn first to the formal eighteenth-century constitutive language and subsequent evolutionary construction of presidential power in foreign policy and national security.

Neustadt portrays the constitutional framers as devising a government of "separated institutions sharing powers." Officials in the White House and the executive branch enjoy primacy over the legislators in most foreign-policy and national-security matters, but they still must confront authoritative congressional challenges on the budget, war powers, commercial matters, human rights, and other issues.

States also matter. Quite apart from the interests that governors, other state and local officials, or private-sector interest groups may articulate, states are institutionally represented equally in the US Senate, where their senatorial agents can try to facilitate, constrain, or block policies advanced by members of the executive branch. House members are also important players, of course, particularly since budget appropriations bills begin in that chamber. Trade and other commercial matters, defense spending, and armed intervention are among the issues that matter to constituents and thus quickly rise to the top of both Senate and House agendas.

That senators typically allocate relatively more time and energy to foreign policy than members of the House (who typically are more concerned with matters of direct importance to their districts) is a reflection of the constituted senatorial position as agent of an entire state rather than of people in particular counties, municipalities, or districts. Senatorial prerogatives in the Constitution on rendering advice and consent on treaty ratification as well as confirming ambassadors and other government officers appointed by the president provide a unique, privileged senatorial link to foreign-policy processes not enjoyed by the House.

The choice of the Senate for this role rather than the House (or both houses of Congress) stems from the fact that the Senate was constituted to represent equally the interests of states as a whole, while the House was more directly representative of people in districts within each state. In constituting the American republic it was action taken by delegates representing states that effectively relinquished their prerogatives, surrendering primacy on foreign policy to officials in the federal government as their single agent. In principle the states could have had their own foreign policies had they not formed a union and ratified first the Articles of Confederation in 1783 and six years later the US Constitution, both documents effectively centralizing the conduct of foreign policy.

The president's formal authority (and that of the executive branch) in relation to Congress on foreign policy comes to us not only from a reading of the Constitution, particularly Article II, but also from a few decisive cases in which the Supreme Court refereed between what the justices customarily refer to as the other two "political" branches. The historical winner in these matches is clearly executive branch officials, which the court sees as having the lead on foreign-policy matters. This is not just for functional reasons: that under direction of the president as chief executive, the secretary of state and other cabinet officers and their staffs are better equipped to conduct foreign policy than some 535 elected members of Congress separated in two houses. The issue is also rooted more deeply in the eighteenth-century British practice in which the monarchy still retained special prerogatives to represent the country's interests in foreign relations.

Foreign policy primarily being the Crown's responsibility at the time of the American Revolution, the Supreme Court has reasoned that the foreign-policy baton was passed directly from the monarch to the president and executive branch to perform the same function in the American republic.[6] A reading of Article II in the US Constitution sustains this interpretation. "Executive power" in foreign-policy matters is given explicitly to the president—authority to make treaties, serve as commander-in-chief of the armed forces, appoint ambassadors and consuls, receive ambassadors and other officials from foreign countries, and commission all officers in government service in the military, foreign service, or other agencies.

For its part, the Senate has the lead on foreign policy within the legislative branch for two principal reasons. First is its designation as advising and giving consent to the president on the making of treaties requiring a two-thirds vote to allow ratification. The second stems from the Senate being the body that represents each state equally. Indeed, had the federation or union of 13 (now 50) states not come about, each state would have had its own foreign policy. That they surrender this power to the federal government, their interests as states directly represented in the US Senate, is reflected in early Supreme Court decisions[7] and has been sustained since.[8] Moreover, formal congressional authority on foreign policy, as with domestic matters, rests heavily on its holding of the purse strings—the revenue-raising or appropriations power specified in Article I, Section 7.

## TREATY MAKING AND THE CONDUCT OF FOREIGN POLICY

John Jay tells us in Federalist Paper No. 64 (1788) why senators and the president have the upper hand over members of the House on making treaties and conducting foreign policy. In making this determination, Jay observes that senators as agents of states "will all have an equal degree of influence" in the Senate since "all States are equally represented in the Senate, and by men the most able and the most willing to promote the interests of their constituents."

Throughout much of its history, justices on the Supreme Court have avoided becoming involved in most executive–legislative disputes. Usually very parsimonious in their decisions on the distribution of constitutional power and authority among the branches, they nevertheless on occasion have assumed the role of arbiter between the other two "political" branches and the states as well. In a relatively few landmark cases over more than two centuries, the justices have underscored executive and senatorial prerogatives, specifying rules on whether treaties or statutes prevail when there are conflicts between the two or with the states.

That treaty matters are primarily the province of the executive branch becomes clear in one early Supreme Court case[9] on a dispute relating to the border between the Spanish and Louisiana territories, the latter purchased by treaty from France 23 years earlier. Writing for the Court, Chief Justice John Marshall notes that "in a controversy between two nations concerning national boundary, it is scarcely possible that the courts of either should refuse to abide by the measures adopted by its own government." Even more to the point, Marshall adds that "the judiciary is not that department of the government to which the assertion of its interests against foreign powers is confided."

Marshall notes that in Article VI the "Constitution declares a treaty to be the law of the land," but so are statutes. He makes an important distinction between self-executing treaties (the terms of which stand on their own without follow-on legislative action) and non-self-executing treaties (which call for legislation to bring them into force). As Marshall puts it: "A treaty is, in its nature, a contract between two nations, not a legislative act." That said, the treaty as a "contract" made by the executive branch is "equivalent to an act of the Legislature whenever it operates of itself."

When it is self-executing, its terms stand on their own and thus do not require any follow-on legislation to make the treaty effective. By contrast, in non-self-executing treaties that require legislative action before coming into force, "the treaty addresses itself to the political, not the Judicial, Department." In such cases, the Court cannot act on a dispute until enabling legislation is passed since for such non-self-executing treaties "the Legislature must execute the contract before it can become a rule for the Court."

Much later we learn from the Supreme Court that although both treaties and statutes are constitutionally regarded as the law of the land, when the two conflict, it is the statute that prevails when its passage is later in time.[10] In this regard, justices on the Court reasoned that a treaty "depends for the enforcement of its provisions on the interest and the honor of the governments which are parties to it." If these fail, "its infraction [soon] becomes the subject of [follow-on] international negotiations and reclamations." Indeed, when a treaty "requiring legislation to carry its stipulations into effect" conflicts with statutes that are "within the power of congress, it can be deemed in that particular [circumstance] only the equivalent of a legislative act, to be repealed or modified at the pleasure of congress."[11] On the other hand, the same legislative prerogative does not exist at the state level since the supremacy clause precludes actions by state authorities that thwart or block treaty obligations made at the federal level.[12]

## The War Powers Conundrum: Competition between the Branches

Federalism and separation of powers fractionates political authority, profoundly affecting the institutions and processes in both domestic and foreign policy. Differences tend to be muted when the same party controls both political branches, but branch conflict is never completely eliminated even then.

Nowhere is this conflict among the branches more apparent than in war powers. Presidential authority as commander-in-chief to "make war" in Article II, Section 2 of the Constitution competes directly with congressional authorities to declare war, appropriate moneys for war, and make rules for the armed forces to follow in Article I, Section 8. Continuing battles on the Potomac between the executive and legislative branches over war powers and other matters is by constitutional design. Motivated to avoid concentration of military power in one branch (or, worse, in one person, as had happened when Oliver Cromwell served as "Lord Protector" in mid-seventeenth-century England), the framers separated war powers between the executive and legislature, forcing them to come together in a shared responsibility—"shared power," as Neustadt puts it—were they to go to war.

This arrangement was clearly part of the civil–military design lest there ever arise another Cromwellian-style dictator prone to use the Army as a power base to establish authoritarian rule. Appropriations for "armies" cannot be for longer than two years,[13] thus allowing in principle a newly elected Congress to dismantle any standing army put in place by the preceding Congress and presidential administration. Moreover, the militia (the national guard) for each state is left under day-to-day local control (formally under the command of the governor) unless called to federal service "to execute the Laws of the Union, suppress Insurrections, and repel Invasions" under the president's authority as commander-in-chief.

Presidents throughout the American experience have reserved the right to order armed interventions when they see circumstances warranting such short-term actions. Sustained combat operations were always subject to a declaration of war from the Congress, which retained full budgetary authority to appropriate funds for these purposes. Ratification of the UN Charter in 1945 upon "advice and consent" of the US Senate provided a loophole presidents could use to commit US forces to actions conducted under UN Security Council auspices without a declaration of war from the Congress. The first such action was US armed intervention in Korea in 1950, dubbed by President Truman and administration officials as a UN Chapter Seven "police action" rather than a "war" requiring congressional declaration. For its part, Congress fully funded the operation.

An important precedent had been set that contributed further to the expansion of executive power. Not since 1941 has Congress declared war. Wars or armed interventions since then have been conducted under resolutions passed by both houses of Congress. Notwithstanding quarrels by the executive branch about its constitutionality, the 1973 War Powers Act requires congressional authorization of armed interventions within 60 days.

## Presidential Power in Foreign Policy and National Security

We conclude that the American presidency enjoys extraordinary authority in foreign policy and national security, less so on domestic matters, where members of the legislative branch are more prone to guard their prerogatives from executive encroachments. Although presidents develop their own domestic-policy agendas they seek to advance, their influence —their ability to persuade—always seems relatively greater in foreign policy and national security matters.

Frequently frustrated by the difficulties they face trying to advance their positions on domestic issues, presidents from one administration to another tend to turn instead to their more powerful niche, the decisions and actions they take on foreign policy. Given the presidency's eighteenth-century constitutional origins, it is not surprising that strong presidential prerogatives in external matters compare to those then held by the British Crown. Indeed, the American presidency can be understood metaphorically as if it were an elected but term-limited monarchy with greater presidential power in foreign than in domestic affairs, in which the legislature usually has the upper hand. Domestic and foreign affairs are shared powers between the branches, but in the latter, the executive clearly has primacy.

## NOTES

1. Richard Neustadt, *Presidential Power* (New York: John Wiley & Sons, 1960) was the original edition.
2. The Nixon campaign apparently communicated with South Vietnamese officials to block any agreement until after the election, thus disadvantaging Democratic Vice President Humphrey's campaign.
3. The Reagan campaign allegedly urged Tehran to wait until after the US election to release the hostages lest President Carter reach agreement with the Iranians (an "October surprise"), thus swinging the election to his favor. See Gary Sick, *All Fall Down: America's Tragic Encounter With Iran* (Bloomington, IN: iuniverse, 2001).
4. Robert McFarlane, the National Security Adviser, claimed both the president and vice president participated in decisions related to this end-run around the congressional prohibition on any appropriated funds going to the Contras. See his *Special Trust* (New York: Cadell & Davies, 1994).
5. In post-Cold War interviews Soviet economists indicated that as much as 35% of Russian and 50% of Ukrainian GDP had been allocated to defense. Conversation with Charles Wolf (RAND Corporation) at Bowdoin College, June 1992.
6. *United States v. Curtiss-Wright* (1936).
7. *Gibbons v. Ogden* (1824).
8. Treaties "made under the authority of the United States" trump separate rights claimed by states. *Missouri v. Holland* (1920).
9. *Foster & Elam v. Neilson* (1826).
10. The "Head Money" cases (1884): *Edye v. Robertson, Edye et al. v. Robertson,* and *Cunard Steam-Ship Co., Ltd. v. Robertson.*
11. The "Chinese Exclusion" case, *Chae Chan Ping v. United States* (1889).
12. *Missouri v. Holland* (1920).
13. Article I, Section 8. In practice, appropriations are for one year at a time.

CHAPTER 8

# POLITICS ON THE POTOMAC—
# THE DOMESTIC POLITICAL MILIEU

Interests drive politics. Foreign policy is no exception. But interests do not exist separately as some abstract, purely objective factor external to policymakers. It is their understandings of whose interests and what interests are at stake that matters. Interests and the goals or objectives that flow from them are constructed subjectively by individual policymakers, shared and developed inter-subjectively in the discourse within and across policy elites. It is hard to identify anything more subjective than calculations of interest. I take up in this chapter how ideational and material understandings of interests play among policy elites in the crafting of foreign policy in Washington—politics on the Potomac.

Ernst Haas saw ideas grounded in interests as motive or driving forces in politics.[1] Put another way, non-material ideas, as interests, drive politics at least as much as understandings of material interests do (see figure 5). Some interests are material, but other interests relate explicitly to values or norms, as in commitment to a cause—ideational interests— whether or not one sees anything material to be gained or lost in this pursuit. It is only when, as advocates, we promote our ideas on their own merits—trying to separate ideas from interests—that we find ourselves on the utopian path. Ideas standing alone apart from interests do not drive politics, however splendid or radiant they may be. For ideas to matter politically they need to be tied to interests understood or held by those who influence or make policy. In the absence of that linkage, even the best ideas go nowhere.

**Figure 5. Ideational or material interests and foreign policy.**

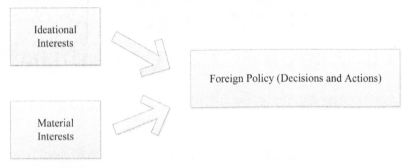

Interest is itself an ideational construct. What we understand to be interest varies from individual to individual, entity to entity. As a practical matter, of course, material and ideational interests tend not to stand apart but rather are often linked or blended, so that sometimes it is difficult to tell one from the other. Although difficult to separate empirically in most cases, it is, however, useful analytically (as shown in Figure 5) to treat ideational and material interests understood by decisionmakers as separate factors influencing the making and implementation of foreign policy. In the American case these internalized understandings of interest come about in a very fragmented policymaking space, given awareness by agents of the structural implications of both separation of powers and federalism.

## INTEREST-BASED FACTIONS AND US FOREIGN POLICY

Factions form around interests—or so thought James Madison, whose concern in Federalist Paper No. 10 is with the "mischief" that factions can cause in the pursuit of their own narrow interests at the expense of others. The republic would be in particular danger were a majority faction to trample the rights or interests of other persons. To eliminate factions one must either deny the liberty they need to exist (which Madison clearly rejected as unwise) or somehow make interests in society the same (which he saw as impractical). Put in schematic form, as in figure 6, we can see the causal logic that underlies Madison's theoretical understanding.

Figure 6. The Madisonian understanding of factions in a liberal society.

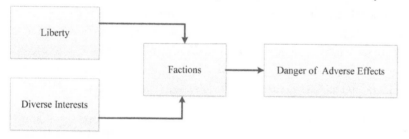

Since the problem ought not be solved on the causal side,[2] the only thing left to do is to contain what Madison saw as the adverse effects of factions. The federal remedy is to fragment their policy space by dividing jurisdictions within the republic among component states, counties, municipalities, and districts within states. For a faction to become a threat to the whole republic, it has to organize itself, gain a following, and secure access across all of these state and local jurisdictions.

The federal remedy of dividing power contains the effects of factions emerging within separate jurisdictions, making it more difficult for them to sway the entire republic. In Madison's own words:

The influence of factious leaders may kindle a flame within their particular States, but will be unable to spread a general conflagration through the other States. A religious sect may degenerate into a political faction in a part of the Confederacy; but the variety of sects dispersed over the entire face of it must secure the national councils against any danger from that source. A rage for paper money, for an abolition of debts, for an equal division of property, or for any other improper or wicked project, will be less apt to pervade the whole body of the Union than a particular member of it; in the same proportion as such a malady is more likely to taint a particular county or district, than an entire State.[3]

We have already identified Madison's dim view of the nature of human beings—"the infirmities and depravities of the human character"—as well as Hamilton's observation on "the ordinary depravity of human nature."[4] Stated somewhat more positively, Madison and Hamilton in an oft-quoted passage come together in Federalist Paper No. 51 to represent the central problem they faced in constituting government, which they understood as "the greatest of all reflections on human nature":

If men were angels, no government would be necessary. If angels were to govern men, neither external nor internal controls on government would be necessary. In framing a government which is to be administered by men over men, the great difficulty lies in this: you must first enable the government to control the governed; and in the next place oblige it to control itself.

Given this task, they add: "A dependence on the people is, no doubt, the primary control on the government; but experience has taught mankind the necessity of auxiliary precautions." The added precautions would take the constitutional form of separation of powers—"opposite and rival interests" compensating for "the [human] defect of better motives."

Quite apart from containing factions in domestic politics, the federal formula of dividing powers among government entities also has substantial implications for foreign policy, particularly when combined with separating powers among branches of government. It is also in Federalist Paper No. 51 that we see Madison and Hamilton representing federalism and the separation of powers as constituting a "compound republic" that constrains not only factions in the body politic but also government itself. Lest either legislative or executive power get out of hand (as had happened in the seventeenth-century English experience under Cromwell), these two "political" branches are constituted as independently as possible to keep each other in check. The judiciary as the third branch is added to the mix as guarantor of the rule of law and a check on the other two branches.

Although the framers added this separation-of-powers remedy to keep the branches in balance and government from becoming too powerful at the expense of liberties enjoyed by the citizenry, the net effect is a highly complex policy space or context within which policy elites and the factions or interest groups that relate to them compete for influence. Given multiple points of access to government entities by those advancing particular interests, it is a conservative recipe if not always for gridlock, then for incremental, small shifts from the *status quo*, making it extremely difficult to effect radical (or sometimes even minor) changes.

## IRON TRIANGLES AND GRIDLOCK

Madison's and Hamilton's shared vision of day-to-day politics expressed so clearly in Federalist Papers Nos. 10 and 51 was indeed profound, although neither could have anticipated just how far their conservative remedy would take American politics. Factions as interest groups, namely their leaders and other agents, do influence the making and implementation of American foreign policy by advancing their interests through the relationships they establish with each other within policy elites and with government officials in both of the political branches. The latter, whether in or out of office, also may be part of one or another of these elites.

Access to officials and their staffs as conveyors of influence is the goal, contributions to campaigns greasing the way in some cases even to direct involvement in drafting and marking up bills of interest. This is the work of "K Street," where many of the lobbyists representing factional interests have their offices. Factions coalesce when interests are compatible. They also come together in political parties in efforts to drive the national agenda.

Factions are not just the work of the private sector. Coalitions and counter-coalitions readily form among elected officials and career civil servants. These coalitions typically also include private-sector interest groups—what Hugh Heclo called "issue networks."[5] As depicted in figure 7, these coalitions can harden into "iron triangles"[6] of private-sector interest groups represented by K-Street lobbyists, congressional committees and subcommittees—particularly their chairs and staffs, and executive departments that form around particular issues, which are difficult if not impossible to break. Coalitions of factions in effect become institutionalized.

**Figure 7. "Iron Triangles" in American security policy.**

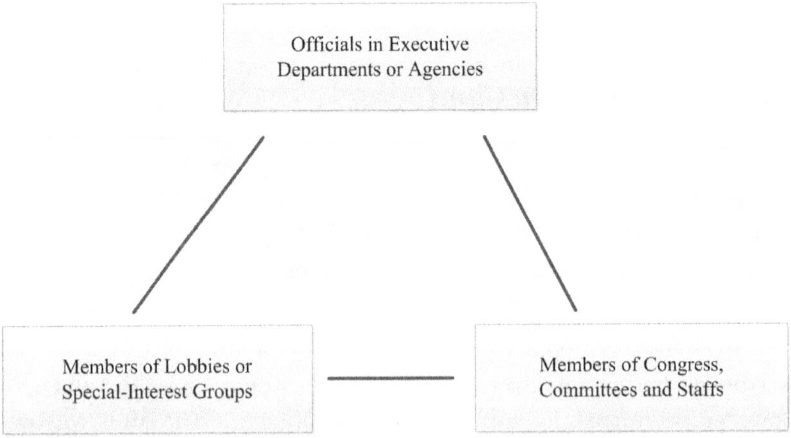

Coalitions or issue networks supporting defense contracts are among the strongest iron triangles one can find. If we unpack them, we find the

K-Street representatives of defense industries closely linked to members and staffs of the Armed Services, Appropriations, and Budget committees in both houses as well as civilian and military officials in the Department of Defense. Triangle "partners" are best served when an Armed Services committee or subcommittee chair or political ally also sits as chair of the defense subcommittee of the Appropriations Committee.

This network is bolstered further when major contractors assemble 2,000 or more subcontractors for a particular defense program distributed in as many of the 50 states and 435 congressional districts as possible to assure widespread support. Given these circumstances, it is not surprising that defense contracts are so difficult to break even when the national security priorities policymakers hold would seem to dictate otherwise. When defense officials want to trim or eliminate particular weapons systems, they run into fierce opposition by other legs of the triangle, so firmly grounded as they are in the body politic.

By contrast, issue networks that form around the State Department tend to be far less cohesive. In part this is because State lacks the glue that defense contracts provide, cementing Department of Defense officials, congressional leaders, and private-sector interests within issue networks. State also lacks the kind of pro-foreign policy constituencies comparable to the strength of pro-defense and pro-military supporters in the homeland that customarily support defense spending in general, DoD programs and contracts in particular. The pro-Israel and other ethnic lobbies do exercise influence, particularly on Capitol Hill and the White House, but even they have a more difficult time cultivating officials in State, who tend to be (and often see themselves as) detached from the demands of domestic politics.

Pressures on officials in State come from diplomats in Washington and foreign consulates in major American cities, and through its global network of embassy and consular contacts with officials, representatives of NGOs, and firms, as well as private citizens in other countries. On Middle East policy, for example, Foreign Service and other career officers in State (labeled "Arabists" by their critics) have in the past often resisted what they have seen as one-sided, pro-Israel policies that do not balance American commitments to Israel with concern for American interests in the Arab world.

Likewise, what are seen, for example, as one-sided pro-Poland or pro-Greece positions face equal challenges by officials in the European Affairs office, who prefer to take a broader, regional view of US interests, influenced as they are by understandings drawn from engagement with both government and private-sector leaders and other officials throughout the world. Indeed, on security-related foreign-policy issues these national or ethnic lobbies may be more likely to find a receptive ear in the Department of Defense than in State, where Foreign Service officers and other officials tend to see US interests in global terms as well as in relation to particular countries or regions.

Whether due to established issue networks or consensus across government departments, foreign policies tend to remain intact across administrations. New administrations can bring changes, of course, but the norm—at least until the Trump administration—has typically been one of continuity. Sometimes new thinking can result in substantial change, as in Richard Nixon's dramatic departure from the norm by altering ties to Taiwan and starting the normalization process vis-à-vis the People's Republic of China (see chapter 2).

Such instances are not the norm. More commonly, we find major departures in foreign policy only when external shocks force rethinking and policymakers coalesce on a new course of action. The nationalist and unilateralist orientations of the Trump administration stand as an exception to this general rule of continuity in foreign policy across administrations. The list of reversals in policy pursued by previous administration is long whether on matters of trade, immigration, arms control, climate change, and relations with alliance partners. President Trump's short-term, transactional approach to almost every issue—"making a deal"—short sells mid- and long-term interests sustained by previous administrations.

Decisive shifts in policy in the twentieth century were relatively rare. Exceptions include entry into World War I after the German sinking of the passenger ship Lusitania in 1915, entry into World War II after the Japanese attack on Pearl Harbor in 1941, and initiation of wars first in Afghanistan and then in Iraq after the *al-Qaeda* attacks in 2001 on the World Trade Center in New York and the Pentagon in Washington, DC. Each of these was an instance of major shock empowering policymakers in the White House and executive branch to make a decisive departure from the *status quo* in American foreign and national security policy. These dramatic shifts in policy stand as exceptions that underscore the more general rule in American foreign policy before the Trump administration took office: a fairly high degree of constancy across presidential administrations.

## PARTISAN IDENTITIES AND FOREIGN POLICY

Political parties in the United States are mechanisms for winning elections and serving the interests of their members, particularly their agenda-setting elites. Put another way, parties tend quite simply to be instruments used by elites to serve their purposes. The driving influences on politics reside among these policy-oriented elites that constitute political parties and set their agendas.

As social constructions developed over more than two centuries, the Democratic, Republican, and other "third" parties reflect the often diverse and changing interests of their members as they seek to win elections and pursue domestic and foreign policies on their behalf. Political parties are shells that contain and are empowered by factions and coalitions within them, their agendas constructed and reconstructed as the interests of their leaders and followers shift. Indeed, interests and the composition of parties change over decades, as do the policies their leaders advocate.

Quite apart from interests are the identities people construct over time with particular parties. To many Americans, identifying with a party is like joining a church, a particular denomination or religious sect, which depends on the good faith and loyalty (and contributions) of members. As with religious affiliations, party identities are often passed within families from generation to generation. Even those who are formally unaffiliated with any party and claim to be independents usually are oriented more to one party than another. Typically representing some one-third of the electorate, the unaffiliated "center" can be decisive not only in elections but also in the popular support an elected official relies upon while in office.

Political parties matter not just for electing presidents and members of legislatures but also as legislative mechanisms for organizing coalitions of regional and other interested factions that can influence the making and implementation of American foreign policy. Partisans hold congressional leadership positions: Speaker of the House, majority and minority leaders in both houses, whips, committee and subcommittee chairs, and ranking minority members on these committees. Even the vice president acting in his role as presiding officer or "president" of the Senate is a decidedly partisan position. This becomes clearest in those few instances when a tie vote is resolved in effect by the executive branch through the office of the vice president. Having this legitimate presence on Capitol Hill also affords the vice president as spokesperson for the White House an opportunity to influence not only fellow partisans but also other senators in the opposition.

As with domestic politics, two-party competition also affects American foreign policy—an historical legacy marked by Democrats and Republicans since the Civil War, Whigs and Democrats before the war, and Federalists and Democratic Republicans in the early years of the republic prior to the War of 1812. Third parties come and go; they add issues to the national agenda and sometimes upset electoral outcomes by taking votes from one or the other of the major parties but at the end of the day two parties remain. This idea of two broad, catch-all parties—each bringing together a diversity of interests and factions coalescing under a single partisan umbrella—is an historical legacy, a well-established construction integral to American political culture and sustained in single-member district and state-wide elections by a winner-take-all, first-past-the-post formula.

Regional and other interests matter, even as a pragmatic orientation to find bases for compromise typically accompanies the building and maintenance of pre-election coalitions within American parties on the issues of the day. The South's position in one or another of the parties has been the means to that end—initially holding the balance as a southern-led party (the Jeffersonian Democratic-Republicans in the early nineteenth century), then in the powerful southern wing of the Democratic Party from the time of Andrew Jackson until the 1980s and early 1990s when, in a realignment, much of the South finally shifted its identity to the Republican Party with which it was more ideologically aligned.

Influence on particular issues, of course, is not unique to the South. Other regions also matter, as do interests that coalesce across regions. Nevertheless, the South historically has been extraordinarily effective in forging unity around key economic and social issues, acting as a regional block through the agency of partisan leaders in the Congress, particularly the Senate. Control of the White House, though helpful in advancing Southern causes, has not been essential so long as the South retained the regional balance of power in the Congress.

Except for the Civil War and the reconstruction period of occupation by the North that followed, regional interests in the South have held the balance of power in American politics for much of the time since the earliest days of the republic—if not in the executive branch, then in the Congress, notably the Senate. Indeed, it was Lincoln's Republican victory in 1860 that threatened the southern states with the loss of their power position in national councils that contributed to their decision to secede from the union.

Holding the balance does not always mean being in the controlling position that a majority in the Congress offers. Quite apart from whether a regional grouping can get its way, it can use its position legislatively to block initiatives it opposes. The South's power within the Republican Party since the 1980s and 1990s has been the principal instrument of regional influence on both domestic and foreign policy, which is the same pattern for exercising influence in national councils when southerners predominantly were Democrats (as they were for much of the 19th and 20th centuries).

Moreover, southern legislators maximize their position by voting typically as a block to a greater degree than other regions typically do. As Democrats, southerners (being politically more conservative than many fellow partisans from other parts of the country) often crossed party lines, coalescing and voting with Republicans on many issues. Now that most southern legislators vote as Republicans, building cross-regional coalitions of conservatives within the same party has proven to be even easier to construct than earlier southern Democratic outreach across the political aisle to garner Republican support for bills of mutual interest.

The same political culture that accepts partisan competition on domestic issues prefers parties to come to consensus on foreign-policy matters. In practice, of course, stopping partisan differences at the waterfront or "watersedge" defined by the Atlantic and Pacific shores is by no means easily achieved. Early in the country's history, pro-British Federalists challenged the more pro-French orientations of the Jeffersonian-influenced Democratic-Republicans. Tariffs favored in the nineteenth and twentieth centuries by industrial or capital interests in the Whig and later the Republican parties were challenged by agricultural interests, particularly among southerners in the Democratic Party (earlier, the Democratic-Republican Party). Reducing or eliminating tariffs not only meant less costly import of manufactures but also a means to avoid foreign discrimination against US cotton and other agricultural exports.

Entry into two world wars was resisted within both parties, particularly by Republican rural and western constituencies that before and after World War I opposed intervention in European conflicts. Invoking nationalist, non-interventionist guidance from George Washington's farewell address to legitimize their position, isolationists in the 1930s, drawn in particular from these Republican and southern Democratic ranks, held sway.

Bipartisanship is strongest, however, when threats to national security lead both parties to rally around the flag, meeting public expectations that partisan differences be set aside. Much as the German sinking in 1915 of the passenger ship Lusitania (and the continuation of submarine warfare) allowed the Wilson administration to take the country into World War I, it took the shock of the Japanese surprise attack in 1941 on Pearl Harbor to break the isolationist sentiment, allowing the Roosevelt administration to get a declaration of war from the Congress. Intense conflict with the Soviet Union in the Cold War also produced a degree of bipartisanship on foreign policy not usually present in the absence of significant threats to national security.

In the post-Cold War period, bipartisanship waned with substantial debates typically along party lines over whether to intervene militarily for humanitarian or other purposes in Kuwait, Somalia, Yugoslavia, Central Africa, and Haiti. It took the shock of the 9/11 attacks on the World Trade Center and the Pentagon to garner bipartisan support for intervention in Afghanistan in 2002 to topple the Taliban regime, which had given sanctuary and an operating base to al-Qaeda. Although the subsequent intervention to effect regime change in Iraq initially enjoyed bipartisan support that muted debate in the Congress, when the security-based rationale on alleged weapons of mass destruction there began to unravel, so did bipartisan support for the venture.

As they do on domestic issues, lobbyists also take on foreign-policy issues that affect their interests. Put another way, K Street matters on Capitol Hill as well as in the executive branch. Campaign contributions grease the skids to assure access to members of Congress and their staffs and to the White House.

## PARTISAN NARRATIVES: STEREOTYPING POSITIONS ON FOREIGN POLICY

There is much partisan stereotyping on matters of war and peace, commercial, social, and other foreign policies. By no means is partisan stereotyping new in the American historical experience. After all, partisan identity depends on inferences and selective use of facts to sustain these constructions. Labeling one's own party or an opposing party as anti-war may be accurate as a snapshot taken at a particular point in time, but such generalizations do not capture the complexity of relations between both popular and elite interests within a party that do change over time. It is interests that matter more than the parties constructed and adapted to serve their purposes.

Nevertheless, partisans do establish their own identities and contribute to those of their opponents through the use of generalizations or stereo-types. In practice their actions may not be so dissimilar. From their earliest days, Democratic-Republicans and the Democrats who succeeded them had few inhibitions about using force if doing so was understood to be in the national interest. But it was the Republican Party that went to war in 1860 to foil southern secession, thus preserving the union. The post-Civil War, late-nineteenth and early twentieth-century period of Republican primacy saw expansion of American commercial influence accompanied by military interventions in the western hemisphere, particularly in Central America and the Caribbean. The Spanish-American War in 1898 not only ended Iberian presence in the Western Hemisphere but also extended the American sphere westward across the Pacific to the Philippines.

Splits in the Republican Party and Theodore Roosevelt's decision to run on a third-party ticket led to Democratic victory by Woodrow Wilson in 1912, his re-election following in 1916. By the end of World War II, however, the conservative voice within the Republican Party began gradually to change its position. Capital was becoming global in its reach and advantaged by open trade and investment markets facilitated by the emergence of the dollar as a world currency. Victorious in wars in both European and Pacific theaters, American security interests also were redefined in both political parties as being global in scope. No longer isolationist as it had been in the 1920s and 1930s, the Republican Party became deeply committed to the pursuit of US national security and other interests on a truly global scale.

Before both world wars, Republicans tried to avoid entanglements outside of the Americas, particularly in Europe. This was most pronounced in the rejection of the League of Nations after World War I and the isolationism that became even more pronounced during the inter-war period. The GOP saw itself as the party of both business and the peace upon which it depended. Democrats were accused by Republicans of selling out to the Soviets in the Yalta and Potsdam agreements at the end of World War II, agreements that facilitated the establishment of a Soviet sphere in Eastern Europe. As if that were not enough, Democrats were said to have "lost" China to the communists when Mao and his regime came to power in 1949. Indeed, Republicans claimed to be the party that could restore the peace, as President Eisenhower did with Korea in 1953 and President Ford also did after the defeat in Vietnam in 1975, taking steps to heal the nation then deeply divided.

Prior to the 1970s, Democrats were often labeled stereotypically by their Republican opponents as the party that gets the country into wars —a reference to Democratic presidents in the twentieth century in office when wars began: Wilson in World War I, Roosevelt in World War II, Truman in Korea, and Kennedy and Johnson in Vietnam in the 1960s.

The last of these wars, however, reversed the stereotype as Democrats became central to the peace movement of the late 1960s and early 1970s. After the Vietnam War ended in 1975, the anti-war legacy remained with the Democrats for more than a quarter of a century, they constantly becoming stereotyped as the party of peace or war avoidance—portrayed by their Republican opponents as weak on defense. The Republicans, in turn, assumed the mantle of a party seen as more oriented to national defense and more willing to go to war when necessary to secure the country's interests. Nevertheless, although this more pacific orientation remains in place in the left wing of the Democratic Party, its centrist and center-left segments proved quite willing to intervene militarily abroad in the 1990s and in the first decade of the twenty-first century.

Since the invasions of Afghanistan and Iraq in 2002 and 2003, Democrats have challenged Republican claims to superiority in national security matters. Indeed, at the outset, post-9/11 interventions in Afghanistan and Iraq enjoyed broad bipartisan and popular support as being in the national interest. It was not parties *per se* but rather understandings of interests by elites within both parties that mattered. Although erosion of support for the war in Iraq was initially more apparent in the Democratic Party, Republicans in Congress were understandably less willing to take on their fellow partisan in the White House. Over time an interest-based bipartisan consensus emerged to draw down and reorient the commitment in Iraq. Driving the consensus was the loss of American lives and financial costs of the war, balanced against regional stability and material interests, especially assuring the continuing flow of oil to world and US markets.

The Reagan–Bush realignment of the Democratic and Republican parties in the 1980s and 1990s—white southerners in large numbers switching allegiance from the Democratic to Republican Party—had no appreciable effect on the broadly shared understanding that engagement with the outside world serves US interests. Indeed, post-World War II Republican policies of the Eisenhower, Nixon, Ford, Reagan, and both Bush administrations proved to be as internationalist as their Democratic counterparts in the Roosevelt, Truman, Kennedy, Johnson, Carter, and Clinton years. Leaders and members of both parties in the twenty-first century have sustained these internationalist understandings of interest until the advent of the nationalist Trump era.

## NOTES

1. *Nationalism, Liberalism, and Progress*, Vol. 1 (Ithaca, NY: Cornell University Press, 1997), pp. 3 and 25.
2. Eliminating diversity of interest is as impracticable as removing liberty would be unwise. Federalist Paper No. 10.
3. Federalist Paper No. 10.
4. Federalist Paper No. 37 (Madison), No. 78 (Hamilton).
5. "Issue Networks and the Executive Establishment," in Anthony King (ed.), *The New American Political System* (Washington, DC: American Enterprise Institute for Public Policy Research, 1978), pp. 87–124.
6. Gordon Adams, *The Iron Triangle: The Politics of Defense Contracting* (New Brunswick, NJ: Transaction Publishers, 1981). Cf. Grant McConnell, *Private Power and American Democracy* (New York: Alfred A. Knopf, 1966).

CHAPTER 9

# ELITE UNDERSTANDINGS OF POWER

Foreign policymakers and academic theorists live in very different worlds. The action-oriented policymaker necessarily is attentive to the in-box, the here and now, what needs to be done today and tomorrow, following up on what happened yesterday. By contrast, the theorist is attuned to the long term, thinking conceptually, measuring or reflecting on what happened yesterday, years and even centuries before. It is not as if the twain never meet, but they rarely do.

Their vocabularies are different. If the policymaker is focusing on what to do and how to do it, then the theorist is asking why, trying to explain, or even anticipating what will be done next. The policymaker, who is always short of time, is less prone to consult the theorist, particularly when the latter seems taken up by abstractions that seem to have little if any relevance to the problems confronting the former. Riding on a different track, the theorist finds the here-and-now focus of the policymaker on the mundane to be intellectually uninteresting.[1]

Yet both lines of inquiry are important, even if neither is drawn to the other. The two also have more in common than they are aware of or, perhaps, willing to admit. American foreign policymakers may or may not identify as being realists, much less structural realists, but many nevertheless share realist assumptions (even if unstated) and see international politics and the making of foreign policy in realist terms. Others, in the language of international relations theorists, may be liberal internationalists, neoliberal institutionalists, or constructivists,[2] even if such terms are foreign to them. Whether or not consciously realists, liberals, constructivists, or something else, policymakers nevertheless tend to have internalized the set or sets of assumptions, material and ideational understandings, and theories offered by one or another of these camps.

To realists, power is a material factor—the capabilities a state has at its disposal.[3] Joseph Nye sees these capabilities as diverse, falling into two broad categories that he defines as "hard" and "soft" power.[4] Nye is among the few who have moved from academe to become foreign policymakers and then moved back to the academy, sometimes with a foot in both camps. Not surprisingly his work as a theorist tends to be more policy-oriented than other scholars who have not had to deal with the day-to-day exigencies of the policymaking world. Even his definitions of what he means by hard and soft power make sense to the policymaker. Indeed, they are policy-oriented definitions.

Hard power to Nye is the stuff of guns and money—military and economic capabilities—a common denominator all realists share, but Nye goes beyond the material. Indeed, his policymaker focus is evident in his discussion of "soft power" that "rests on the ability to set the political agenda in a way that shapes the preferences of others." He is speaking inter-subjectively here, relating policymakers among themselves at home as well as with those in other countries. He notes how "soft power arises in large part from our values . . . expressed in our culture, in the policies we follow inside our country, and in the ways we handle ourselves internationally."

Consistent with classical realism, which includes both material and ideational understandings of power in international politics, Nye argues that "hard and soft power are related and can reinforce each other" in the effort "to achieve our purposes by affecting the behavior of others."[5] Indeed, he refers to "smart power" as "learning better how to combine . . . hard and soft power."[6]

In this regard, he sees "public diplomacy" as explaining American positions to publics and policymakers abroad, multilateralism in alliance and institutional settings, and the "almost infinite number of points of contact with other societies" that Americans enjoy as instrumental in the exercise of this smart power. It is the understandings policymakers have of both the potential soft power and the balance they strike between the soft and hard dimensions that determine just how "smart" American power may be.[7]

It is difficult to understand how a country can have military capabilities without a productive economy that makes fielding a military possible. It is the aggregate size of the economy that enables the organizing, training, and equipping of armed forces. Even if states are highly developed economically and enjoy substantial levels of income, as is true in many European countries, the size of their armies, navies, and air forces is still limited by the size of their economies.

The armed forces of Finland, Sweden, and Switzerland, for example, necessarily will be smaller than those fielded by Germany, France, the UK, and Italy (not to mention the United States), which have much greater gross domestic products. Of course, just because a country's GDP—an indicator or measure of its material capability or power— enables its policymakers to build a large military does not mean that they will choose to do so. For a variety of historical or other reasons policy elites in some countries may choose to have smaller militaries than they otherwise can afford.

With a GDP second only to those of the United States and China, Japanese policymakers have limited their military spending (and thus the size and capability of their military forces) to about 1 percent of GDP. In the Japanese case, allocating fewer resources to defense than they could is part of policymaker avoidance of any return to the militarism exhibited in World War II and the years leading up to it. This commitment to avoidance operates as a self-limiting norm constraining policy elites that have held power since the end of World War II and that thus far remains in place, notwithstanding challenges by some. How much to spend on the military remains a subjective choice quite apart from the material capabilities an economy brings.

Policymaker understandings of economic capability do precede any decisions they might make in relation to the size and capabilities of any armed forces they might wish to acquire. The kind of economy that policymakers understand they have at their disposal also influences the kind of military a country likely will acquire. It is not as if the economy or how it relates to others as abstractions "out there" explains policy; it is policymaker understandings of these as factors that contribute to decisions made and actions taken. Overestimating these capabilities can be as problematic as underestimating them. Interpretations by policymakers of feedback from their decisions and actions may lead them to reassess their relative economic and other capabilities. It is a learning-by-doing process.

We observe policymakers in highly developed, high-income countries that, compared to China, have relatively smaller populations (for example, Canada, Japan, most European countries, and the United States) tend to choose development of militaries that are technology- or capital-intensive, relying more on advanced equipment as being to their comparative advantage. Chinese policymakers, by contrast, have relied heavily on the labor-intensive military forces that they have in abundance. This is their comparative advantage, but they also increasingly have incorporated advanced military technologies and weapons systems as their level of economic development has increased significantly in recent decades. For their part, policymakers in less-developed countries also tend to rely on labor-intensive forces, adding new weapons systems and related military technologies when—or in some cases regardless of whether—they can afford to do so.

For its part, the United States has over 1.3 million persons in its armed forces on active duty—about 0.36 percent of the American population (the Army with some 472,000 soldiers on active duty). More than 807,000 additional national guard and reserve forces bring total armed forces personnel to more than 2.1 million (about 0.66 percent of the US population), but US military capabilities are really a function of what a $20 trillion, highly developed economy can buy or produce.

So important to American policymakers is the military component of power that they are consistently willing to spend more than 40 percent of the world's total expenditure for defense—in some years defense spending is greater than all other countries in the world combined! Total US defense spending in 2020 on the order of $750 billion (about 3.75 percent of GDP), President Trump has urged NATO allies to spend at least 2 percent of GDP on their militaries. Prior administrations made the same plea that the allies meet the 2 percent agreed NATO floor on defense spending, but President Trump put added pressure on countries he saw as free riding on US defense coattails, threatening that the US would consider withdrawing from the alliance if others did not pay their fair share for collective defense.

High-technology weapons systems are not just for the inherently capital-intensive Air Force and Navy but also enhance substantially the capabilities of what are necessarily the more labor-intensive ground forces found in the Army and Marine Corps. US military capabilities are thus very much a function of how much policymakers choose to draw from the American economic base. Apart from access to capital and high technology upon which the US military depends are the higher levels of education, training, and technical skills found more readily in the populations of societies with high-income, capital-rich economies.

Material factors matter in ways sometimes overlooked. American policymakers often have taken for granted the privileged position the United States has enjoyed due to the aggregate size of its economy and the role of the dollar in international finance. Although always subject to challenge, the dollar's position as principal medium of exchange and its role as primary reserve currency have meant that American decisionmakers have relatively few worries about how the country finances its foreign policy and the overseas commitments of its military forces. Purchases abroad to sustain US war efforts are made in dollars, the national currency, readily convertible into any other currency. Even pricing oil in dollars has privileged the United States not only in the finance of imports for domestic use but also in the use of the national currency to pay for fuel consumption, food, and other logistics outlays by military forces deployed throughout the world.

Money is, after all, a social construction universally established as both a store of material value and medium of exchange. The relative value or exchange rate of the dollar in terms of other currencies is driven by supply and demand, which reflect the subjective preferences people in the private sector, government, or central banks and other financial institutions have that influence their decisions to buy or sell in a truly global monetary marketplace. People's understandings of the dollar's purchasing power, its use in financing purchases and investments, the overall strength and growth of the US national economy, and requirements for dollars directly influence the dollar's exchange rate, which facilitates or constrains economically the conduct of US foreign policy.[8]

## POLICYMAKER UNDERSTANDINGS OF RELATIVE POWER

By contrast to Nye, structural realists are content with power's material definition. Economic and military capabilities translate into power.

Because the "soft" tends to flow from the "hard" realities of power politics, structural realists tend to treat power as an integral whole, not dissecting it analytically into component categories. Moreover, to these thinkers the power of a particular country available for use by foreign policymakers is relative to the power or capabilities of others. Given this understanding that the power of the United States is measured relative to the capabilities of countries, we need not leave the concept "out there" as a structural factor exogenous to states and their decisionmaking agents. Instead, we can take power and make it part of the subjective and inter-subjective understandings internalized by policymakers "in here."

Policymakers may understand power—whether hard, soft, or both—as if it were an absolute quantity, or they may see it as relative to the power of others. The meanings American policymakers internalize about the power of the United States or American capabilities (hard or soft) relative to other countries does affect their sense of what can be done; in other words, the art of the possible in the conduct of foreign policy.

No other country even comes close to matching the size of the $20 trillion US economy, which is some 1.6 times greater than China's and almost four times Japan's, the next in line. Only when one sums all of the European Union economies does one find a competitor with the same economic capabilities, if measured in the aggregate. Although Russia retains a pretense to great power status that its leaders act upon, in fact its economy is miniscule—$1.6 trillion, about 8 percent the size of the US economy.

It is not power or relative power in the abstract that matters to policymakers, but rather what they understand about how power and relative power position facilitate or constrain the making and implementation of the foreign policies they formulate—which doors they see power opening and which doors they see as obstacles blocking or obstructing the decisions and actions they take. Those who miscalculate their relative power positions in the world "out there" likely soon will learn "in here" that they have exceeded their limits as others rise to thwart the challenge posed.

## UNDERSTANDINGS OF STRUCTURAL REALISM AND BALANCE-OF-POWER POLITICS

Structural realism—that the distribution of power influences the conduct or behavior of states—has been under assault in academic circles, a reaction against its alleged system determinism. Power, to structural realists like Kenneth Waltz, is a material factor that underlies international politics. Some states have more power; others have decidedly less. This is not hard for policymakers or anyone else to understand.

What matters is the particular understanding policymakers in the United States and their counterparts in other countries have of American power, whether in absolute or relative terms. Power is not an abstraction to the policymaker. It is a subjective and inter-subjective concept in which human interpretations matter. Thus one hears policymakers say that failures in the implementation of foreign policy (as in loss of a war in Vietnam or setbacks from time to time in the Middle East) undermine the country's power position, with adverse effect on the capabilities its agents have in serving the national interest. Power to the policymaker is an interpretive concept, its practical meaning a function of how it is understood at home and abroad.

Critics tend to discount the role of material structure in international relations, regardless of whether the power distribution defining structure is unipolar, bipolar, or multipolar. The danger in this critique, however, is that some opponents go too far, effectively eliminating material structure (power and its distribution) from their theoretical formulations altogether. Rather than eliminate structure merely because it is exogenous or external to state and non-state actors and their human agents, we instead incorporate it at the human level within or as part of the decisionmaking calculus that precedes foreign-policy decisions and actions. Material structure does not drive policy directly. It becomes effective when human agents at home and abroad internalize the understanding and thus make it so.

Although how we understand structure does not stand alone as a single explanatory variable for all behavior among states, it nevertheless does contribute to our understanding of how state actions are facilitated or constrained by the structural "realities" their agents face—what they see and understand. Whatever these realities "out there" might be, what matters more is how policymakers comprehend them and judge their effects. Even if policymakers and the elites of which they are a part do not use terms like structure, they do question the current and future status of American power in relation to other countries. They may ask themselves how likely it is for the US to remain the world's only superpower and, if so, for how long. When, if ever, will China match or surpass US capabilities? Related to this inquiry is the strategic question policymakers ask about what can be done to avoid erosion of American power.

Policymakers entertain structural realist questions in their own, very practical language. They are prone to ask themselves about the durability of the *status quo*. Will the world still be unipolar, with the US remaining the dominant power a decade or more from now? Is the world returning to bipolarity—this time the United States vs. China (much as during the Cold War when the US and USSR were two superpowers at the top of the world's power hierarchy)? Or should policymakers prepare themselves to deal multilaterally in an increasingly multipolar world with such players as China, a more unified European Union, a Russia assuming a dominant role in its spheres of influence, a more assertive Japan, and rising powers like India and Brazil? Even if policymakers do not use structural-realist or other theoretical vocabulary, the practical understandings they have of structure as it relates to the US position do affect their thinking, decisions, and actions.

## UNDERSTANDING THE DISTRIBUTION OF POWER: IMPLICATIONS FOR POLICY CHOICE

Internalized structural understandings of a country's power position relative to the capabilities of others have important implications for the making and implementation of foreign policy. The distribution of power is not a structure "out there," but rather one internalized "in here" within the circle of decisionmakers who have a sense of what they are or are not able to do. Miscalculations—either overestimating or underestimating these relative capabilities—likely will have consequences that lead them to reassessments and new understandings about what is or is not possible.

When we underscore the importance of the subjective or inter-subjective, we are not suggesting that policymaker understandings necessarily are correct or somehow divorced from the world "out there." Their understandings "in here" matter in terms of the decisions they make and actions they take, but they really do not live in a fantasyland entirely of their own making.

Just because we say, for example, that the desert sands are cool at midday does not make them so. Thinking it is cool, we step barefoot onto the sands and quickly discover how hot they really are. Our understanding of desert temperatures changes as we learn from direct experiences. So it is with power. If the understandings American policymakers hold either overstate or underrepresent US power relative to other states, they typically will pay a price by pursuing policies that either fail or are suboptimal, considerably less than the best.

Perceptions or understandings by American policymakers at a moment in time are not the only facts that matter. "Others" in both domestic and foreign policy elites have a way of tempering their perceptions or correcting their misperceptions in an on-going inter-subjective process. In much the same way as what they say and do affect the perceptions and understandings of others abroad, American policymakers change or adjust their understandings as they learn from the "realities" often imposed on them by words and actions of their counterparts in other countries. Adaptation or learning by agents is a part of on-going foreign policy decisionmaking processes. What matters is how decisionmakers as agents for their states comprehend interests and the capabilities and limits to the power or capabilities they employ in pursuit of objectives.

When decisionmakers see themselves as enjoying a concentration of power superior to all others, or what they may describe structurally as a unipolar world in which a single state (theirs) has a dominant position, they may exhibit the kind of assertive, if not hegemonic, behavior one expects to see a monopoly firm practicing in the marketplace.[9] They still do have a choice, informed by other shared meanings, on whether to use this dominant position to advance multilateralism and pursue cooperative or collaborative approaches or to fall back on narrower, unilateralist bases for action.

Understandings of material structure are not the only factor, but they are certainly an important part of any theory that would explain American foreign policy. When the decisionmakers have as part of their normative frame a general understanding that positive-sum approaches will advance their own agendas even as others also have something to gain, they are not surprisingly more prone to engage peacefully with their counterparts in other countries. Peaceful engagement and multilateralism can become commonly accepted shared norms governing the ways and means by which international politics are conducted.

On the other hand, some policy elites may be informed by a different set of values more zero-sum in construction, tending to make them more prone to tell their counterparts abroad: "It's our way or the highway!" Multilateralism in this understanding means little more than follow the leader, get on the leader's bandwagon, or get out of the way. This mode of multilateralism was more prevalent in neoconservative policy-elite circles dominant in the early years of the first Bush administration during the lead-up to war in Afghanistan and particularly in Iraq.

We have seen a return to this mode of transactional, zero-sum calculations in the Trump administration's nationalist orientation. From this perspective, any gains made or losses taken by others are incidental and thus not central to the lead country's policy calculations. Others are free to accept a particular course of action, but it doesn't matter much to the lead country if they don't. Any "multilateralism" thus becomes in this context merely a thin veneer to disguise the adverse impact of what is an essentially unilateral foreign policy pursued because policymakers see themselves as having the power to do so.

This was the dominant brand displayed in the US approach to building a multilateral coalition to invade Iraq. Although some in the policymaking elite (mostly in the State Department and in the military) did reach out to others in a more collaborative, positive-sum fashion, the overall effort was driven primarily by the secretary of defense and vice president, who were the principal advisers upon whom the president relied. In Secretary of Defense Rumsfeld's characterization, the mission should drive the coalition, not the coalition the mission. The US would set the objectives and others were welcome to come along for the ride.

Beyond such domestic remedies as increasing the size and capabilities of the armed forces, American policymakers are prone to reach out for allies and coalition partners when they find external challenges or threats either beyond the capacity or willingness of the United States to deal with single-handedly. So it is when policy elites in other countries see themselves as disadvantaged by American decisions and actions. Aside from diplomatic efforts to persuade the United States not to pursue certain courses of action, they may choose individually or collectively with others to constrain or dissuade American decisionmakers—balancing behaviors designed to offset American power.

Balancing behaviors calculated to affect American foreign policy choices may or may not take military form. Although policy elites in countries like Iran and North Korea have sought nuclear weapons for national pride in an effort to be taken seriously as regional powers, they also see them as a deterrent to attacks by the United States or others. As a way of curbing American power, insurgencies with popular bases of support operating in and from countries like Iraq, Afghanistan, and Pakistan use force in small-unit or terrorist attacks against the United States and the regimes it champions.

Most countries do not seek nuclear weapons or resort to insurgencies or other military measures to balance American power. Given the American preponderance of military power, other policy elites are likely to seek diplomatic remedies. Subjective and inter-subjective exchanges are generally viewed by these policy elites as more effective means by which to persuade American policymakers to pursue or not pursue a particular course of action. They seek to moderate American power and influence the decisions of American policymakers. Failing that, they may choose not to support American initiatives, as when French and German policymakers opted out of the American call for intervention in Iraq in 2003 after both had supported American-led efforts the year before in Afghanistan. Notwithstanding threats from Iran or its surrogates alleged by the Trump administration in 2019, European governments made clear they would opt out of joining the United States in any war with Iran.

Economic measures are also a potent form of balancing behaviors, as when countries choose to substitute the euro or other currencies for the dollar in commercial transactions or the reserves they maintain. Policy elites in other countries tend not even to consider resorting to boycotts, blockades, or other belligerent forms of economic balancing, given the relative magnitude of the American economy, the dominant position the United States sustains in global commerce, and, as exemplified by the global financial crisis that began in 2008 and afterward, the dependence by parties abroad on continued trade, investment, and other transactions with American firms.

Belligerent measures lack viability as policymakers in other countries understand they have far more to lose than gain in relations with the United States by using such tactics. On the other hand, more subtle financial or commercial pressures can be used in efforts by policymakers in other countries either to influence their American counterparts to take particular actions or to dissuade them from taking an alternative policy course.

The unilateral imposition of tariffs on Chinese exports to the United States by the Trump administration predictably led the Chinese to retaliate with tariffs targeted in particular against US agricultural products produced by farm interests in the president's domestic political base. Trump's trade war with China was accompanied by strong nationalist, America-First rhetoric, as had also been the case with imposition of tariffs (or threats to impose them) levied against Canada, Mexico, and European Union countries.

## THE TAPESTRY OF IDEATIONAL AND MATERIAL CONSIDERATIONS

Although we cannot discount, much less ignore, understandings of power and its distribution that are in the heads of policy elites, power and balance of power are by no means the only things that count. We necessarily add other factors or considerations in our theoretical quest to explain and make the foreign-policy world and its politics more intelligible.

Ideas (to include ideas or understandings about power and its distribution) do matter. Only if we were to construe the material and ideational as if they were mutually exclusive are power and its distribution necessarily at odds with the more voluntarist formulations that see decisionmakers as decisive agents. Indeed, the perspective represented here is not just for realists of one stripe or another. It is also compatible with the scholarship of those who put relatively more emphasis at different levels of analysis on human agency.

The ideas human beings formulate, the social constructions that inform our view of the world, and the shared meanings within and across policy elites define the domain of actions and interactions in world politics. That said, specifying the relation and causal order between the material and ideational understandings as well as how much allowance is made for human action remain core questions in theory development.

These are, of course, not new questions. We find them in one form or another in both ancient and modern writings on matters of war and peace. The worldviews and understandings of theorists like Thucydides, Machiavelli, Hobbes, Grotius, Locke, Rousseau, and Kant resonate with present-day thinking about international relations and world politics by capturing one or another side of current debates. We use their names as a helpful shorthand for identifying recurrent modes of thought.

Even if members of one or another policy elite have never heard, much less read, the work of any of these writers, the ideas policymakers hold are often linked to insights originally pursued or developed by one or another of these theorists. These ideas selectively have become part of the collective understanding members of a particular policy elite may hold on power and its relation to the making and implementation of foreign policy.

## NOTES

1.  E.H. Carr, *The Twenty Years' Crisis, 1919–1939* (New York: Harper Torch-books, 1940, 1964), ch. 1.
2.  On constructivism, see Mark V. Kauppi and Paul R. Vioti, *International Relations Theory*, 6th ed. (Lanham, MD: Rowman and Littlefield, 2020), ch. 6.
3.  Kenneth Waltz sees power as "the combined capability of a state" and "a defining characteristic of structure," which is "the distribution of these capabilities among states." *Realism and International Politics* (New York and London: Routledge, 2008), p. 79.
4.  *The Paradox of American Power: Why the World's Only Superpower Can't Go It Alone* (Oxford and New York: Oxford University Press, 2002), pp. 4–12.
5.  Nye, *Paradox*, p. 9.
6.  Nye, *Soft Power* (New York: Public Affairs, 2004), p. 32.
7.  Ibid., p. 147.
8.  I develop this thesis on the importance of the dollar for the conduct of US foreign and national security policy in Paul R. Viotti, *The Dollar and National Security: The Monetary Component of Hard Power* (Stanford, CA: Stanford University Press, 2014).
9.  Paul R. Viotti, Jr. extends Waltz's focus on conflictual models to coopera-tive or collaborative microeconomic models. Papers presented to annual meetings of the American Political Science Association, San Francisco (2001) and Chicago (2007).

# Afterword

When it comes to explaining foreign policy (decisions and actions the US takes in relation to the outside world), we are drawn inevitably back to the decisionmakers themselves. Ideas grounded in understandings of interest drive American foreign policy. We look both internally and externally to these ideas, grounded as they are in the understandings decisionmakers at home and abroad have about both interests and material capabilities or power and normative concerns that drive their choices and facilitate or constrain these decisions.

The theoretical challenge is how we connect material and ideational factors in the world "out there" to the decisionmakers who incorporate them as part of their decisionmaking calculus "in here." We find that interests, norms, the distribution of power in an anarchic world, and other factors on a domestic level that facilitate or constrain decisionmaking do so when understandings of these factors are internalized by the human agents who actually make policy. Integral to explanation of foreign policy are the understandings that these decisionmakers hold and that typically are shared in the policy elites with which they identify. We look to these ideas, shared meanings, and norms accepted by individuals in leadership positions and positions of influence at particular points in time. The answer to this theoretical challenge, then, lies not "out there," but rather "in here": within and among the decisionmakers themselves.

Liberal, conservative, and neoconservative or militant international-ists—not to mention nationalists—have decidedly different understand-ings "in here" of the world "out there" and, as a result, provide different answers—whether to pursue peaceful engagement, containment, armed intervention and warfare or some combination of these—informed as they are by the subjective and inter-subjective exchanges among policymakers within and across policymaking elites at home and abroad. What brings internationalists together is their conviction that the US has so great a stake in world politics that it cannot withdraw into a domestic, nationalist (much less isolationist) shell.

International relations theorists address a world of state and non-state actors and the interactions among them.[1] Ideas found in theories of international relations that are internalized by foreign policymakers can affect the different ways they and the policy elites to which they belong comprehend the world around them. Understandings about how international (and domestic) politics work, correct or otherwise, do cross the academic and policy divide. In this reciprocal flow, theorists draw from the experiences of policymakers, the latter informed directly or indirectly by major currents in scholarly work. It is not the bibliography policymakers can cite, but rather the extent to which ideas contained in this literature shape the understandings that contribute substantially to the decisions they make and the actions they take. If theory or studies by academics are to be taken seriously, their practicality and thus their value to the policymaker have to be demonstrated.

We have departed throughout this volume from theoretical explanations that put causality external to policymakers, making them instead the focus in explanation of foreign policy. International politics as a whole or international *system* is not our dependent variable. It is foreign policy that requires us to delve into the understandings of human agents who make and implement decisions. States and their policymaking agents coexist and interact with each other and with other units in diverse and complex patterns of interaction. To say the least, states-as-units have not yet withered away, however desirable they may or may not be. Their human agents still have much to do.

## Looking Forward: A Return to Internationalism?

The president and policy elites in the Obama administration brought American foreign policy back to a liberal-internationalist orientation—putting primary emphasis on constructive or peaceful engagement, albeit still containing adversaries and using force as deemed necessary. The Trump administration upended Obama's approach, substituting a new nationalism and reversing much of what the Obama administration had achieved. A central question is whether this new nationalism—effectively endorsed by Republican leaders driven by sentiments in their predominantly southern or rural-populist base—will prevail.

The decision in October 2009 to award President Barack Obama the Nobel Peace Prize just nine months into his administration was a mark of approval by at least some international elites for a substantial shift from the militant internationalism pursued by the Bush administration. Indeed, President Obama's addresses in Washington at his inaugural, later in Cairo, at the United Nations in New York, and elsewhere made clear his liberal-internationalist preference for multilateralism, international institutions, and peaceful engagement as the preferred modes for dealing with other countries, whether "friends" or adversaries. This approach departed markedly from the first five years of George W. Bush's administration, in which neoconservative, militant-internationalist elites skeptical of peaceful engagement were prominent and the last three years, which witnessed a return to a conservative internationalism somewhat more willing to engage but more comfortable with containment and other force options for dealing with adversaries.

To say the least, the Trump administration has taken a different position. Beyond rejection of the liberal and conservative consensus on internationalism in general and multilateral institutionalism in particular, policy has taken a transactional focus that seeks to maximize short-term gains at whatever expense to selected others. Both adversaries and long-standing allies and partners are left in a quizzical position—

never knowing decisively what position the nationalist president and his advisers (some of whom have been militant internationalists) will adopt.

Although containment of adversaries, armed intervention, and warfare seem likely to remain part of the American approach to foreign policy, the historical record suggests to this author that peaceful engagement is most promising as a course of action for the coming decades, particularly for a country with the enormous capabilities or power still enjoyed by the United States. Moreover, constructive or peaceful engagement can go beyond merely being a tactic to use with "friendly" countries and adversaries. It is also an opportunity for the United States to further the institutionalization of multilateralism and other cooperative and collaborative international norms on which it may need to rely more heavily if and when the country no longer possesses the decisive power advantages it now enjoys.

## NOTES

1. On our understanding of how these images and interpretive understand-ings inform international relations theorists, see Paul R. Viotti and Mark V. Kauppi, *International Relations Theory*, 6th ed. (Lanham, MD: Rowman & Littlefield, 1987, 2020).

# INDEX

# About The Author

Paul R. Viotti is Executive Director of the Institute on Globalization and Security, University of Denver, where he is also a professor in the Josef Korbel School of International Studies. Professor Viotti holds a PhD in Political Science from the University of California, Berkeley, an MS from The George Washington University, an MA from Georgetown University, and a BS from the US Air Force Academy. His previous publications include *US National Security: New Threats, Old Realities*, *The Dollar and National Security*, *American Foreign Policy*, five editions of *International Relations Theory*, five editions of *International Relations and World Politics*, and three editions of *The Defense Policies of Nations*. He has served as President (1993–2003) and Vice Chair of the Board (2003–2016) for the Denver Council on Foreign Relations.

# CAMBRIA RAPID COMMUNICATIONS IN CONFLICT AND SECURITY (RCCS) SERIES

### General Editor: Geoffrey R. H. Burn

The aim of the RCCS series is to provide policy makers, practitioners, analysts, and academics with in-depth analysis of fast-moving topics that require urgent yet informed debate. Since its launch in October 2015, the RCCS series has the following book publications:

- *A New Strategy for Complex Warfare: Combined Effects in East Asia* by Thomas A. Drohan
- *US National Security: New Threats, Old Realities* by Paul R. Viotti
- *Security Forces in African States: Cases and Assessment* edited by Paul Shemella and Nicholas Tomb
- *Trust and Distrust in Sino-American Relations: Challenge and Opportunity* by Steve Chan
- *The Gathering Pacific Storm: Emerging US-China Strategic Competition in Defense Technological and Industrial Development* edited by Tai Ming Cheung and Thomas G. Mahnken
- *Military Strategy for the 21st Century: People, Connectivity, and Competitipauon* by Charles Cleveland, Benjamin Jensen, Susan Bryant, and Arnel David
- *Ensuring National Government Stability After US Counterinsurgency Operations: The Critical Measure of Success* by Dallas E. Shaw Jr.
- *Reassessing U.S. Nuclear Strategy* by David W. Kearn, Jr.
- *Deglobalization and International Security* by T. X. Hammes
- *American Foreign Policy and National Security* by Paul R. Viotti

- *Make America First Again: Grand Strategy Analysis and the Trump Administration* by Jacob Shively
- *Learning from Russia's Recent Wars: Why, Where, and When Russia Might Strike Next* by Neal G. Jesse
- *Restoring Thucydides: Testing Familiar Lessons and Deriving New Ones* by Andrew R. Novo and Jay M. Parker
- *Net Assessment and Military Strategy: Retrospective and Prospective Essays* edited by Thomas G. Mahnken, with an introduction by Andrew W. Marshall

For more information, visit www.cambriapress.com.